Social wo people with learning difficulties

Making a difference

Susan Hunter and Denis Rowley

First published in Great Britain in 2015 by

Policy Press
University of Bristol
1-9 Old Park Hill
Bristol
BS2 8BB
UK
t: +44 (0)117 954 5940
pp-info@bristol.ac.uk
www.policypress.co.uk

North America office:
Policy Press
c/o The University of Chicago Press
1427 East 60th Street
Chicago, IL 60637, USA
t: +1 773 702 7700
f: +1 773 702 9756
sales@press.uchicago.edu
www.press.uchicago.edu

© Policy Press 2015

British Library Cataloguing in Publication Data
A catalogue record for this book is available from the British Library.

Library of Congress Cataloging-in-Publication Data
A catalog record for this book has been requested.

ISBN 978-1-86134-878-4 paperback
ISBN 978-1-86134-879-1 hardcover

The right of Susan Hunter and Denis Rowley to be identified as the authors of this work
has been asserted by them in accordance with the Copyright, Designs and Patents Act
1988.

Cover design by Policy Press
Front cover: image kindly supplied by www.alamy.com
Printed and bound in Great Britain by CMP, Poole
Policy Press uses environmentally responsible print partners

SOCIAL WORK IN PRACTICE series

Series editors: **Viviene Cree**, University of Edinburgh and
Steve Myers, University of Salford

This important series sets new standards in introducing social workers to
the ideas, values and knowledge base necessary for professional practice.
These core texts are designed for students undertaking professional
training at all levels as well as fulfilling the needs of qualified staff seeking
to update their skills or move into new areas of practice.

Editorial advisory board:
Suzy Braye, University of Sussex

Jim Campbell, Goldsmith's University of London

Gina Hardesty, Independent Consultant

Ravi Kohli, University of Bedfordshire

Jill Manthorpe, King's College London

Kate Morris, University of Nottingham

Joan Orme, University of Glasgow

Alison Shaw, Policy Press

Charlotte Williams, RMIT University, Australia

Published titles in the series
Social work - Viviene Cree and Steve Myers

Social work and multi-agency working - Kate Morris

Youth justice in practice - Bill Whyte

Radical social work in practice - Iain Ferguson and Rona Woodward

Religion, belief and social work - Sheila Furness and Philip Gilligan

Communicating with children and young people - Michelle Lefevre

Social work and lesbian, gay, bisexual and trans people - Julie Fish

Supporting people with alcohol and drug problems - Sarah Galvani

Social work in the community - Barbra Teater and Mark Baldwin

Residential child care in practice - Mark Smith, Leon Fulcher and Peter Doran

Effective writing for social work - Lucy Rai

Practice research partnerships in social work - Christa Fouché

Contents

List of tables and figures

Tables

Figures

Acknowledgements

With thanks to all those people with learning difficulties from whose generosity, understanding and friendship we have benefited over the years. Thanks also to Policy Press, and in particular to Viv Cree for her perseverance and support.

Introduction

For any social worker, the history and evolution of the ways in which social workers have tried to support people with learning difficulties make fascinating, challenging, and at times, chilling, reading. It is a story that is *fascinating* in its reflection of social history and the major public policy debates of the last 150 years. The story is not a straightforward one, however – within it there are eddies, sometimes shock waves, and occasional triumphs.

- The Industrial Revolution and its fragmenting impact on communities and their vulnerable members.
- Theories of evolution and the legacy of the eugenics movement still reverberate in today's debates on genetic engineering and designer babies.
- There are ongoing struggles for human rights and for the recognition of minority rights for marginalised groups within our society.
- Fundamental and contentious issues remain, such as who controls the right to life and the right to die.
- There has been an increasing 'professionalisation' of support, and technical, managerial solutions for social problems, and notably, the courage of individuals in the face of day-to-day adversity and the inspiration of their achievements so stunningly exemplified in the 2012 Paralympics.

For social workers, this history makes *challenging* reading because the professional values of social work aspire to anti-discrimination and advocacy, together with and on behalf of people in our society who are marginalised and devalued for a variety of reasons. The social justice and equality agenda in disability policy is central to social work's declared professional 'mission' and professional values (BASW, 2002), but is elusive to its collective grasp and problematic in individual day-to-day practice.

It is reading at times in that much of it is about well-intentioned efforts to support and 'rehabilitate' individuals at risk of being marginalised in a rapidly industrialising society that is increasingly dependent on technical and cognitive skills. However, these were efforts that ultimately led to the enforced isolation, segregation and oppression of men, women, and not infrequently children with learning difficulties, in what were called 'mental handicap hospitals' in the UK. The impoverishment and indeed misery of those who lived their lives in institutions that were created and run in the name of progress and expert care have found a contemporary voice in first-hand accounts by Jimmy McIntosh, Jimmy Laing (quoted in Laing and McQuarrie, 1992), the Lennox Castle Stories (2012) group, and more academic accounts by Blatt and Kaplan (1974), Atkinson (1997), Traustadottir and Sigurjonsdottir (2008) and others.

Former residents of Lennox Castle Hospital in Scotland named their account of life in hospital 'Lest we forget' because of the continuing prevalence, even today, of scandalous behaviour towards people with learning difficulties, both in service settings and in the community. How can it be that a society that is increasingly 'professionalised' and 'regulated' continues to fail to protect vulnerable people? A failure to protect not only those in the new institutions, as described in the final report on Winterbourne View Hospital in Bristol (Flynn, 2012) and in our mainstream health services, as described in the Mencap reports *Death by indifference* (2007) and *Death by indifference: 74 deaths and counting* (2012), but also those living in our midst in the community, as described in the serious case review of the murder of Steven Hoskin (Flynn, 2007) and the killing of Francecca Hardwick by her mother Fiona Pilkington after years of torment and bullying by local young people (IPCC, 2011).

Although, in general, services and opportunities have become better for people with learning difficulties, and we have, over the last few decades in particular, moved from segregation in institutions to the notion of full and inclusive citizenship, much still needs to be done, and many committed professionals are working tirelessly in alliance with people with learning difficulties and their families to create better services and better lives. As before, however, the path of progress is not clean and linear. For example:

■ While some people with learning difficulties are being listened to, are really involved and are being influential, others are being ignored, with their human rights disregarded and abused.

■ UK policies have become more supportive of the visions outlined in the following aspirational policy documents – *The same as you?* (Scottish Executive, 2000) and *The keys to life* (Scottish Government, 2013) in Scotland, *Valuing People* (DH, 2001a) and *Valuing People Now* (DH, 2009a) in England, *Equal lives* (Northern Ireland Executive, 2005) in Northern Ireland, and the *Statement on policy and practice for adults with a learning disability* (Welsh Assembly Government, 2007) in Wales – but many of the recommendations have not been fully implemented.

■ Although generic policy changes have been implemented that are congruent with the forward-looking ideas emerging in services for people with learning difficulties, there are still many examples of policy undermining the position of people with learning difficulties (for example, the tick-box approach to Work Capability Assessments introduced by the firm Atos), and there are examples of bad interpretation of universalism as a cynical exercise in reducing specialist service costs.

■ There are many good practice examples, but we have also seen the emergence of bad practice, and the continued prevalence of poor and even abusive practice in essentially invisible supported living and residential service settings.

■ Human rights legislation and international accords formally protect the rights of people with learning difficulties, but the same human rights legislation is not always used to challenge circumstances where practice that appears abusive is known to occur .

We believe that these tensions will continue to exist for the foreseeable future.

Reading the reports of the recent scandals and tragedies, and considering the ongoing contradictions experienced by people with learning difficulties, raises the question of where social work as a profession is situated in relation to this narrative.

Social work practice with adults has undergone profound changes since the introduction of community care legislation in 1990, particularly in the statutory sector. Its traditional focus on prevention and support has been overtaken by more procedural responsibilities embodied in care management and assessment, care packaging, and commissioning and review processes. Indeed, some commentators have suggested an erosion of professional values in the face of increasingly managerialist service cultures (Jordan, 2004; Ferguson, 2007). Having said that, the self-advocacy movement has become notably more assertive in demanding full citizenship and rights for its members (see, for example, People First [(Scotland], 2012). The requirement of many people with learning difficulties for sustained and possibly life-long social and personal support is caught uncomfortably between a service emphasis on procedural interventions, and a professional ethic based on equality and social justice. The current policy agenda of personalisation, with its emphasis on flexible and responsive service outcomes (DH, 2012; Scottish Government, 2013), provides a further opportunity to realise aspirations held both by professionals and people with learning difficulties, to achieve a better life. However, the impact on these aspirations of current and planned austerity measures is not yet fully known, although they have been described as 'savage' for people with difficulties (*The Guardian*, 2012; Demos, 2012). These tensions in the evolution of professional social work practice, in government policy attempting to 'modernise' services and to respond to economic turbulence, and in the reasonable expectations of service users for a better quality of life, pose a significant challenge to the profession of social work. The dilemmas contained in the agendas of inclusion, safeguarding, equity and justice fundamentally challenge social workers' understanding of how the needs and expectations of people with learning difficulties should be framed and met, and how social workers can engage with them in creating both better services and better lives.

This book is based on the notion that improving and modernising services, which has been a declared aim of social policy for the last 60 years, is not an end in itself. Rather, it is but one facet of achieving a better life for people with learning difficulties in which they are connected to family, friends and community, and are able to exercise real and meaningful measures of control and choice. We hope that this book is a contribution to the debate, and also a challenge to social work practice. We suggest approaches by which social work can consolidate and develop the modernisation of services and practices. We believe that social work, with its lead responsibilities in community care and safeguarding (Ridley and Hunter, 2010), is well placed to take forward this modernisation agenda. However, we also believe that if such improvements are to be sustained, they must go hand in hand with a broader understanding of how deeply entrenched attitudes to disability in our society really are. History warns us that resilience to change in practice, policy and legislation is such that people with learning difficulties remain at risk of death and abuse in social work services and in our communities. We suggest that practitioners must not lose sight of this, and must engage with an agenda of creating better lives as well as better services.

To this end, the book is divided into three parts, with Part One setting out the key ideas, the historical and contemporary policy context, and the underlying conceptual frameworks.

Part One: Context

Chapter One: Key ideas

In Chapter One, the key ideas that are central to the human rights context, within which social work practices should be located, are set out. Alongside human rights, the chapter features notions of personhood and of good living. The relationship between 'good services' and a 'good life' is raised.

Chapter Two: Contemporary policy context

Chapter Two sets out the historical and contemporary policy context, with both the opportunities and hazards it presents in the lives of people with difficulties. The conundrum of persistent professional failures and scandals in learning disability services, despite significant, progressive service reform over the last hundred years, is explored. The policy shift from service reform to transformational service change is described.

Chapter Three: Conceptual frameworks

In Chapter Three, the underlying conceptual frameworks for these policies and practices are set out, in two groupings: those associated with early frameworks that promoted positive, personalised support such as normalisation and the social model of disability; and those associated with transforming the concept of 'better services' into 'better lives', such as personalisation and co-production.

Part Two: Transitional points

Part Two explores the role of services and the social worker, drawing on person-centred, community-centred and family involvement perspectives. These perspectives are applied to five key transitional points in the lives of adults with learning difficulties, transitional points that present both opportunities and dangers in creating better life experiences.

The transition to adulthood (see Chapter Four) is a key moment for all individuals, but for those with learning difficulties who have been seen historically as 'children' unable to assume adult roles, decisions made by families and professionals at this point can influence lives markedly, and be difficult to 'unmake'.

All those 'normal' expectations of setting up a home (Chapter Five), getting a job (Chapter Six) and having a family (Chapter Seven) flow more readily or with greater difficulty in the light of decisions made and opportunities developed in the late teens and young adulthood.

Consideration of growing older in people with learning difficulties is relatively new in the literature, with one early review finding only 13 references in a literature search (Hogg and Lambe, 1998), but it presents a significant challenge to policies and practices based on concepts of 'independence' and 'choice' (see Chapter Eight).

A common feature at the heart of each of these transitional points is the capacity of the individual to take informed risks and yet to be kept safe. These twin concerns can catch professionals in a pincer movement between 'risk-averse' organisations and individuals' aspirations for 'control and positive risk taking' in their lives. This tension is explored in this Chapter Nine. Practice material is used throughout the chapter to illustrate the discussion.

In Chapter Ten we look at three groups of people with multiple and interconnecting needs who, although their needs are obvious and their numbers relatively small, experience some of the greatest barriers in accessing services, their families have very high levels of anxiety about the future. The chapter includes a commentary on practice in the fields of mental health and criminal justice (still a social work responsibility in Scotland), where the complexities of inter-agency and inter-professional working are prominent, and the public perceptions of people who use health and criminal justice services are generally negative and discriminatory.

Part Three

Part Three (that is, Chapter Eleven) draws the book to a conclusion by asking why it is so difficult to sustain person-centred, family- and community-based practice through a discussion of the challenges for practitioners and managers in this field of practice in creatively supporting 'good lives', yet managing the risks. Some of the themes are then illustrated in 'Simon's story' and, in conclusion, the overall challenges to practice are set out.

As a final point, it may be useful to note what this book is not about. It is not concerned with setting out a classification of learning difficulties – there is a long-standing literature that can be consulted on this, and some associated comments can be found in the discussion of the use of labels and personhood in Chapter One. Neither is the focus on the demographics of 'learning difficulty', which suggests that 20 people in every 1,000 have a mild or moderate learning difficulty, three to four people in every 1,000 have a severe or profound learning difficulty, and a 1 per cent increase in the population of people with learning difficulties is predicted year on year over a 10-year period (Emerson, 2009). However, it is important to note the shifting population profile, reminiscent of the population in general, which includes more babies and children with complex needs and severe difficulties surviving into adulthood, and more adults surviving into old age.

Part One

Context

1 Key ideas

In this chapter we ask you to think about some key ideas that underpin the rest of the book:

- personhood
- a 'good life'
- human rights.

We also briefly reflect on the language and labels used in disability discourse, and how our use of words affects the way that people are seen and how they are treated in society.

Personhood

What makes a person a person? Are some people more equal than others?

Let's start at the beginning. Consider your response to some apparently simple but literally 'vital' questions. Indeed, we would ask you to start this book by writing down your responses to these fundamental questions. Although they are essentially ethical questions, they have an impact on the many practical matters that are addressed later in this book, including the ways in which we, as individuals and as professionals, relate to people with learning difficulties – examples such as the murder of people with learning difficulties, their abuse in regulated services as well as in the community, their experience of enforced sterilisation and terminations, their over-representation in the prison population and the under-responsiveness to their needs by the healthcare system – all these indicate the importance of addressing what it means to be a person:

- Are all human beings people?
- Are all people 'equal'?
- Or are some, to use Orwell's words, 'more equal than others'?

It might seem odd to begin our exploration of ethical issues in the way that we relate to and support people with learning difficulties by looking at the question of what makes a person a person, but this question is important for three reasons. First, because we are clear in our minds that whatever we do in relating to people with learning difficulties should start from the same place as how we relate to anyone else – from recognising the ways in which we are similar to one another, rather than the ways in which we are different. Second, because some influential thinkers have, from time to time, written in a somewhat cavalier way about people with learning difficulties. For example, Peter Singer, one of the best-known living philosophers, once considered the possibility of using people with severe learning difficulties to replace animals in medical experiments. In doing so, he drew attention to the likelihood that using 'mentally handicapped' human subjects would be more cost-effective (Singer, 1979; Fairbairn 2008).

Think spot

Are people with learning difficulties as valuable as people without learning difficulties? Write a paragraph or two explaining your answer. Then write a little bit about how you think society should change, because of what you believe. Specifically, how do you think social work practice should change?

Have you come across people who have a different view to yours – who, for example, might believe that Peter Singer has a point? Try, for a moment, to imagine yourself into the shoes of such people, thinking about their reasons for their beliefs, trying to make them your own (for a short time). Then write a paragraph or two, as if you are these people, explaining why you hold these views.

Singer is not alone in holding disturbing attitudes towards people with learning difficulties. For example, in his book, *The end of life*, James Rachels (1986), another applied philosopher, compares people with learning difficulties unfavourably with those he considers to be 'normal'. Rachels believes that 'complex lives' are worth more than 'less complex' ones. He also assumes that people with learning difficulties necessarily lead simpler, that is, less complex, lives than people who do not have learning difficulties.

Rachels believes that in a situation of forced choice – such as when there are insufficient medical resources to go round – we should choose people with complex lives over people with less complex lives. And this, he seems to think, means that we should choose what he calls 'normal' people over 'retarded' people (Fairbairn, 1991).[1]

Third, this question is important because these ideas are not historical vestiges left behind as our society becomes more forward thinking. They prevail not only in philosophy, but also in local and national politics, as the following examples show.

The strange case of Councillor Collin Brewer

On 3 May 2013, Collin Brewer, an independent councillor in Cornwall, was re-elected despite having to apologise for suggesting that disabled children should be 'put down' to save money. In an interview with the Disability News Service (DNS) on 8 July 2013 (Pring, 2013a), he re-stated his belief that there was a good argument for killing some disabled babies – those with high support needs – because of the cost of providing them with services (Pring, 2013b). But he also explained why he had raised the issue of the cost of supporting disabled children in a comment he had made to a member of staff of Disability Cornwall in 2011. He said: 'I had just been to a council meeting which was discussing finance. When you are talking about having to close toilets, facilities for everyone, and perhaps the coastal footpath for everyone, then I have got to question individual budgets to individual people.' He did call for more facilities for disabled people to be built in Cornwall, to save the cost of sending them to expensive out-of-area placements, and also praised the move away from the use of 'massive institutions' for people with mental health conditions, but he then compared the £250,000 that it would cost to keep 10 public toilets open with similar sums paid out to support just one disabled person.

When asked by DNS whether there might be a good argument for killing a disabled child with high support needs, because it would free up more resources for the wider community, he said: 'I am not making that judgement. There may be a case. I haven't a clue how much they cost.' He went on to say: 'When people complain to me about the state of our finances, I say, "well, we can't afford to do it." We might be forced to close our beaches. That's a service to us all. It is a dilemma and it is going to get increasingly a problem with budget cuts.' He also said that he had concerns about the 'burden' of disabled people who are left to rely on council services after their parents die. He said: 'Who shoulders the burden after they have looked after them for so many years?' (Pring, 2013a).

Disability Cornwall commented that it was no surprise to them that his views were occasionally echoed by others, but that it was particularly frightening that these views are held by people who have the positions and power to make life-and-death decisions. 'It is a sad indictment of our so-called "civilised" society that disabled children are increasingly discussed within a context of affordability, as if they were goods on a shelf that can be picked up and discarded at will, dependent upon what's in the public purse' (quoted in Grant, 2013).

What is the difference between 1930s Germany and modern-day Britain?

Wolfensberger (2005) and others[2] draw attention to some common features between the experience of people with learning difficulties in Nazi Germany and their experiences in the UK and the US in modern times. They point out how in the early part of the 20th century the extreme eugenics movement advocated killing those who were judged to have 'lives not worth living'. In the 1930s, there were huge cuts to state institutions, causing overcrowding. At this time, Nazi propaganda emphasised the cost of caring for people with mental health problems and disabled people. In 1939, parents of the disabled child Gerhard Kretschmar wrote to Adolf Hitler to ask him to permit their child to be killed. Hitler agreed, and immediately set up Aktion T4, a committee whose job it was to organise more such killings. When the Second World War started, parents were told that their mentally and physically disabled children were being sent to special treatments centres, but the reality was that they were being killed without their parents' knowledge. This programme was soon extended to adults, starting in Poland, and then in Germany. Under this programme, at least 200,000 disabled people were murdered over six years, through lethal medication, starvation or the gas chambers.

Explicit comparisons have been made between these historical events and the experience of disabled people in 21st-century Britain.[3]

On 9 May 2013 DNS pointed out:

> We have propaganda pushing the idea that sick and disabled people are scroungers, work-shy, lazy. This propaganda is coming from government ministers, their special advisers, and tabloids like the Daily Express, The Sun, and the Daily Mail. Even broadsheets like the Times and the Telegraph have contributed. Such propaganda has even been raised by MPs [Members of Parliament] in the Work and Pensions Select Committee and ministers told to stop. The propaganda is working too, with hate crimes against disabled people up in vast numbers. We have many people fighting to legalise assisted suicide, inadvertently promoting the idea that life for some people is not worth living.

The authors are clearly fearful that if euthanasia becomes legal, there will be pressure on some disabled individuals to stop being a burden on other people. Other pressures include:

- Cuts to local authority care budgets, for example, in one local authority in England the cuts mean that anyone whose care costs more than sending them to an institution will lose some care. The politicians argue that it is a choice because people can choose to move to a care home, or have some of their care provision cut. But what to cut? Eating? Washing? Dressing? Using a toilet? The net result is loss of care, or institutionalising people.
- Sick and disabled people being judged as fit to work and told to claim Jobseeker's Allowance and to look for work or to undertake unpaid work experience for large companies.

In 1930s Germany, the government itself ordered the rounding up and killing of disabled people. In modern-day Britain, the government can claim that it is not its fault, even that it should not happen, but that private companies and the chasm of bureaucracy between various government departments are what kill people. Starvation, homelessness and neglect are what will kill people. The implementation is different, but the result is the same.

A 'good life'

People with learning difficulties have the same aspirations as anyone else. Like every other citizen, they aspire to:

- have a home
- have loving relationships with family and friends
- control the basic elements of their lives
- attain sufficient financial means to live with dignity
- pursue their dreams and passions
- make a contribution to society.

Etmanski (2000) describes this set of aspirations as 'a good life'. He suggests that for the vast majority of people, an absence of meaningful relationships would prevent anyone from living a good life. It is certainly true that most of us find it impossible to imagine a good life without the benefit and support of genuine relationships. However, for many people with learning difficulties, this is their bleak reality. Although much progress has been made, we need to do more to respond to the challenges that those with learning difficulties face. Improvements such as accessible buses and taxis, lifts labelled with braille, events translated into sign language and other similar measures reflect the progress that has been made, but they are not enough to ensure that disabled people have a real sense of belonging.

Over the last 50 years the disability movement has been driven by the 'rights paradigm', the belief that rights were the means by which citizenship would be attained for disabled people. While the rights of disabled citizens have been increasingly entrenched in the laws, policies and institutions of the UK, true citizenship, as reflected and evidenced by participation, contribution and acknowledgement of our fellow citizens, has remained elusive for many people with learning difficulties. As a result, disabled people have not had the opportunity to fulfil their obligations as citizens (Styan, 2004).

Think spot

A good life for all?

As well as thinking about what a good life might mean for you, think about whether a good life is an entitlement for all of us or an 'added bonus':

> Can everyone expect to have a good life?
> Does every citizen actually achieve this?
> What are the limiting factors for any citizen?
> On what basis are some people excluded from aspects of a good life?
> How can someone with learning difficulties take advantage of what everyone expects?

If you agree that people with learning difficulties should be able to aspire to, and achieve, a good life, it follows that in your practice as a social worker you must ask yourself how you can apply that standard in the work you do with people with learning difficulties. Put simply, if we were to design services and support for people with learning difficulties based on the socially valued analogue, that is, what we ourselves expect as the parameters and the limitations of a decent life,

> What would we design?
> What would we attend to?
> Would services look different?
> What would we offer?
> What services would we eliminate?

Think about it...

> How would you live up to the standards that you expect for yourself, yet avoid the pitfalls of the past?
> Could you be idealistic, visionary and at the same time, practical?
> Could you arrange things in such a way that you would use 'service resources' where and when needed, but also encourage the use of natural supports?
> How would you avoid supplanting local people – replacing what they naturally want to do as friends and neighbours – with formal services?

Duffy (2011, p 8) states: 'A good life is not something you give someone else. A good life is built upon combining connections, capacities, community resources and personal control including financial resources.'

In Canada, family carers have been at the cutting edge of the movement to plan and create better futures for people with learning difficulties. The founder of PLAN (the Planned Lifetime Advocacy Network), Al Etmanski (2010, p 2), describes the importance of the work of the family movement as follows:

As families, we hold the values and strengths inherent in our innovation of day to day tasks and visioning, our resilience in building relationships and ongoing advocacy, and our abundance to draw upon the resources around us. Even in an uncertain future, this doesn't have to be scary, just approached with eyes wide open and hands clasped in shared experience and encouragement.

Think spot

What makes your life worth living?

People everywhere know what matters in our lives, and consistently come up with ideas that are no different from the kinds of ideas that the great philosophers of the past and the important thinkers about community care, social care and community life, have come up with. The wisdom is all around us, but we insist on ignoring it. Take two or three minutes, and write down the answer to the following questions:

> What makes your life worth living?
> What gets you up and out of bed in the morning?

> What drives you on?
> What fuels the good things in your life?

Limit yourself to no more than eight statements, and put them in order of importance, then ask someone who knows you well to comment on your answers.

In our experience, asking these questions of a wide range of people, both inside and outside the world of services, the answers are nigh on universal – with family life and the support of friends virtually always at the top of people's lists.

Human rights

We believe that human rights are the foundation of services and supports for people with learning difficulties. We all have these human rights just because we are human, but not all of us have the same experiences of realising these rights. As a result of our circumstances, or because of our identity, some of us face barriers to achieving these rights. Some barriers are physical, such as those still faced regularly by people who use wheelchairs, and sometimes they can be different kinds of barriers because services, although used by disabled people, are not adapted in ways that make them useful.

Human rights legislation and guidance

The Universal Declaration of Human Rights (UN, 1948) states that human rights are based on a 'recognition of the inherent dignity and of the equal and inalienable rights of all members of the human family ... and that all human beings are born free and equal in dignity and rights' (UN, 1948, p 1).

The Human Rights Act 1998 came into force in the UK in October 2000, and it brought into effect expectations of the European Court of Human Rights with which all public bodies have to comply. It places a legal obligation on the government and public authorities to respect the basic human rights of all citizens.

The Act sets out the fundamental rights and freedoms to which individuals in the UK have access, including a right to life, the right to freedom from torture or degrading treatment, the right to liberty and security, the right to freedom from slavery and forced labour, as well as the right to a fair trial, and that there should be no punishment without law. It also covers respect for private and family life, home and correspondence, as well as freedom of thought, belief, religion and expression.

It makes clear the right to marry and to start a family as well as to be protected from discrimination, and to the peaceful enjoyment of one's property. It also provides for the right to education and to participate in free elections.

The United Nations (UN) Convention on the Rights of Persons with Disabilities (2007) was formally ratified by the UK in 2009. It applies to everyone who has a long-term physical, mental or intellectual disability.

The Convention is an agreement between different countries whereby those that sign up must ensure that the rights of disabled people are respected and upheld. It means that countries will not treat people differently or unfairly because of their disability, and that disabled people are to have the same rights as everyone else. It is not about giving individuals new legal rights, but it can be used with the laws already in each country to change things for disabled people.

The European Court of Human Rights explains this as having the right to having a life, saying what you think, having the best possible health, and having the opportunity to be educated and to live in the community. It also makes clear that government and other public organisations have a duty to work together to make this a reality by, for example, producing information in ways that disabled people can understand.

The Equality Act 2010 covers nine protected characteristics that cannot be used to treat people unfairly: age, disability, gender reassignment, marriage and civil partnership, pregnancy and maternity, race, religion and belief, sex, and sexual orientation.

The Act sets out the different ways in which it is unlawful to treat someone, including direct or indirect discrimination, harassment, victimisation and failing to make a reasonable adjustment for a disabled person. It prohibits unfair treatment in the workplace, when providing goods, facilities or services, when exercising public functions, in the disposal and management of premises, in education and by associations (such as private clubs).

Source: Scottish Government (2013, p 144)

A report focusing specifically on the human rights of adults with learning difficulties, entitled *A life like any other?* (House of Commons and House of

Lords Joint Committee on Human Rights, 2008), stated that the Human Rights Act 'provides a legal framework for service providers to abide by, and empower service users to demand that they are treated with respect for their dignity' (pp 21-2). In 2013, the new Scottish learning disability strategy report, *The keys to life* (Scottish Government, 2013), placed a central emphasis on the human rights of people with learning difficulties.

These legal underpinnings of human rights are written and designed to ensure that all citizens are able to live the lives of their choosing, and that everyone, regardless of status, can participate equally in community life. It is worth noting that all UK governmental policies and legislation in respect of people with learning difficulties apply to all ethnic groups. However, people from black and minority ethnic (BME) communities experience additional barriers, and 'specific, focused and determined action is required' to ensure the implementation of these rights (Foundation for People with Learning Disabilities, 2012).

The concept of providing individually tailored and personalised support is underpinned by the Universal Declaration of Human Rights (UN, 1948), and is further supported by the European Convention on Human Rights (Council of Europe, 1953), and is incorporated into domestic law through the Human Rights Act 1998 and by various other international human rights treaties.

Chetty et al (2012, p 10) point out that:

> Human rights-based and person-centred approaches therefore share the same starting point – the personal experiences of the individual – and the same end goal – empowering individuals to fulfil their potential by giving them the authority, capacities, capabilities and access needed to change their own lives, improve their own communities and influence their own futures.

The right to participation

All of us have the right to participate in decisions that affect our human rights. For governments and other public bodies to adopt a human rights-based approach to the development of policy and practice, it is necessary for them to commit to, and to implement, a high level of meaningful participation, not only by those individuals affected by the policies and practices, but also by the communities, civil society and others with a stake in their development.

Several Articles in the Convention on the Rights of Persons with Disabilities confer protection of the right to participate in decisions, the right to access support for participation, and the right to access information.

The right to a private home and family life and to access information

Article 8 of the European Convention on Human Rights (Council of Europe, 1953) is concerned with the right to respect for private and family life, home and correspondence. It includes a right to participate in decisions that affect our human rights.

All citizens have a right to live in a safe environment. People with learning difficulties are vulnerable to hate crime – both abuse and neglect. They may require assistance to be able to report incidents easily. Indeed, *Valuing People Now* (DH, 2009a) stated that people with learning difficulties from BME groups, and newly arrived communities and their families, often face 'double discrimination'. They tend to experience insufficient and inappropriate services, which may be caused by:

- policies and services that are not always culturally sensitive;
- wrong assumptions about what certain ethnic groups value;
- language barriers;
- discrimination (Foundation for People with Learning Disabilities, 2012).

As part of the right to freedom of expression, disabled people have a right to accessible information, that is, they have a right to information in a form and language that enables them to participate in decisions that affect their human rights. In addition, the Convention on the Rights of Persons with Disabilities requires the promotion of 'other appropriate forms of assistance and support to persons with disabilities to ensure their access to information' (UN, 2007, Article 9(2)(f)).

Agencies must strive to ensure that individuals and communities are confident that action will be taken to support them to achieve the right to a private home and family life and to access information.

The right to live independently and to be included

Chetty et al (2012, p 12) point out that the European Court of Human Rights states that Article 8 of the European Convention on Human Rights (Council of Europe, 1953) encompasses 'the right to personal autonomy, personal development ... as well as [the right] ... "to conduct one's life in the manner of one's choosing".'

Article 19 of the Convention on the Rights of Persons with Disabilities (UN, 2007) encompasses the right to live independently and to be included in the community. This means that disabled people have the right to the same choice and control over their lives as non-disabled people. It infers that governments should do everything they can to ensure that disabled people have as much choice and control as possible in order that they can enjoy these rights.

The adoption and implementation of personalisation and self-directed support are at their most potent when combined with a serious-minded commitment to human rights.

The right to have relationships with others

Article 8 of the European Convention on Human Rights (Council of Europe, 1953) extends to a right to establish and develop relationships with other human beings, and to conduct one's life in a manner of one's choosing (Chetty et al, 2012).

Not surprisingly, there are strong parallels between fundamental human rights, as enshrined in statute and guidance, and the qualities that Etmanski (2010) came up with in his attempt to define 'a good life', as can be seen in Table 1.1.

Table 1.1: Human rights and a good life – the same thing?

Human rights	A good life
The right to participation	Contributing to community life
The right to a private home and family life and to access information	Home and a home life
The right to live independently and be included	Choice and control
The right to personal development and to establish and develop relationships with other human beings	Friendship and relationships
	Financial security

People First (Scotland) (2012) informed the Scottish Human Rights Commission of a situation where a man with a learning difficulty had a Sexual Offences Prevention Order that was much more restrictive of what he could do than would be imposed on anyone else who had committed a similar offence. The Commission responded by saying that it did not believe that the man's rights were being unfairly removed. Can you imagine what their reasoning might be?

You may be interested to hear that the first thing the Commission said was to re-assert that there are, indeed, relevant rights for everyone to have their physical integrity protected, and that this included the right to be protected from a sexual offence. All members of society have a right to be protected from an individual who is assessed as being a risk to them. The Commission pointed out that everyone has the right to liberty, but that this is not an absolute right. Citizens do not have an absolute right to be free, and in certain closely defined circumstances, the state has a legitimate interest and, in some instances, an obligation, to restrict a person's liberty. One of these instances might, for example, be where there is a risk of a repeat offence.

However, where there is a requirement that a person is accompanied when they go out, and there is a limitation on their freedom of movement, what needs to be ascertained is:

- that there is a legal basis for the restriction of the person's liberty: this need not be an individual court order relating to that person, but it could be, for example, a statute that gave a duty to protect others from the risk of harm;
- that this restriction is really necessary and proportionate, whether this restriction is the least that is necessary to achieve the aim of keeping people safe from the risk of harm;
- that the person who is subjected to the limitation on their freedom of movement should know why this restriction is being imposed, and further, that they should have the chance to have that reviewed over time.

We think that there are three key elements in the task of achieving a human rights culture:

- empowering people to understand what their rights are, and to claim their rights where necessary;
- improving the ability of those who are supposed to uphold our rights to be able to do that;
- ensuring that they are accountable for the realisation of human rights.

In the recent past, two sets of reporting – one on the London 2012 Paralympics and one on the increase in hate crime (Rose, 2012; Gravell, 2012; Bowcott, 2015) – demonstrate the persistent currency of the debate. The positive and extensive coverage of the Paralympics in the mainstream press and television has been seen as a boost to attitudes towards disability, with the creation of positive regard and roles for disabled people. Yet at the same time, there has been a marked increase in reported hate crime, reflecting ingrained and systemic disregard for the rights of the same group of people. Social workers find themselves addressing both these strands of experience within our society, and require a keen awareness of both in their professional interventions. Laying the foundation for this awareness is an appreciation of attitudes to people with learning difficulties and alongside the history of disability services. We explore this further in Chapter Two.

Language and labels

All of us group and label other people. The history of legislation and support services for people with a 'learning disability' is littered with negative and stereotyping words, which have been used to categorise and to separate people from the rest of society. And the problem is not a new one either.[4]

Many of the words we use start off well, but come in the end to be considered offensive, and so using the right words, or at any rate, trying to use the right words, is important. The problem lies in deciding what the right words are.

It is not unusual to experience controversy over how useful and accurate our existing terms are, and also to find that there are similar strong feelings about any proposal to change the words we use. Some people prefer to err on the side of change while others see change as irrelevant, confusing or simply unnecessary political correctness.

After long argument and debate, the American Association on Mental Retardation (AAMR) officially became the American Association on Intellectual and Developmental Disabilities (AAIDD) as recently as 2007 (Hatton, 2012). The fact that there has been such international controversy and concern over names, labels and vocabulary should alert us to the necessity to take serious care in deciding on the labels we use to describe the men and women who use social work services.

A label is not a person; a person is not a label

Labels and categories are essential components in service provision. We use the labels as tools for communication, organisation and reflection rather than as accurate descriptions of the individuals with whom we are working. And yet, although professionals know that these labels never fully describe individuals, they are often bandied around as if they do.

Labels are not value-free. They carry with them expectations of behaviour. They affect other people's perceptions, expectations and responses — often a range of stereotypes that pre-define an individual with that label. In explaining them, we make links to a variety of other labels.

Labelling is done to people by those in power

In this area of work there are many people and professions involved, including education, social work, nursing, psychiatry and psychology. Perhaps as a result of this, the debates around language and labels tend to be further confused by the various parties competing for 'naming rights'.

Labelling is nearly always done by those in power, and can be thought of as an exercise in establishing and imposing control. Professionals attach labels to individuals and groups for administrative purposes (Rowley, 2007). Although they may not like to think of themselves in this way, people who work in direct care and support services are members of a powerful social group. For this reason alone, social work and other allied professionals need to be sensitive to the language they and their colleagues use (McLimons, 2007).

Sharing power as a basis for partnership

By offering some resistance to these powerful labelling processes, self-advocates and their allies can influence the public perception of people with learning disabilities. This can have a positive effect on attempts at inclusion (McLimons, 2007).

At the heart of any ethical consideration of these issues is the degree to which individuals involved engage in the debate. The views and contributions of self-advocacy leaders are sometimes rejected by powerful professionals who openly declare that they 'don't really have learning difficulties' and should not be listened to because they are not 'representative of people with real learning difficulties'.

Language and definitions used in UK laws

Different individuals, groups, professional disciplines and non-professional alliances understand the terms 'learning disability' or 'learning difficulty' (or, for that matter, 'intellectual disability' or 'developmental disability') differently. Whatever words are ultimately decided to use, there will still be problems. In the education sector, for example, 'learning difficulty' is used to describe people with educational difficulties, such as children with dyslexia.

'Learning disability', 'learning difficulty' or other related terms appear in a wide range of legislation:

- community care
- mental health
- criminal justice

- local government
- benefits
- child care and family.

Within these contexts, *similar words* may be used with *different definitions*. It is therefore important to clarify the specific context in which any classification occurs, and to remember that classification in one particular context does not imply classification in any other (BPS Professional Affairs Board, 2000).

The main term used in both Scottish and English law and guidance is 'learning disability'. For example, both *The same as you?* (Scottish Government, 2000) and the *Health Needs Assessment report* (NHS Scotland, 2004) use the following definition – learning disability is a significant, life-long experience that has three components:

- reduced ability to understand new or complex information or to learn new skills (in global rather than specific areas);
- reduced ability to cope independently;
- onset before adulthood (before the age of 18), with a lasting effect on the individual's development.

While the Department of Health in England (DH, 2001a) describes the components of 'learning disability' as:

- significantly reduced ability to understand new or complex information, to learn new skills;
- reduced ability to cope independently which starts before adulthood with lasting effects on development.

All three criteria noted in the Scottish definition must be met for a person to be considered by the British Psychological Society to have a learning disability (BPS Professional Affairs Board, 2000). While considering this definition, it is of course essential to always consider that everyone is an individual, and will have individual needs, preferences and ambitions (NHS Scotland, 2004).

This definition is widely used within adult services. Within services for children, the broader terms of 'learning difficulties' and 'special needs' are commonly used. These encompass a wider range of children who require support for learning for any reason, including specific developmental disorders such as dyslexia, problems with speech and language, or sensory impairments. Children with such needs do not often have associated learning disabilities as defined above, although they may require support for learning in specific, rather than global, aspects (NHS Scotland, 2004).

Additionally, in Scotland, people on the autism spectrum were included in *The same as you?* (Scottish Government, 2000), to ensure that there was no omission of people who wished to access a service in order to have their needs met. However, a proportion of people on the autism spectrum do not have significant learning disabilities.

Gunn (1996, cited in BPS Professional Affairs Board, 2000, p 23) notes: 'It is important to understand the definitions used in each Act and to remember that these terms have a specific legal meaning which may not be the same as the meanings given to them in general or professional conversation.' Clarity of definition is therefore important when considering the needs of people who use a range of inter-related services, for example, at times of transition.

Labels as a passport to access services

Labels can facilitate or hamper the lives of people with learning difficulties. There is a tension between the need to acquire a label as a passport to support and resources, and the need to avoid being labelled in order to have a chance of being viewed as the same as everyone else.

Effectively, many people and their families have to choose between:

- accepting labels that can help them gain access to specialist support – at the cost of diminished roles and rights;
- rejecting those labels in order to gain greater citizenship rights – even at the cost of diminished access to support that could help them to live better lives.

As part of the process of creating change, language must not only be persuasive, but it must also reduce the likelihood of misinterpretation, and reflect the views of those it is applied to.

Language on its own is not enough to create change, but it is the linchpin through which action for change is formulated and evaluated. It needs to keep moving forward, as part of a process of reflection and action.

Even if we do not make changes in the language we use at a legal or policy level, we can be committed to keeping the process more human by being respectful in our written and spoken descriptions of people. Somewhere between the extremes of 'political correctness' and the vagueness of everyday communication we must find forms of address that protect people who use services and professional staff, while simultaneously promoting a culture of mutual respect.

The report, *A life like no other* (Healthcare Commission, 2008), broke new ground in how it addressed this issue. The Healthcare Commission chose to use the term 'learning difficulties' rather than 'learning disabilities'. It stated:

> We are well aware of the range of debates around terminology that have taken place over a number of years, but our reason here is simple. Whenever we consulted with people with learning difficulties during the audit it was clear to us that this was the term they preferred. Its use here is therefore a reflection of the inclusive nature of the process we followed.... In this report when we refer to people with learning difficulties we are referring to the group of people that healthcare services refer to as people with learning disabilities. (Healthcare Commission, 2008, p 12)

Although our personal preference would be to take a similar approach to that taken by the Healthcare Commission, and to use the term 'people with learning difficulties' to mean what healthcare and social work services usually refer to as 'people with learning disabilities', we accept that at present the predominant term in all the constituent policy documentation in the UK is 'learning disabilities'. We have therefore used both 'learning difficulties' and 'learning disabilities' in this book, depending on the context.

Conclusion

Overall, things have got better. Over the last few decades we have moved from institutionalisation to the notion of full citizenship, but the change process is not clean and linear. For example:

- Some people with learning disabilities are being listened to, being really involved, and are being influential ...

    but

- some people with learning disabilities are being ignored, with their human rights disregarded and abused.

- There are many examples of good and innovative practice ...

    but

- we have also seen the emergence of bad practice and the continuing of poor and even abusive practice in essentially invisible supported living and residential service settings.

- Human rights legislation and international accords formally protect the rights of people with learning difficulties ...

    but

- the same human rights legislation is not used to challenge circumstances where practice that appears abusive is known to occur.

- The laws of the UK have become more supportive of the visions outlined in the aspirational policy documents, such as *The same as you?*, *The keys to life*, *Valuing People* and *Valuing People Now* ...

  but

- some laws have not yet been fully implemented.

- Wider generic policy changes have been implemented that are congruent with the forward-looking ideas emerging in services for people with learning difficulties ...

  but

- there are many examples of policies that undermine the position of people with learning difficulties (for example, work capability assessments), and there are examples of bad interpretation of universalism as a cynical exercise in reducing specialist service costs.

Notes

[1] We are grateful to our friend and colleague, Gavin Fairbairn, for these examples, and for helping to develop our thinking about personhood and people with learning difficulties.

[2] See www.latentexistence.me.uk/whats-the-difference-between-1930s-germany-and-modern-day-britain/

[3] See www.latentexistence.me.uk/whats-the-difference-between-1930s-germany-and-modern-day-britain/

[4] In fact, in Scotland the debate is so old that it is enshrined in an Act of 1475 in the old Scots tongue (Brieves of Idiotry, James III p 8 c 66), which distinguishes between 'idiots', 'fools' and 'furious persons'.

2 Looking back: what can we learn from the past?

In this chapter we review some of the kinds of negative life experiences that people with learning disabilities have had to endure, and we reinforce our belief that there continues to be a risk that institutional practices may present themselves in new guises in the present time. We believe that re-visiting the past is necessary to prevent re-invention and re-assertion of these abusive ideas and practices.

History repeats itself – The Winterbourne View hospital scandal

The first years of the new millennium were a defining period in the history of services for people with learning disabilities. The closure during these years of the few remaining NHS long-stay 'mental handicap' hospitals, many of which were built in Victorian times, signalled a new era of optimism characterised by services that aspired to be socially inclusive rather than exclude people hitherto 'warehoused' in such institutions – out of sight and out of mind. These closures drew a line in the sand – never again were disabled people who were vulnerable to be treated as less than human and subject to the scandalous practices of the 1960s and 1970s that had taken root in these institutions and that had led to their ultimate closure (Martin, 1984; Stanley et al, 1999; Butler and Drakeford, 2005). So for people with learning difficulties, their families and professionals alike, the television *Panorama* programme about Winterbourne View hospital was more than shocking; it was a body blow that 'recalled the endemic abuses which are known to have existed in the long-stay hospitals of the past' (cited in Flynn, 2012, p 14).

'Undercover care: The abuse exposed', *Panorama,* **BBC One, 31 May 2011**

This programme shocked the nation.

[Secretly filmed] BBC One's *Panorama* showed patients at [Winterbourne View hospital] near Bristol being slapped and restrained under chairs, having their hair pulled and being held down as medication was forced into their mouths. (Cafe, 2012)

During five weeks spent filming undercover, *Panorama*'s reporter captured footage of some of the hospital's most vulnerable patients (with severe learning disabilities and autism) being repeatedly pinned down, slapped, dragged into showers while fully clothed, taunted and teased and showed one senior care worker at Winterbourne View asking a patient whether they wanted him to get a "cheese grater and grate your face off?" (Cafe, 2012).

[A clinical psychologist] ... labelled some of the examples seen on film "torture".... The hospital's owners, Castlebeck, have apologised and suspended 13 employees. (BBC News, 2011)

Of the 11 individuals subsequently prosecuted, five received custodial sentences and six received suspended sentences. Winterbourne View was later closed down. In March 2013 Castlebeck, owners of Winterbourne View, went into administration.

Moving on from institutions and institutional practices

In this section we take a brief look at the history and discrediting of institutional care for people with learning difficulties, with a view to understanding just how 'devastating' the 'scandal that unfolded at Winterbourne View' (DH, 2012b, ministerial foreword) was in the context of a presumed modernised and humane service system. This 'scandal' constitutes a reminder for professionals as well as politicians, of how fragile the apparent progress of the last 50 years can be in the face of persistent and discredited service models, and negative attitudes to people with learning disabilities.

Notwithstanding the events at Winterbourne View, it is fair to argue that the current professional context in which social workers set out to support people with learning difficulties has undergone a transformation during the last hundred years (Brignell, 2010). Some of these changes reflect broad societal changes in attitudes towards a whole range of minority groups who are seen to be 'on the margins' of society, including people with learning difficulties. They also reflect changing views on social responsibility with regard to welfare and citizenship, which can be discerned in the development of universal services such as pensions, education and a national health service, which have come to be seen as a benchmark for how industrialised and civilised societies provide for their people.

Essentially, the story of learning disability services over the last 150 years is one of service and practice evolution: from the creation of 'asylums' to support and 'rehabilitate' people who might be seen as casualties of the Industrial Revolution; to institutions and hospitals whose founding positive inspiration dissipated and decayed in the wake of the moral panic of eugenics; to the optimism of new models for community living based on the rights of individuals to be included in society and to participate fully. By way of shorthand, this evolution is often referred to as 'deinstitutionalisation', particularly in relation to hospital closure and the redevelopment of larger residential units into smaller-scale accommodation.

However, in addition to deinstitutionalisation and modernisation, there has also been an aspiration for 'transformational change' in services, from segregated Victorian institutions, to not only community-based support models, but also to ones that 'empower people' (Rowley, 2008). A comparison of the titles of two major government policy documents relating to learning disabilities illustrates the ideological journey travelled: from *Better Services*, in the words of the 1971 White Paper (DH, 1971), to *Valuing People* in 2001 (DH, 2001a). In other words, this is a journey that started with improving professional services to one that is now person-centred rather than service-led, and embraces user-defined outcomes (Miller, 2012) to achieve not only a better quality of life, but also a 'good life' (Etmanski, 2000; Johnson et al, 2010).

In broad terms, it is a good news story. Indeed, UK policies have been described as 'remarkably progressive' and as 'a source of envy' in other countries (Greig, 2008). While there may be gaps between aspiration and reality (see Whitehead, 2008), the policy intent of increasing user choice and control is explicit. That said, and despite the notable trends from deinstitutionalisation to inclusion, progress cannot necessarily be assumed to be linear, and might be better described as an 'ebb and flow'. The abuse of people with learning difficulties by service professionals at Winterbourne View, as described above, bears testimony to this.

In this chapter we explore the resilience of outdated service models despite advances in contemporary social policies and the underpinning legislation. A key note of caution that we hope readers will draw from this text is that practitioners would be wise to remain alert to the resurgence of discredited models and practice under another guise. The present period of austerity and welfare cutbacks may compound the pressure to resurrect such congregated and segregated service solutions in the name of economies of scale.

Table 2.1 draws attention to how seams of service thinking and provision can co-exist over time, even though some may go underground, and some become more prominent than others at different times. The key policy trends since the creation of the Victorian institutions are organised roughly along chronological timelines, but overlapping is evident. These themes are characterised as:

- containment and menace
- reform and scandals
- deinstitutionalisation
- community-based initiatives
- co-existence and inclusion
- community care, mainstreaming and inclusion
- risk and protection
- personalisation
- austerity.

Table 2.1: Competing paradigms

	1900-60s	1970s	1980s	1990s	2000s	2010s
Containment and menace	➡	➡			➡	➡
Reforms and scandal		➡	➡			➡
De-institutionalisation		➡	➡	➡	➡	
Community-based initiatives		➡	➡			
Co-existence and inclusion				➡	➡	
Community care, mainstreaming and inclusion				➡	➡	➡
Risk and protection			➡	➡	➡	➡
Personalisation		➡	➡	➡	➡	➡
Austerity			➡		➡	➡

Before moving on to a discussion of these trends as discrete items, it is worth noting the following points on the interaction between the various timelines:

■ *Institutional resilience:* the policies of segregation and containment of people with learning disabilities that characterised the early part of the 19th century persisted under the umbrella of specialist segregated services, both medical and social, until the scandals of the 1960s and 1970s, when policies of deinstitutionalisation emerged. Despite over two decades of community care policies, ideas of menace and lack of human worth have resurfaced since the new millennium in the shape of institutional models such as Winterbourne View (Flynn, 2012), scandals in other mental health and general health resources, and reports of widespread hate crime and its tragic consequences (Gravell, 2012).

■ *Deinstitutionalisation:* the process that started in the 1970s never reached completion as intended, and continues to this day. Bearing in mind the history of scandals and hospital closure policies, the government's response to the Winterbourne serious case review report (DH, 2012b) is ironic to say the least. The Minister for Social Care announced that there was to be a 'dramatic reduction' in the number of people with learning difficulties kept in hospitals; that all placements were to be reviewed within one year, and all those 'inappropriately' placed would be transferred to community-based services by the following year (Rose, 2012). As history makes clear, this is not the first time that such government assurance has been made.

■ *Mini-institutions:* although the NHS long-stay 'mental handicap' hospitals closed, arguments about whether any hospital beds should be retained as assessment and forensic beds were commonplace. Many of the community health and social care-based resources that were developed bore more of a resemblance to mini-institutions in the community than homes; they may have been on a domestic scale, but were not domestic in nature.

■ *In the community, but not of the community:* community care and inclusion initiatives have had notable successes – for example, see *An ordinary life* (King's Fund, 1980) and the *All Wales Strategy for the development of services for mentally handicapped people* (Welsh Office, 1983) – but institutional thinking has not been left behind. The increasing complexity of day centres attempting to be all things to all people illustrates this point well. Most people using these centres want jobs, but most spend their time in the centres, with occasional excursions into the community on segregated activities. This is beginning to change as local authorities are closing down centres in favour of dispersed social activities and voluntary work in mainstream resources, but supported employment has remained on the periphery of options in adult services.

■ *Abuse (risk and protection):* it took the discrediting of eugenics thinking and the emergence of minority rights for the hospital 'scandals' to be conceptualised within the risk and protection framework that was already well established in relation to children. It seems likely that assumptions were made that the risks of institutional abuse and lack of protection would fall away as community living took hold. Legislation was passed and policy developed that modernised ideas about what was meant by 'capacity', strengthening the rights of vulnerable individuals to be involved in decision making and planning about their lives and the support required. However, independent and supported living in the community has proved to carry its own risks of financial and personal abuse – at times life-threatening, as in the case of Steven Hoskin, who was murdered in a brutal and callous way by two of his 'friends' in the town where he lived (Flynn, 2007). This, in turn, has led to protective legislation and more robust guidelines, enabling professionals to work in partnership and to intervene in the lives of adults at risk of harm (DH, 2009b).

■ *Personalisation:* this is the current policy buzz word for placing people at the centre of planning services and support, and putting them in control of their lives. Like other trends here, its history stretches back to the 1990s, when the disability movement campaigned for 'direct payments', so that people could employ personal assistants (PAs) to support their independent living. Its success has been patchy as eligibility is narrow, professionals less than well informed, and the requirements of being an employer are onerous. Initiatives such as In Control and self-directed support aim to make 'individual budgets' (Community Care, 2007) more widely available over a wider range of service arrangements, and in Scotland, self-directed support has become the default option for those eligible for community care (Scottish Government, 2013). The advent of the widespread use of self-directed support has properly increased concerns about exposure to abuse of vulnerable adults living in the community (Lymbery and Morley, 2012), but also, and worryingly, the prospect of risk-averse health and social care services and practitioners placing constraints on the activities and aspirations of disabled people.

■ *Austerity:* whether current policy aspirations for independence, choice and inclusion can be fulfilled in a period of unparalleled reductions in welfare benefits and local authority services remains to be seen. Only serious optimists would imagine that such policies could survive better than the deinistitutionalising ones in the 1970s that were affected by the oil crises of the time. Debates about economies of scale and efficiency will undoubtedly resurface, bringing with them pressures to resurrect congregated services and/or increased expectations on family care.

Containment

The main contemporary disability policy documents in England, Wales and Scotland, respectively – *Valuing People* (DH, 2001a) and *Valuing People Now* (2009, 2011); the *All Wales Strategy for the development of services for mentally handicapped people* and *Associated guidance* (Welsh Office, 1983, 1984), and *Fulfilling the promises* (National Assembly for Wales, 2001); and *The same as you?* (Scottish Executive, 2000) and *The keys to life* (Scottish Government, 2013) – use the language of rights, independence, choice and inclusion to set the agenda. In these documents we read that people with learning difficulties can lead 'rewarding lives' in a society where everyone is 'valued' (DH, 2001a, Prime Minister's foreword), leading 'normal lives' where services provide 'support' (Scottish Government, 2000, ministerial foreword).

This is a very different discourse from a hundred years ago when the Mental Deficiency Act 1913 was written in terms of 'idiots', 'imbeciles' and the 'feeble-minded', and set out to prevent the 'racial disaster of feeblemindedness' (Wood Committee, 1929) through certification and segregation in colonies. Concerns about the loss of liberty expressed in parliamentary debate at the time were overwhelmed by the feared consequences of failing, in the words of the Home Secretary, Winston Churchill, to cut off this 'stream of madness' that was thought to hold 'disastrous consequences for the entire community' (Churchill, 1913; Wormald and Wormald, 1914).

The 1913 Act and the eugenics movement, with its fear of 'degeneracy in the nation's gene pool', set legislation and policy in the direction of 'containment' for the next 50 years. People with learning difficulties were either 'certified' and institutionalised in 'colonies' away from families and communities, or, if they were living with families and offered services at all, they were segregated within 'special' services, and scant attention was paid to enhancing their life opportunities. The advice from professionals, reported historically by parents following the birth of a disabled child, was 'to send them away and have another baby'. Furthermore, it was not until the Mental Health Act 1959 that 'decertification' was enacted, with a distinction between 'mental illness' and 'mental handicap' – the term that replaced the perceived stigmatising terminology of 'idiocy'.

Recently trained professionals may not have experienced the Victorian institutions that characterised services through much of the last century, so in order to appreciate the power and the injustice of these institutional experiences, it is important to read some of the autobiographical material that is now available.

Think spot

When were you born? In England in 1976 50,000 people were in institutions, and 4,000 by the year 2000. The last NHS 'mental handicap' hospitals mostly closed in 2006.

>   Did any of the people with learning difficulties whom you know live in such institutions?
>   What do you know about their experience?
>   Make a point of selecting and studying one piece of autobiographical or biographical material from the following:

> > Blatt, B. and Kaplan, F. (1974) *Christmas in purgatory: A photographic essay on mental retardation*, Boston, MA: Allyn & Bacon (www.disabilitymuseum.org/lib/docs/1782card.htm).

> > Atkinson, D. and Williams, F. (1990) *Know me as I am*, London: Hodder Education.

> > Ingham, N. (1999) *Gogarburn lives*, Edinburgh: Living Memory Association (www.livingmemory.org.uk/shop.html).

> > Mitchell, D., Traustadóttir, R., Chapman, R., Townson, L., Ingham, N. and Ledger, S. (2006) *Exploring experiences of advocacy by people with learning disabilities: Testimonies of resistance*, London: Jessica Kingsley Publishers.

On the creation of the NHS in 1948, the colonies were re-labelled as wards in the NHS 'mental handicap' hospitals. Most people with learning difficulties have always lived with their families (Mencap, 2000), but for those unable to do so, the development of the NHS heralded the possibility of more liberal and informed treatment. However, with its emphasis on sickness, although less toxic than the assumptions of degeneracy associated with eugenics, also consolidated the pre-eminence of the medical model underpinning services, with an emphasis on diagnosis and pathology.

Over time, the medical model increasingly became a source of contention and debate, and its individual deficit explanations were set against arguments based on the social model of understanding disability (Oliver, 1983), which emphasises the structural barriers to inclusion within society faced by people with disabilities. But the medical model created its own narrow worldview that treatment by experts was the solution. It effectively continued to draw attention to abnormality rather than personhood, and reinforced the search for technical and professional solutions to people's problems without creating alliances with community resources, family networks, and drawing on the strengths of the individuals themselves.

The creation of inward-looking services, effectively self-contained communities from cradle to grave, came to be embodied in the dehumanising, self-perpetuating systems so persuasively analysed in Goffman's (1961) book *Asylums*, and discussed in the next section. Here it can be seen how the intention to improve services through more humane hospital treatment, as opposed to the indignities of the workhouse, contained the seeds of longer-term problems, of new institutional patterns, and the limitation of individual deficit models.

Reform and the deinstitutionalisation agenda

Any optimism for improved services and lives supported by the NHS had come under attack by the end of the 1960s, with 18 inquiries in all into scandals at 'mental handicap' hospitals (see Martin, 1984). In the wake of these scandals, such as those at Ely (DHSS, 1969) and South Ockendon (DHSS, 1974), which brought to the attention of a shocked public the mistreatment and abuse of patients in these hospitals, the White Paper *Better services for the mentally handicapped* (DH, 1971) began to rewrite the policy script, establishing targets for the development of services in the community. However, in effect, what was envisaged by the White Paper was a continuum of care in which the balance of care shifted from hospital to community, but *not the basic premise* that some people would always need institutionalised hospital care – in effect, that they would be 'hospital-dependent'.

While the Mental Deficiency Act 1913 had notably introduced compulsory detention in hospital uniquely on the grounds of disability, it did also give local authorities 'enabling' powers to develop resources for occupation, training and supervision for 'defectives living in the community' (Mental Deficiency Act 1913). The resources developed were on a small scale and were called occupation centres, junior and senior (children with learning disabilities did not have the right to education in the UK until 1978; see Warnock, 1978). Progress in developing these centres was slow – there were only 4,000 places across the country by 1939 (National Development Group, 1977), with a modest expansion to 24,537 by the 1960s (Taylor and Taylor, 1986). Nonetheless, most local authorities had developed some adult training centres (ATCs) by the time the-then Ministry of Health (1968) published its model of good practice for ATCs. The day centre model has proved very resilient by changing its shape and intentions, and it is only since 2000 that centres have begun to close and refocus their efforts by supporting people with learning difficulties to use mainstream resources.

Co-existence and inclusion: an 'ordinary life'

Implementation of the reforms was cautious, and although hospitals began to be run down, with some people moving out, few were fully closed, and community accommodation in the 1970s and 1980s still largely took the form of hostels for eight to 20 people. For those individuals living with their own families, and especially those with ageing parents, residential homes for 25–30 people were developed.

In addition to the slow progress towards the targets set for increasing day service provision over a period of 20 years, the number of places in the community in social education centres or ATCs effectively doubled to 47,464 (Taylor and Taylor, 1986). These day centres pursued not only multiple objectives, but also sometimes conflicting ones:

■ social contact and 'occupation' for some service users
■ education and work training options for others
■ safe and reliable respite for families
■ manageability for staff, as numbers swelled.

In the meantime, this diversification of activities did little to address the aspirations of between 65 per cent and (later) 80 per cent (Steele, 1991; Glenn and Lyons, 1996) of service users who repeatedly said that they wanted jobs.

In response to the development of self-contained special needs units for people with profound difficulties within day centres, family pressure groups emerged to campaign for local and inclusive services for their young people irrespective of the complexity or severity of their disabilities.[1]

It became clear that rather than making lasting connections within the community, people in centres were 'making excursions' into the community from a service base that remained segregated, but with greater degrees of refinement in the activities undertaken. Day centres are a further example of the resilience of service structures in the face of pressure for change. In this case, day centres diversified internally, and even developed porous boundaries, but the basic model persisted.

The single most radical piece of UK policy concerning the support of people with learning difficulties up to the millennium emerged in Wales. While it drew on the policy changes outlined in the English White Paper (DH, 1971), much of its inspiration was drawn from a cluster of ideas pivotally developed by Wolfensberger (1972) under the rubric of 'normalisation' (see Chapter Three). The *All Wales Strategy for the development of services for mentally handicapped people* (Welsh Office, 1983) was an ambitious plan for what we now call 'total system change'. This was an early effort by government to achieve whole systemic 'model coherence', but it was not one that was emulated across the UK.

The *All Wales Strategy* adhered to three principles:

■ able to access to community-based services
■ being treated as an individual
■ being given additional support to maximise individual potential.

In the light of current initiatives, such as personalisation and self-directed support, which aim to give individuals greater control over the services they receive through personal budgets in lieu of services, and to promote community capacity building, the Welsh strategy appears to have been well ahead of its time. One reason why it was uniquely successful at the time was the allocation of additional new funds, £26 million per annum, which were made available by the Welsh Office over a 10-year period in order to create local comprehensive services with multi-disciplinary community mental handicap teams. Funding for new services was explicitly tied to meeting the three principles, and at the time, amounted to a significant departure in UK policy implementation.

Simultaneously, a radical shift, sometimes referred to as a paradigm shift, was gaining traction throughout the UK based on the work of the King's Fund's 1980 Ordinary Life Programme, and of Wolfensberger's (1972) 'principles of normalization', which evolved into what he called 'social role valorisation' (SRV), and was later reworked by O'Brien (1987) to constitute a 'framework for accomplishment'. (These theoretical underpinnings are discussed in more detail in Chapter Three.)

Community care, mainstreaming and inclusion

Community care officially came of age with the enactment of the Community Care Acts in all four jurisdictions of the UK in the 1990s, such as the NHS and Community Care Act 1990. Together with a raft of associated legislation that followed,[2] these Acts can be seen as the most comprehensive pieces of legislation to drive forward the reforming and deinstitutionalising initiatives of the previous 30 years.

In policy and practice terms, it is also the period during which inclusion, not simply presence, in the community began to emerge as a significant service narrative. The legislation made an explicit presumption in favour of community-based provision over institutional care, stating that care should be planned collaboratively with service users and their carers in an individually tailored way, thereby giving them legitimacy to be involved in the process of planning and choosing their care. Essentially, it offered the potential for people, including those with complex support needs, to create lifestyles in tune with their particular needs and preferences in an inclusive manner. However, the policies set out in the legislation contained a number of tensions – political and professional – that created conflicting agendas with which social workers have struggled ever since.

The tensions arising from the political agenda behind the Acts arose from the promotion of a quasi-market economy in welfare, the so-called 'mixed economy of care' (Le Grand, 1991; Means et al, 2002). The assumption was that this would deliver greater effectiveness and efficiency by:

- limiting local authorities to commissioning services from the independent sector rather than providing those services;
- targeting services at those in *greatest* need through care management, creating packages of care to support individuals living in their own homes rather than in expensive residential care.

From a professional point of view, there was much that was positive about the legislation, which reflected the importance of:

- enabling choice of services and service provider, and promoting the consultation and empowerment of service users and carers in decisions about future plans through care management and packages of care that were individually tailored rather than service-led;
- seeking to provide support and 'care' for people in situ in the community.

On the less positive side, tensions arose from the practice consequences for local authority social workers who became assessors for and commissioners of services rather than providing direct, ongoing support to individuals. Some commentators have argued that this led to managerialist practices within local authorities, which have subsequently 'deprofessionalised' social work (Postle, 2002; Jordan, 2004; Webb, 2006; Ferguson, 2007).

In relation to people with learning difficulties and the increasingly long drawn-out process of closing hospital accommodation, specific central government provisions were made for 'bridging funding' – that is, double funding, allowing hospital provision to be run down gradually as community accommodation was expanded. This funding ran in tandem with the major initiatives mentioned earlier – *Valuing People* (DH, 2001a) and *The same as you?* (Scottish Government, 2000) – and was critical to the success in finally closing the hospitals in the following decade up to 2010.

As originally conceived (Challis and Davies, 1986), care management could have provided a framework, and direct payments the means, for people with learning difficulties to consider employment alternatives to day centre attendance by employing PAs to support them in the workplace as well as in the home. However, it became bogged down in bureaucratic and managerialist gate-keeping activity, partly in response to reduced resources, but also in response to risk-averse practices in local authorities. This early attempt to 'transform' services through greater choice in community-based service provision and greater service user control brought into sharp focus the question of informed decision making and risk taking.

Choice and risk: striking a balance between autonomy and protection

With this intention to maximise self-determination and individual control over matters that centrally affect the lives of service users, and with increasing community presence, choices and freedoms, has come a new concern about risks of exploitation – financial, sexual or physical – and more generally, abuse in the form of bullying and harassment.

While it is well documented that the institutions of the past presented their own risks (Martin, 1984; Stanley et al, 1999; Butler and Drakeford, 2003), solutions were available to services to intervene protectively once the abuse was recognised. Within the community, particularly with regard to adults living on their own, such intervention is complex, legally and procedurally, and requires sophisticated skills and understanding. However, legislation and policy guidance has now been modernised and permits professional intervention in the lives of adults who do not have the capacity to make decisions for themselves. (A detailed discussion of this legislation can be found later, in Chapter Nine.) These measures relating to capacity and compulsory measures require assessment and intervention to pay attention to 'least restrictive' provisions, to the individual's previous known preferences, and to the views of their carers.

The wider societal concern with risk assessment and management has significant implications for social workers taking protective measures, and also brings with it responsibilities not to generate a 'risk-averse' climate of practice.

Finally, the most recent evolution of policy that exemplifies this tension between autonomy and protection is the emergence of personalisation and self-directed support.

Personalisation

Personalisation is not a new idea in policy or practice terms, having its antecedents in direct payments and in person-centred planning (Glasby and Littlechild, 2009; Hunter et al, 2012a). So individualised funding is one aspect of personalisation, but has become the pre-eminent focus in policy terms.

The foundations were laid in the 1990s for what is now termed 'self-directed support' through the Community Care (Direct Payments) Act 1996. This allows local authorities to provide eligible users with money – direct payments – rather than services, so that individuals can buy their own services ('cash for care'), often through employing their own PAs. This initiative built on the Independent Living Fund (ILF), which was created in response to the campaigning of disability activists in the independent living movement and those who developed the social model of disability (see Chapter Three).

While the introduction of direct payments constituted an unparalleled attempt to give service users power and control over their lives, over how they were supported and by whom, the outcomes have been disappointing. Research consistently highlights:

■ the limited uptake of direct payments;
■ the bureaucratic and 'red-tape' disincentives for service users becoming employers and for professionals who have been resistant to change;
■ the limited spread of direct payments across service user groups, people with physical disabilities being the most likely to use them (Witcher et al, 2000; Ridley and Jones, 2002; Scourfield, 2007; Ridley et al, 2011).

As *Community Care* magazine notes (2007), the numbers of direct payments made in 2011–12 were up from 4,392 in the previous year to 5,409, but were insignificant compared with the 63,485 people receiving home care in the same period. Also, the direct payments allocated tend to reflect individual need as assessed by professionals, usually social workers.

Nonetheless, the development of direct payments and the modernisation of a 'new script for public services' (Leadbeater, 2004) did set the scene for the introduction of personal budgets, which has culminated in major legislation in the shape of the Health and Social Care Act 2012 and the Social Care (Self-directed Support) (Scotland) Act 2013.

Notably, there has been an additional and pioneering strand in the development of personalised funding and support with regard to people with learning difficulties through the In Control initiative (Poll et al, 2006). The focus here is broader than the employment of a PA – with its focus on outcomes rather than needs, it promotes a wider range of activities, drawing more intentionally on community resources. Central to the self-directed support model is that:

■ it really helps people to be in control of their support if they know how much money they can spend on it;
■ a related resource allocation system (RAS) is available to aid transparency and fairness;
■ self-assessment should be part of the process;
■ assessment should be 'outcome'-focused[3] rather than need and service-focused (Miller, 2012);
■ tracking expenditure and enhancing security may be less burdensome than under the direct payments model (CIPFA, 2007).

In Control has had a major impact on the development of personalisation and personal budgets, especially in England (see Glendinning et al, 2008). Some key aspects are summarised below.

> With the In Control initiative, people who are entitled to support make their own initial determination of their needs using self-assessment, with a seven-step model to being in control (see www.in-control.org.uk).
>
> A funding model known as the RAS, that seems fair and reasonable to meet people's needs, is developed locally. Individuals have a clear indication of their entitlement and are offered a choice of managing the funding themselves, or through:
>
> - payment to a third party
> - payment to a trust
> - payment to an organisation, or
> - payment to an Individual Support Fund.
>
> Planning in this self-directed support model is individualised, with help available for service users to make creative use of the community resources if they wish to plan their own support.

Self-directed support has been described as an evolving concept that is often confused with direct payments (Ridley et al, 2011). However, as the Social Care (Self-directed Support) (Scotland) Act 2013 makes clear, it is but one of four options, alongside:

- Individual Support Funds, where local authorities contract with providers on an individual's behalf;
- the local authority selecting appropriate support; or
- a mixture of all these options.

There has been favourable service user feedback on the use of personal budgets and their ability to deliver improved services (see, for example, *Community Care*, 2007). However, one of the main protagonists of the In Control initiative has recently apologised for the 'perversions' in implementation that have emerged under the pressure of local authority cutbacks (Duffy, 2012). Duffy observes that a number of complications have arisen that threaten to undermine its enabling aspirations. He acknowledges that RAS, a process meant to be enabling and transparent, has become complex and procedural in practice, due, in his view, to lack of senior management trust in frontline worker judgement. Support plans were intended to be the professional underpinning of the service user's self-assessment in order to meet the legal requirements for a professional community care assessment, but have been reported as being used to constrain rather than liberate planning.

These pressures were further exacerbated in England by setting a target date of April 2013 for all of those eligible to be in receipt of an individual budget (later reduced to 70 per cent). Further, *Community Care* magazine's 2012 survey on the 'state of personalisation' reported that 82 per cent of professionals said that their paperwork had increased as councils require panels rather than social workers to sign off support plans (*Community Care*, 2007).

Ironically, the emergence of such constraints on the original vision was witnessed when care management was introduced, with the result that the privileging of service user choice and the devolution of care budgets to frontline workers and their seniors never took root. It seems that once again professional determination by social workers to counter some of the trends undermining personalisation and to weather the challenge of national implementation in a climate of austerity is in danger of being diluted. The other major challenge to the roll-out of personalisation in the context of budgetary cuts and reductions in services is the issue of risk and risk taking.

Personalisation, risk and austerity

With personalisation comes an adult safeguarding concern about how adults who might be deemed 'at risk of harm' are supported and protected (SCIE, 2010; Hunter et al, 2012a). The inherent tension between matters of empowerment and protection has resulted in twin-tracking these policies rather than an intersection in implementation. Both English and Scottish studies have found little awareness in the professionals responsible for implementing self-directed support of the implications for adult support and protection concerns, commenting that lead officers for adult safeguarding seem to be 'bystanders' in the implementation of self-directed support, with few system or practice linkages between the two strands of activity (Manthorpe et al, 2009; Hunter et al, 2012b).

This carries the obvious hazard of retrenchment from personalisation in the face of 'scandals' and 'tragedies' that are inevitable, as there is no such thing as a risk-free life for anyone with or without disabilities. Adding to the mix, the greatest retrenchment in public service finance since the Depression in the UK (Portes and Reed, 2014) and in Europe, for example the Netherlands (DAA News Network, 2011), creates a strong possibility that more segregated and congregated services, which have the appearance of greater safety and economies of scale in their favour, will resurface. As noted elsewhere (Hunter et al, 2012a), cuts in public sending will occur irrespective of the care model in place, but local authorities may be tempted to use self-directed support as a vehicle for cuts, thereby potentially discrediting the model before it has really had time to gather momentum (Bovaird and Loeffler, 2012).

Conclusion

This brief 'look back' over the history of policy evolution and service development shows how positive initiatives to promote a better life as well as better services for people with learning difficulties can turn sour and deteriorate, so that attempts to improve the quality of their lives end up compounding the problems they set out to resolve.

The development of day services is a prime example of a service that set out to support individuals in the community, but which did so in a way that kept them separate and largely segregated from that community. The sad events at Winterbourne Hospital show how some models viewed as antiquated and even inhumane simply go underground to resurface in due course, and continue to do so. Other models lose their way under pressure from the economic climate of the day. While care management reflected a particular ideological and political stance of the-then government in the early 1990s, it responded to the economic restrictions of the time in a bureaucratic and ultimately self-defeating way. The same potential pitfall faces the implementation of self-directed support at a time when the impact of cuts in public sending matches that of cuts during the Great Depression.

For these reasons, social workers cannot afford to be complacent that transformational change will occur because government policies and ideologies have changed, that discredited models have been permanently laid to rest, and that considerable professional and personal commitment will not continue to be required to ensure that change is sustained. Alliances with like-minded professionals and politicians are understood, but working alongside service users is just beginning to be understood. Service users and their families are in for the long haul; social workers would do well to join them.

The next chapter briefly elaborates the key theoretical ideas underpinning these trends, in particular those of normalisation and SRV, the 'five accomplishments' and the social model of disability, concluding with some brief reflections on the impact on practice.

Notes
[1] See www.inclusionalliance.org.uk/index.html?pid=16

[2] The Carers (Recognition and Services) Act 1995, the Community Care (Direct Payments) Act 1996 and the Community Care and Health (Scotland) Act 2002.

[3] See www.jitscotland.co.uk

3 Underlying conceptual frameworks

In this chapter we set out some of the key conceptual frameworks that have underpinned and informed the development of legislation, policy and practice in supporting people with learning difficulties.

We examine the ways in which they have assisted practitioners and providers by providing a critique or critical response to the negative experiences of people with learning difficulties using services. In particular, we look at:

- normalisation/social role valorisation (SRV)
- the framework for accomplishment (the five accomplishments)
- the social model of disability
- personalisation
- co-production and community connecting.

The chapter concludes with some reflections on the implications of contemporary policy trends in co-production and individual funding, and raises questions about choice and participation where a person's capacity to make decisions is in question.

The evolution of the policy, legal and ideological context in which services for people with learning difficulties services have developed over the last century has been accompanied by the development of a number of influential conceptual frameworks. The list above is not comprehensive; for example, inclusion and universalism are two other important sets of ideas that are not explicitly examined here, although they do provide the context for much of the discussion.

Our list of conceptual frameworks above falls naturally into two groupings. The first three ideas – normalisation, the five accomplishments and the social model of disability – can be seen essentially as a response to, and a critique of, the institutional model of services, not only the old long-stay 'mental handicap'/learning disability hospitals, but also other prevailing community-based congregate services. They are essentially concerned with reform and improvement of existing services.

Arguably, the second set of ideas is much more challenging. Personalisation and co-production have emerged and grown in strength, as the process of deinstitutionalisation and 'community presence' has failed to fully deliver on participation and community integration. Taken together they are concerned with achieving radical transformational systems change.

Normalisation and social role valorisation

The concept of normalisation (Wolfensberger, 1972) emerged from earlier work in Scandinavia (Nirje, 1969). It was (and is) a seminal idea in the field that informed all subsequent developments, and it is still a philosophy that is both referred to and argued about today. The impact of Wolfensberger's thinking about the importance of deinstitutionalisation and how to achieve it, and his legacy for current thinking, cannot be underestimated. Although not without his critics, it is worth exploring normalisation and its successor, SRV, in some detail here. These two frameworks – normalisation and SRV – explicitly set out to counter the social devaluation of people with learning difficulties based on negative perceptions of them within mainstream society. The concept grew out of practices in Scandinavia that developed services based on normal patterns and routines of life, such as going to work or school, and living in more homely settings within institutions. Wolfensberger developed the ideas in the US as a model for relocating people out of institutions and into the community (Wolfensberger and Glenn, 1975).

Central to Wolfensberger's concept is the idea of the 'culturally valued analogue'; in other words, seeking to ensure that people with learning difficulties are afforded the expectations, activities and resources used, and, importantly, valued by ordinary people. By marrying practical service innovations with sociological theories of deviance, he developed the concept of valued social roles for people with learning difficulties (and other marginalised groups), and proposed that it was essential to offset the social devaluation typically experienced by people with learning difficulties. This eventually became known as social role valorisation (Wolfensberger, 1983).

Power of negative images to create and reinforce exclusion

While Goffman (1961) explored the impact of institutions on 'patient' behaviour, Wolfensberger conducted historical work (1969) that explored the development of institutions in Europe. This led him to conceptualise a model for thinking about the 'juxtaposition' of models of services and staffing with various 'images' of disabled people. So, for example, he suggested that if society viewed people as a 'menace', the service model would be one of containment and the staffing orientation that of a 'warder'. On the other hand, if people were viewed as 'eternal children', the model would be protective, parental and perhaps educationally based. He devised eight historical categories and their service derivation, an adapted version of which can be seen below, in Table 3.1a.

Table 3.1a: Historical images of disabled people

Image – 'myth'	Service model	Staffing model
Sub-human	?	?
Menace	?	?
Object of ridicule	?	?
Object of dread	?	?
Object of pity	?	?
Holy innocent	?	?
Diseased organism	?	?
Eternal child	?	?

Source: Adapted from Wolfensberger and Glenn (1975).

Think spot

It is evident that most of the above historical images of people with learning disabilities are negative and some paternalistic, with what would now be seen to be unacceptable service outcomes and staffing regimes.

Replace the question marks in the service and staffing model boxes in Table 3.1a with your own ideas of the appropriate models for supporting citizenship. Reflect on how your ideas sit with current practice.

Wolfensberger's conclusions about the service and staffing models associated with each of these historic images are shown in Table 3.1b below, along with his suggested ninth category, a blueprint for our times, that of 'citizen'.

Table 3.1b: Historical images and service/staffing models

Image – 'myth'	Service model	Staffing model
Sub-human	Warehousing	Warden
Menace	(Extermination) camp	'Hang-man'
Object of ridicule	Bedlam	Handlers
Object of dread	Containment	Custodians
Object of pity	Care	Carers
Holy innocent	Spiritual	Guardians
Diseased organism	Hospital	Medical, nursing staff
Eternal child	Home; nurture	Parents
Citizen	Inclusion	Personal assistants

Source: Wolfensberger and Glenn (1975).

Using positive discrimination to counter the experience of exclusion

Normalisation supporters argued that in order to counteract these negative images, it was important to create 'socially valued' roles and 'normative' lifestyles for people. In other words, that if the legacy of services had been to 'devalue' people with learning difficulties, then services should aspire to re-value them by supporting them to fill valued roles in the community as homeowners, taxpayers, employees, volunteers, partners, parents – all the roles that most of us value in our lives. It was argued that filling such roles had such a positive impact on other people's perception and expectations that the person's disabilities became invisible, or at any rate, significantly less important, to others. Proponents of SRV believed that people with learning difficulties would internalise this new enhanced set of role expectancies, thus creating a virtuous circle of change. SRV and 'normalisation' achieved widespread practical application through an evaluation framework called PASS (Programme Analysis of Service Systems) that helped develop and design intervention at the neighbourhood and governmental levels as well as individual and family ones.

Prevailing positive influence of normalisation/social role valorisation

The frequency with which ideas based on normalisation are still found today attests to how useful practitioners have found them, although service evaluation research suggests that the there is a 'marked gap between what is being delivered and the aspirations of empowerment and social inclusion that underlie current policy' (Emerson et al, 2005, p 122). The gap between the rhetoric and the lived experience is important as it reminds us that the institutions are only the beginning of the problem we are trying to tackle; in other words, community living may harbour 'institutions without walls' (people experiencing hidden forms of institutionalisation). When judging 'quality of life' or improvements in quality of life, the challenge is to cease relying on the institutional lived experience, but rather to base further development and improvement on a combination of the lived experience of the general population and the preferences of people with learning difficulties themselves.

Critique of normalisation/social role valorisation

The language of normalisation was open to misinterpretation as 'something done to people' rather than services. It has been criticised from a feminist and cultural standpoint (Brown and Smith, 1994), and in particular, from the service user/carer perspective (Szivos, 1992). There were continuing questions about exactly whose ordinary life standards were to be used, and whose norms were to form the basis of judgements about quality of life (see, for example, Kelley and Walmsley, 2010). Particularly contentious, and understandably so, was the added value given to integrating people with learning difficulties with non-disabled people at the expense of recognising the importance of 'affiliation' and collective strength between people with learning difficulties. Proponents of collective advocacy find this aspect of normalisation thinking unacceptable. Nonetheless, these ideas continue to have a profound impact on the thinking of professionals across disciplines, and to have currency within the more recent discourses of inclusion citizenship and human rights.

Frameworks for accomplishment

In 1987 O'Brien and Lyle conducted some research on the features that make a good quality of life, and as a result, they produced their framework for accomplishment. They suggested that there were five areas of life that were widely accepted as being influential in shaping everyone's quality of life, and that they were likely to be areas in which people with learning difficulties were disadvantaged. They suggested that in order to help people with learning difficulties achieve an ordinary or inclusive life, services needed to ensure that they enabled them to gain or maintain accomplishments in these five vital areas of life.

Five frameworks for accomplishment

- Community presence – to be to be in the community, not separate from it.
- Attention to skill development or competences for living well.
- Choice and control – along with the necessary support.
- Respectful interaction that promotes positive self-worth and dignity.
- Participation in community activities through having a range of satisfying relationships.

Source: O'Brien and Lyle (1987)

This reconfiguration of Wolfensberger's ideas into five service objectives for achieving an ordinary and an inclusive life was, and continues to be, enormously influential in the many significant developments and improvements in the lives of people with learning difficulties. It was, for example, significantly influential in the development of the All Wales learning disability strategy, referred to earlier in Chapter Two (Welsh Office, 1983).

Normalisation and the five frameworks for accomplishment were models designed by professionals with the intention of assisting them to think and develop services differently. The operation of these models and associated evaluation methods included service users, but they were not user-led. By contrast, the social model of disability was fashioned at the heart of the user movement by user-activists.

Social model of disability

Alongside normalisation and the five frameworks for accomplishment that were influential throughout the 1960s, 1970s and 1980s, the social model of disability, developed by physical disability activists during the 1980s, has had a comparable and profound impact on how professionals think about disability to the present day. This model was developed by the disability movement to counteract what it termed the 'personal tragedy' (and medicalised) model of disability. It distinguished between 'impairments' found in individuals, and the 'disability' that arises from barriers within society, such as inaccessible buildings and prejudicial attitudes that limit the participation and achievements of disabled people. It thereby defines disability as a form of social oppression.

This model has also had its critics, with attention drawn to the absence within the model of consideration of identity and of the 'lived experience' of individuals, with particular reference to cultural and gender representations (Corker and French, 1999; Thomas, 2004). Indeed, Shakespeare and Watson (2002) described the rallying call, 'disabled by society, not our bodies', as a shibboleth that had served its purpose. Nonetheless, it has been an effective movement in politicising and increasing the confidence of people with disabilities to have their voice not only heard, but acted on; in refocusing policy and service development on social barriers to integration; and demonstrating the practicality and efficacy of allocating individual personal budgets with which people could buy their support and services. The impact of the model is reflected in legislative successes such as the Community Care (Direct Payments) Act 1996 and the Disability Discrimination Act 2005, as well as in service innovations such as independent and supported living.

Strongly associated with the notion of individuals controlling their own living arrangements was the idea of independent and collective advocacy to offer support to individuals engaged in this process. The legacy of this movement remains prominent today in the:

- increasing use of PAs to provide individually tailored support;
- widespread use of individual budgets to fund that support (in particular, direct payments and personal budgets);
- continuing emphasis on a model of 'support' to live a good and inclusive life rather than 'readiness' to live such a life;
- development of current policies of self-directed support.

If the first set of ideas about reform was developed in counterpoint to deinstitutionalisation, the second set offers conceptual frameworks for driving forward how services can shift their focus from individuals being simply present 'in the community' to individuals being fully included and engaged as part 'of the community', and infer the need for change at all levels of the welfare system – individual, organisational and governmental.

While normalisation, SRV and the five frameworks for accomplishment and, to a lesser degree, the social model of disability, focus on service reform and mechanisms for engaging with service users within that reform, co-production and personalisation are both concerned with 'transformational change' (ADSW, 2009). *Putting People First* (HM Government, 2007) talked about services being 'co-produced, co-developed and co-evaluated', and stated that real change 'will only be achieved through the participation of service users and carers at every stage' (HM Government, 2007, p 1). This is not simply a technical 'bolt-on' to an existing service system, but rather an attempt at radical transformation.

Co-production

As a term, 'co-production' has been used in the US and broad public service management (Pestoff, 2006) since the 1970s. However, within adult social care, it is most closely associated with the policies and practice of personalisation. In co-production, the individual who uses services is seen as 'part of the problem-solving team, not as a problem' (Hunter and Ritchie, 2007, p 12), one who brings assets in the form of resources and skills to the table. As in person–centred planning, the individual is seen as the 'expert' in their own problem. Another description often used is to 'work with rather than do unto users' (Cummins and Miller, 2007, cited in Needham and Carr, 2009, p 1). This apparently simple statement conceals notable complexity in terms of who is involved, and in terms of levels of co-producing.

Co-production can occur between individuals, in face-to relationships; collectively, between groups of users with each other and with professionals; or between organisations or agencies. It can also occur on a scale of intensity that has been categorised from 'compliance' to 'support' to 'transformation' (Cummins and Miller, 2007). In other words, co-production may be limited to consultation and defining the problem; it may expand to local authorities creating mechanisms to enable and encourage user participation in broader organisational as well as individual care decision making; or recognise people's expertise and assets as an important aspect of the collaborative process that is concerned with broad quality of life concerns as well as 'clinical' ones.

The key characteristics of such an approach are shown in Table 3.2 below.

Table 3.2: From service domination to co-production

From	To
Locus of power with professionals	Locus of power with people who use support
Professional assessment of need	User-defined outcomes
Professional-led mechanisms for service development	New user-led mechanisms for service development
Users as passive recipients	Active participation by people who use services
A 'consumer' in a mixed economy of care	Being an active citizen
A service focus (or even individualised funding)	Capacity building and embedding within community networks

Source: Adapted from Hunter and Ritchie (2007)

Personalisation

At present governmental bodies within the UK are committed to rolling out personalisation and personal budgets in particular, across the whole of social care. The scale of the transformation this will bring is potentially enormous. It will turn provision of care and support upside down as individuals start to use their individual budgets to commission the support they want. This may well bear little resemblance to what has traditionally been on offer. Demand will change and, in order to stay in business, provider organisations will need to get much better at understanding the 'distinctive worldview' of those who use services, and work in a more direct relationship with the purchasers of their support.

With a full commitment to personalisation, Rhodes (2010) anticipates radical changes in the role of social work to an enabling one, rather than a gate-keeping function. He also envisages that the state will change to become:

- primarily the distributor of benefit entitlements to individuals;
- a guardian of the 'safety net' – because there will always be people who are overlooked, who self-exclude, or who are abused;
- a committed strategic funding enabler of friendship, family care and of interdependent and empowered communities;
- a patron for various positive functions that it cannot and should not control;
- focused on the structural issues that have the most impact on people in need of care and support – housing, access to employment, access to education, and so on.

Co-production and personalisation are well suited when there is a requirement for long-term support that is highly individualised, 'site-specific', involving different agencies and individuals working together, over time, as needs change (Hunter and Ritchie, 2007). This is fully congruent with the direction of policy and practice in recent years, and sits particularly well within the context of best practice supporting people with learning difficulties. This is well illustrated by the emergence of innovative systems change through local area coordination (LAC).

What is local area coordination?

LAC was originally developed in Western Australia in 1988 to 'build individual, family and community self-sufficiency so that individuals with intellectual disability can choose to live with their families, or in their local community without compromising their quality of life' (Clark and Broad, 2011, p 1). It has a strong person-centred value base, and works with individuals and families in communities.

LAC has subsequently developed across Australia and other countries (including Scotland, as a key recommendation in *The same as you?* [Scottish Government, 2000]), and is now starting in a number of areas in England, including Middlesbrough, Cumbria, Stroud and Derby City, supporting people who are vulnerable through age, disability, sensory impairments and mental health needs.

It has also most recently been developed in New Zealand as a key part of national service reforms (Clark and Broad, 2011).

In Western Australia, LAC was an example of a driver of whole system reform including the development of alternative, 'asset/strength-based' and cost-effective community living support models (Bartnik, 2010).

LAC formed a central role in re-thinking the purpose of services. Rather than asking 'What services or money do you need?', it asks 'What is your vision for a good life, and what are the range of ways you can get there?'.

LAC has been both influenced by and contributed to the development of strength/asset-based community development thinking and practice over the last two decades – which is now having an impact on the unfolding of the health and wellbeing, Joint Strategic Needs Assessments, localism and social care reform agendas.

It is built on the principle that the purpose of social care reform is to strengthen informal supports and community self-sufficiency and to make services more personal, flexible and accountable (Bartnik, 2008).

LAC aims to actively form partnerships with individuals, families, co-producers and local communities to promote self-sufficiency and local solutions to problems. It also aims to form strong partnerships with formal services and professionals.

Source: Adapted from Clark and Broad (2011)

According to the New Economics Foundation (cited in Needham and Carr, 2009), co-production is based on the idea '... that people need to be rooted in mutual support networks, and that not everything can be bought …' (pp 3-4), and that individuals should be 'interdependent citizens' rather than 'consumers', embedded in a wide network of support including personalised services. It follows, therefore, that attention needs to be paid to building social capital and neighbourhood connections that can be drawn on to provide support alongside formal services. Writers in the field of urban regeneration, such as John McKnight (1995), were early contributors to the idea of 'community connecting'.

Co-production and community connecting

Community connecting is about bringing together two distinct but sometimes overlapping approaches: person-centeredness, which, for the purposes of this discussion, we locate within personalisation and community-centred work, both of which we locate in co-production:

■ person-centredness supports people to discover, recognise and contribute their own gifts to others, and is a clear feature of 'deep' personalisation; and
■ community-centred work builds networks, cross–sector partnerships and local leadership to improve access.

As part of the co-production and personalisation agenda, interventions need to be understood not only in the context of how they directly support outcomes for individuals, but also by how they contribute to developing the capacity of communities (Gillespie and Duffy, 2008) as illustrated below in Figure 3.1.

There are lessons to be learned here from the well-established tools of person-centred planning that can be applied in community connecting. In particular, spending time, listening and conversation are tools of change that can equally well be applied in both individually centred work and in community-centred approaches. At the individual level, this might include spending time with the person, learning what life is like for them by getting alongside them in all sorts of different situations, and doing a range of different activities with a variety of people, at different times of the day and week.

> Community connectedness says I don't care about your deficiencies, I insist on your contribution. (McKnight, 1995, quoted in Outside the Box, 2005, p 78)

In the same way, it is also important to spend time with, listen to and get to know other people in the neighbourhood – other people can add valuable

Figure 3.1: Community connecting: combining person-centred and community-centred approaches

Person-centred approach   **Community-centred approach**

- Know the person.
- Recognise their gifts and what they bring to others.
- Provide support for people to be in control.
- Support to plan for the future and type of support they may need.
- Build connections between people.

- Link people together with common interests.
- Open access and remove barriers.
- Apply broad definitions of access.
- Intentionally bring under-represented groups to the forefront.
- Act on the experience of people to create change.
- Influence community planning and allocation of resources.

Community connecting

Source: Adapted from Goldsmith and Burke (2012, pp 7-8)

information about what seems important to the person, what makes them tick, what makes them happy or sad or angry, as well as what their past has been like, offering helpful insights and ideas about what is going on in the community, what its strengths are, and what the individual and community have to offer and can gain from each other. Enlisting help from other people at this stage can be a foundation for encouraging people to become involved later in developing opportunities and making connections.

By listening and learning from other people, rich, colourful details can be added to the picture of both the individual and the community. Completing a relationship map is a helpful way to illustrate who is part of the person's life, and therefore who can be enlisted to support them (Kennedy et al, 2002).

The individual level is picked up in more detail again in the following chapters, but the focus here is on the community level, since much of community development thinking has been lost from a social work agenda increasingly preoccupied with targeted service delivery, care management procedures and service infrastructures.

The principles of community development are remarkably similar to those discussed above:

- *empowerment:* increasing the ability of individuals and groups to influence issues that affect them and their communities;
- *participation:* supporting people to take part in decision making;
- *inclusion, equality of opportunity and anti-discrimination:* recognising that some people may need additional support to overcome barriers they face;
- *self-determination:* supporting the right of people to make their own choices;
- *partnership:* recognising that many agencies can contribute to community development (adapted from Scottish Executive, 2004).

How such an approach can underpin co-production is illustrated below.

Partnership building in community development

In the Building Inclusive Communities project in Kent, it was recognised that strong partnerships were vital to creating maximum impact and reaching more people within different networks. Three kinds of partnership building were identified:

1. **Local involvement and co-production:** engaging all members of the community, not just those who are active, and finding ways to generate new opportunities together, based on pooling knowledge and resources in a new way.

2. **Building social capital:** there are many definitions of what this means, but many have as a central tenet the value of social networks. Social capital has been described as 'the ability of people to work together for a common purpose in groups and organisations' (Fukuyama, 1996, quoted in Gilchrist, 2009, p 10).

3. **Designing, re-shaping, generating and checking:** looking at what already exists and how this can be re-modelled or re-shaped in the light of new demands, needs and customer expectations.

Public services such as leisure centres should see the potential economic benefits of becoming more accessible to new customers. The project's experience of visits to premises showed that already accessible environments were not being widely promoted, and that this was an area that could be improved with little expense. However, this does demand action by partner agencies: to prioritise time to do this and to explain to senior managers why the work is important. There is a need to make the case, not just on moral or social grounds, but also on the economic benefits of attracting new paying customers.

Source: Goldsmith and Burke (2012, p 16)

The Kent project found a clear need to invest in well-trained workers with a community development background who were able to move between sectors, generate shared work plans and improve the current evidence base. The project also identified the need for strategic community development approaches to achieve greater participation at all levels, including a strong and more diverse leadership base to turn the vision into tangible and measurable objectives within community planning (Goldsmith and Burke, 2012). It is worth reflecting on whether current social work education training can adapt to offer opportunities for future social workers to acquire and develop skills and knowledge in these pivotal areas that are central to a co-production-based approach.

In the context of co-production, the reinforcement of social capital is envisaged to include contributions from all members of the community, including those traditionally seen as 'service-dependent' and as net recipients of support rather than as contributors. So community connecting is characterised by reciprocity between 'neighbours', a natural interaction within community living and not a service.

Most of us of us would like to live in an area where people look out for one another, and where there is a degree of 'community spirit'. This elusive and intangible concept can be promoted by recognising and celebrating the contribution of all local people, including people with disabilities, in achieving a better quality of life in our neighbourhoods.

There are many ways in which any of us can make a contribution to improving life in the locality in which we live. Most of these are unpaid and almost taken for granted things that we do, such as volunteering, being a member of a social or sports club, being a member of a residents' or tenants' association, or just being a good friend. We contribute just by being part of our community and being with other people. In turn, we benefit by gaining in confidence and social skills. The rest of the community benefits from our ideas and experience, and from the personal qualities we bring to our connections.

Since 1990, one organisation, KeyRing, has consistently supported people with learning difficulties to live in their own 'ordinary' home in 'ordinary' neighbourhoods, the support being 'constructed from the input of a local volunteer (more commonly now, a paid community living supporter), mutual support among network members, and community connections' (Poll, 2007, p 46).[1]

KeyRing and Neighbourhood Networks, its Scottish sister organisation, now support over 900 members in 100 networks. Essentially up to nine individuals, some of whom have been in residential care and some on the margins of professional services, are allocated individual tenancies from housing associations or local authorities, within walking distance of each other, with some support from a community living volunteer who lives in the tenth flat.

At the outset this was seen as an opportunity to help people have more choice and control over where they lived and with whom. Thirty years down the line, the organisation is clear that the strength of the model lies in:

> ... understanding what people want; putting self-reliance at the heart of people's support: enabling mutual support amongst Network Members; and supporting people to make connections with the local community. (Poll, 2007, p 47)

This is a good description of the idea of 'co-production' that promotes individuals' capacity to contribute to solving their own problems. Detailed accounts of how it works and its strengths can be found elsewhere (see, for example, Simons, 1998; Kinsella, 2002; Poll, 2007).

Eventually, KeyRing, under the influence of the community development ideas of John McKnight (1995), called this an 'asset-based approach to community development'. While some people with learning difficulties might need a level of personal support that would not sit quite as easily within this model, for those who are members, KeyRing expects that they will not only use community resources, but also make a contribution to the life of that community. Examples of these kinds of reciprocal relationships between members and their communities are given in Poll's account in Hunter and Ritchie (2007). This is not to deny that there were instances of harassment, but strategies based on community mapping (to establish community capacity inventories) and support to seek redress were developed. Such was the success of KeyRing that Kinsella notes that:

> ... compared to most people with learning difficulties in the community, KeyRing tenants are community resource and relationship rich. (Kinsella, 2002, p 15)

KeyRing – a better life through community contribution

KeyRing members agree to be 'good neighbours' to each other and to share their skills. The network prevents isolation and becomes a safe place for people to learn about building relationships and being involved in a group or community. North Wales had its first KeyRing network in November 2004. The areas where the networks are situated have their fair share of difficulties; sometimes they are seen as undesirable places, but they also have huge and often untapped assets.

Mr M's story illustrates how life can change for people who become better connected with their community. Mr M is 45 years old and has learning difficulties. After his parents died he lived alone, but his home was burgled ten times in three months. He joined a KeyRing network when it was established. At this point, his only identified friends were support workers – the only people he knew were those who were paid to spend time with him. Six years later, Mr M has just held a joint birthday party with another KeyRing member. There were 30 well-wishers at this party. He has been named Volunteer of the Year by his local BCTV (British Conservation Trust Volunteers) group several times for his 'green-fingered' activity on behalf of neighbours and an allotment group, and his intimacy circle now features true friends. Mr M's confidence has gradually begun to grow as he feels safe and valued.

It is difficult to provide a full overview of Mr M's life because much of what he now does is organic and spontaneous. We do know that a number of members and others in the community, including Mr M, get together on a weekly basis to share a meal, and that Mr M now feels secure enough in his home to begin to start the process of buying it.

Of course there are risks and concerns, but these are managed, rather than avoided. There is much goodwill towards Mr M in the community, and if he has a need, the kindness he has previously shown is reciprocated. Mr M isn't a fluke; other people have seen their lives improve through community connections.

Source: Adapted from KeyRing (no date)

So, far from the 'suspicion' with which the aspirations of KeyRing were greeted by professionals in the 1990s, we now have a social care and health policy arena that is underpinned by assumptions that individuals who use services not only require support, but also bring assets to the table, and indeed are active participants not only in developing their own care and support, but also in making a contribution to the communities in which they live (Leadbeater, 2004; HM Government, 2007; Health and Social Care Act 2013; Social Care (Self-directed Support) (Scotland) Act 2013).

Conclusion

This chapter has traced the main theoretical planks underpinning the development of policy and practice since the 1960s, as traditional institutional provision was discredited. The conceptual importance of the legacies of normalisation, SRV, the framework for accomplishment and the social model of disability cannot be overestimated. Ideas of particular significance include that of the 'cultural analogue', that is, using 'ordinary' lifestyles and expectations as a benchmark against which to consider the lives of people with learning difficulties; of the power of images and social roles in processes of exclusion; and of social barriers rather than individual characteristics as obstacles to inclusion, thereby differentiating between 'disability' and 'impairment' respectively. Notwithstanding the critiques of these models, they generated a way of thinking about service reform that led to the emergence of policies of personalisation and co-production that are concerned with 'transformational change' in services. Here, the expertise of service users and carers is privileged in constructing not only their own packages of care, but in drawing on community resources as well as their own, in order to innovate and co-produce broader service development.

However, some considerable challenges exist in realising these policy aspirations, both in the current climate of austerity, and how individuals who have reduced ability or experience of taking major decisions about their lives can be supported to do so. There is also a concern that carers and hard-pressed communities may be faced with increased expectations to provide care as public resources are reduced and eligibility thresholds are raised (Age UK, 2007).

In terms of spending cuts, the Association of Directors of Social Work (ADSW) report on personalisation (2009) captures the tensions at the heart of these developments, suggesting that these are tensions that are likely to increase in a climate of austerity: 'One of the significant challenges ... is the need to meet ever greater demands for services within limited resources and to do so in a more individualised way' (ADSW, 2009, p 1). It has been suggested that under the impact of austerity cuts, 50 per cent of which will fall on local government and benefits, well-intentioned principles of empowerment could be a double-edged sword, and perceived 'not simply ... to improve service quality by "bringing the user in" but also ... to cut costs, by making the user do more for themselves' (Bovaird and Loeffler, 2013, p 6). The possibility that cost-cutting is at the expense of those who need support is an issue that has rightly concerned the user and carer movement, as well as some professionals (SCIE, 2010; Ferguson, 2012).

Even without a climate of austerity, the assumption that everyone who uses services can be in control of their own budget and social care support requires some caution, particularly in relation to people with complex support needs and those people whose 'capacity' or ability to make decisions may be reduced or under-developed. Later in this book, Chapter Nine considers some of the recent developments in legislation and policy that have both modernised the legal concept of capacity (capax), and reinforced supported decision making so that people who arguably need personalised support the most are enabled to get it.

It is our argument that these ideas present an important bulwark against the resurgence of the discredited models described in Chapter Two. However, in addition to arguing that the recasting of the debate in terms of human rights has to be one aspect of the way forward, we now argue in the next chapter for a re-affirmation of the personalised and person-centred professional practice that has been emerging alongside modernised policy initiatives, but one that is firmly embedded within a family and community perspective. Chapters Four to Ten in Part Two present practice scenarios to illustrate this approach.

Note

[1] The authors would like to acknowledge the untimely death of Carl Poll, founder of KeyRing, in 2014. We join all those who have already expressed their admiration for his extraordinary pioneering work and personal commitment to 'changing lives' for the better for all of us: disabled, non-disabled, relatives, professionals, neighbours and friends alike.

Part Two

Transitional points

4 Transition to adulthood

In this chapter we discuss the distinction between the concepts of service transitions and life transitions, and the implications for the experience of users and their families when they encounter services. We point out that unlike life transitions from childhood to adulthood, for example, service transitions are usually implemented at specific points, within restricted time frames, and with reference only to general developmental needs. This clash of timelines is often accompanied by a clash of language and expectations, and has been recognised in policy documents and in the appointment of transition champions to improve outcomes for young people in transition to adulthood. Ten transition challenges are set out for both practitioners and organisations, paying particular attention to achieving innovative options in housing and employment through transition teams, and joint working protocols for adult and children's services.

Martha's story

Martha is nearly 15 years old and has learning difficulties. She attends a mainstream secondary school and receives additional classroom support there. She is shy, and has not made as many friends at school as she and her family hoped she would. A person-centred transition review meeting was arranged to specifically look both at her immediate future and at her longer-term future, and how everyone could work together to ensure that any plans made were rolled out as smoothly as possible. Martha's mum, Dorothy, hopes that her daughter can go on from school to do some courses at a local college.

Going into the meeting, Dorothy's first concern was to get everyone working together to look at Martha's transition from school to college, and from children's to adult services. Dorothy hoped it would be possible to look at some real long-term supported employment options that would be available, and to talk about how these could be implemented smoothly. She was feeling worried about getting forced into discussions about possible future living arrangements as she felt there was still plenty of time to think about that at a later date, although she accepted that this would have to be addressed at some point soon.

It was intended that the transition review should address the following questions:

- What is possible for Martha in the future?
- What does everyone involved want Martha's future to be like?
- What is going to be done to work towards this future?

The review was attended by Martha's family, including her mum and dad, two friends from school, her support workers, her teacher, her speech therapist, a staff member from the Careers Support and Information Service, a social worker and a social work manager.

Some of the actions that came from Martha's review were:

- increasing the number and type of leisure opportunities she could try to access;
- looking at options for 16+ education;
- forming a circle of support; and
- thinking about future living arrangements.

Martha's family commented afterwards that they had not been prepared for the breadth of options, ideas and possibilities that were discussed.

Think spot

Why do you think that was? In what ways do you think the social worker could have prepared Martha and her family better? What do you think will be the main areas of work for the social worker in the next two to three years?

What we mean by 'transition'

There are two quite different ways of looking at transition. First, there is what might be referred to as 'life transition' – what ordinary people variously describe as growing up, leaving school, leaving home, getting a job and having a 'good life' as an adult. This is the process of moving from child to adult status.

Second, there is 'service transition' – the essentially bureaucratic, although nonetheless important, transition between service systems (a kind of border control process involving being passed from the jurisdiction of one set of education/child care/child health professionals to a different and unrelated set of adult education/adult care/adult health professionals).

Service transition (for example, from child to adult services) takes place when it is considered that the young person's needs can no longer statutorily be met by child services, or would be better met by adult services, or because the young person is no longer technically a 'child' and is therefore not eligible for children's services. However, the professional services on offer are not necessarily concerned with or able to address the task of supporting life transition.

We know from wider experience of the vast majority of ordinary families that the crucial task for any adolescent and their family is to move from the protected life of childhood to the autonomous life of an adult. We also know that individuals are unlikely to be at the same stage at the same time (Hudson, 2006), and that support needs to be there when that particular individual needs it. Service transitions, however, are nearly always time-restricted, and are usually not there to help at later points in life, when the person is really dealing with the business of growing up (for example, at the point at which they are leaving college and moving on to the next stage of their life).

It is for this reason that a person–centred approach that supports the young person to gain a good adult life is key to making things better. The purpose of transition planning is not just passing the baton from children's services to adult services, but to support the young person and their family to move on to the next stage of their life.

It is not a surprise, therefore, to find a clash of language, and ultimately a clash of expectations and outcomes reported in much of the literature. For example, two major reports note that most of the young people involved did not understand the term 'transition' (Heslop et al, 2002; Tarleton, 2004). However, it was also apparent that all of them did have clear expectations about what they wanted to do as they grew up. Unfortunately, it is unlikely that that staff were focused on supporting young people in the achievement of these goals and aspirations. Similarly, parents were often unclear what could or should happen at transition, and what their role was. As a result, they felt at best anxious, and at worst fearful about what the future held for their child.

Policy context

The same as you? report in Scotland (Scottish Government, 2000) reviewed services for people with learning disabilities, and highlighted not only the crucial importance of the transition phase between child and adult services, but also the need for partnership between local authorities and NHS boards in planning services.

In England, *Valuing People,* the English national learning disability strategy, reported that people with learning disabilities and their families found the period of transition stressful and difficult (DH, 2001a, p 41). As a result, transition was one of the priority issues addressed in the strategy (DH, 2001a).

One of the requirements set out in *Valuing People* was for local Learning Disability Partnership Boards to appoint a 'transition champion', and to develop a strategy to improve young people's experiences and life outcomes as they moved into adulthood. In most areas of England, Partnership Boards used the information pack for transition champions (Valuing People Support Team, 2003) to help them set up and run training programmes to support the wider use of person-centred reviews. As a result, person-centred transition planning is now more established as the basis of good practice in transition. This approach has been adopted and become pivotal in other strategies, including the Transition Support Programme (HM Treasury and Department for Education and Skills, 2007).

It is no surprise that young people with learning difficulties want the same life outcomes that other young people want, but it is also clear from follow-up work to *Valuing People* that the planning processes that they and their families hope will open up career paths for them instead lead to options with low aspirations and no real prospects. Such plans tend to:

> … lack a clear goal, and are restricted to a day centre or a particular type of college course. Many young people, as adolescents, enter residential provision because (a) local colleges do not perceive themselves as having the necessary skills and (b) there is not close working between social care, education and health. (DH, 2011a, p 4)

Further work carried out to consolidate the vision of *Valuing People Now* resulted in the expectation that all young people with learning disabilities should be able to have person-centred transition reviews and plans; that they should be supported to assert their voice in these reviews; and that plans emerging from the reviews should be based on knowledge of the real options available.

For people with learning difficulties from BME communities, this can be a particularly problematic time. It is estimated that some 20-25 per cent of young people in transition from children's to adult services are from BME communities (Foundation for Learning Disabilities 2012).

Grapevine All Means All project

The Equality and Human Rights Commission funds this project to help young people with learning disabilities from BME communities to understand and take up personal budgets in order to enable them to control how services are delivered, and by whom. This includes helping the young people and their families to define and articulate their wants at a time of transition.

This story is one example of the families they have worked with.

Nobody in F's immediate family speaks English. They are very protective, and worry a lot about her safety. The family has refused services in the past, and it seems that services are unable to provide any support that can meet F's needs while adhering to her family's wishes. F was not allocated a social worker before, during or after leaving school, her family having met three different social workers (two of whom were students). The project worker has begun essential lifestyle planning with the family, enabling their fears to be discussed openly, as well as ascertaining how they want F to be supported. Appropriate solutions have been developed and welcomed by the family. Since then, these have been agreed by the city council as a personal budget that funds F's PA and a series of activities, including a place at college.

Some of the emerging messages for practitioners reported by the project are that:

- families tend to prefer to get their help from one consistent worker rather than from several;
- there was a lack of both information and practical assistance to enable them to get support;
- within some BME groups, particularly Muslim groups, it is not really accepted for women to mix with men after they leave school;
- families fear for the safety of their female relative in mixed gender environments such as adult education centres and further education colleges. Where this is an issue, advocates have supported parents to explore appropriate environments: single-sex social groups, or classes that are predominantly single-sex, for example, sewing, jewellery making, football, as well as specific community groups;
- the main point of contact may be with the relative who does most for the person with a learning disability, often a mother or aunt, who may not be the key decision maker in the household.

Source: Adapted from Poxton (2010)

Contrasting the experience of young people with learning difficulties and their peers

We think it would be helpful at this point to compare and contrast the experiences of young people with learning disabilities with those of other young people who are at a similar stage in life. Typically, young people without a learning disability:

- undertake an informal apprenticeship in choice making and decision making throughout childhood and adolescence by role-modelling on friends, school, family and others;
- receive information from a wide range of sources that is specifically targeted at them;
- have a number of options related to their interests and skills – thus widening their choices;
- have access to support and advice around any choices they make, along with opportunities to change their mind;
- have the opportunity to discuss all of this with friends, as well as with parents and school staff;
- experience many ways to gain in confidence;
- ultimately make the decisions themselves.

On the other hand, young people who have additional support needs tend to have somewhat different experiences. The National Development Team for Inclusion (NDTi, 2013, p 4) reports that young people with learning difficulties have the same personal goals and aspirations as their peers, but need help and support to achieve them. Thus, by contrast, their experiences can be summarised as:

- routinely having limited chances to make decisions or to choose between options;
- being provided with information from both the school and specialist services that is aimed at their parents and not at them;
- being assessed by staff they do not know and who do not know them;
- experiencing assessment that is built round what 'people like him/her' need;
- being offered disability services based on what they cannot do;
- getting few or no choices – and feeling that it is hard to change their mind;
- the discussion happening in meetings, and involving professionals and parents;
- decisions usually being made by parents;
- not getting a chance to try any other options.

Think spot

Fitzpatrick (2006a) suggests the following exercise for comparing the aspirations of a young person with learning disabilities in transition with those of their peers and siblings:

> Make a list with the young person of what they think is a 'good life'.
> Ask their parents, brothers and sisters, friends and other people you respect to do their own lists – what would they want for themselves, or any young person that age, as well as for this person?
> Bring together the people who care about this young person, and have a discussion about what is a good life for this young person:
>> What are the things that appear on all or most of the lists?
>> Has someone seen something about them or for them that other people haven't noticed?
>> What would each aspect of a good life look like in practice?
>> Other detailed questions such as: What would the person be doing? Who would be with them? What would they be wearing? Where would it be happening?

Take some time to reflect on your thoughts and ideas:

> Are they all about disabilities and services?
> If so, how could you help make the transition to adult life more 'ordinary'?
> How is a 'good life' going to be achievable for this person?

Source: Fitzpatrick (2006a)

Ten transition challenges

The list below is our summary of the main challenges faced by young people with learning difficulties and their families in the build-up to, and during, the process of transition.

1. Being fully person-centred.
2. Giving the young person a voice.
3. Starting planning early.
4. Providing good information to the young person and their family.

5.   Offering real options, real choices and real budgets.
6.   Making sure services and supports are well coordinated.
7.   Using the positive experiences of young people and their families.
8.   Extending the life experiences of young people with learning difficulties before leaving school.
9.   Learning from what works well – using outcomes-based evidence.
10. Remembering that there are other transitions in the future.

Addressing the ten challenges at individual and family level

How can a social worker and their managers improve transition practice at an individual and family level?

Being fully person-centred. A number of tools and techniques can be used to improve social work practice. Some of these are drawn from different person planning tools, and also from some of the work on developing planned individual networks or circles of friends. In using these techniques it is essential to keep the person at the heart of everything, and to try to create as many opportunities as possible for the young person to have choices.

The transition process must place the young person and their family at the centre of planning for the future. It must take account of their own views of what they need and want for their future life. It is important that all involved understand how to keep the process person-centred and focused on outcomes for the young person, rather than on service outputs.

Many staff supporting young people in the approach to school leaving have very restricted knowledge of what the young people they are supporting want from adult life, and little practical and up-to-date knowledge about how they might pursue their goals. This is particularly the case for young people with very significant disabilities, who do not communicate with words, and/or who have been labelled 'challenging' (Routledge, 2001).

If there is a real shared commitment, the use of a person-centred planning approach in transition can:

■ move the focus away from satisfying the bureaucratic imperatives of the statutory agencies, and instead make sure that the interests of the young person and their family are central to the process;
■ be used to flesh out and complement the formal assessment tools already used by professionals – enhancing the picture of the young person's life to date and aspirations for the future;
■ improve interagency coordination;

- improve and strengthen the relationship between ⦙
  and local community facilities that might have a rol⦙
  future plan.

Adopting a more person–centred approach and ⦙
undertake or lead their own planning increases thei⦙
and helps address the complaint often made by f⦙
planning is not based around what is important to t⦙

There is a role here for advocacy organisations t⦙
with people, and to provide support and even training, so that families and
self-advocates can take a leadership role in the preparation of their own
plans. The young people and their families will also feel that they are in
control of what is going on if they receive good, accessible information on
direct payments and personal budgets.

Practical examples of productive supports for the introduction of a person-
centred transition approach include:

- making adjustments to traditional meeting and review formats, providing
  help to students who do not communicate with words, and providing
  tailored assistance for people from minority ethnic communities;
- providing more accessible information that will help people make more
  informed choices, for example, videos, easy-read booklets, transition fairs,
  taster sessions that allow people to sample local community opportunities,
  and informal courses about local adult services;
- making independent advocacy available in school;
- providing training for school to support staff, with the introduction of
  person-centred planning in the school.

The importance of efforts to improve the transition experience is underlined
by the stark conclusion reached by Heslop et al (2004, p 108) in 'Bridging
the divide at transition':

> One of the most striking findings from this project was how
> little difference transition planning seemed to make to the young
> people's lives, particularly in relation to employment and housing
> opportunities. This was largely because so few options were
> available. The lack of any real choice or options was a reason given
> by parents for why it was so difficult for their children to participate
> in decision making about their future. It was also for many parents
> the most negative thing about the planning process.

Giving the young person a voice. Young people and their families should be
helped to develop the skills and confidence to take the lead role in transition

ning. Support staff, including social workers, must ensure that young people and their families know that there is nothing wrong with having high aspirations for their son or daughter, and challenging the views of professionals.

Starting planning early. Young people and their families must get clear personal and timely information that explains the stages of transition. As personal budgets become more and more the norm, it is even more important than ever that transition planning is person-centred, and is started early.

Providing good information to the young person and their family. Young people and their families and service professionals often report a lack of timely information about planning, services and budgets, and that this hampers their ability to plan effectively and creatively. Before and during transition planning, young people, families and professionals need access to good information about what is possible and what support is available.

Offering real options, real choices and real budgets. A range of options and choices should be made available to the young person who is leaving school. These should be based on and designed around the informed choices and needs of the young person, and should support them to access universal services and non-specialist opportunities (Routledge, 2000).

Making sure services and supports are well coordinated. Effective transition should bridge the gulf between children and adult services. The risk with current systems is that no one takes responsibility for making sure plans are made and followed through. Because the various partners involved have very different organisational cultures and working practices, it is necessary for someone to take an effective leadership role that encourages the participation of the various partners, ensures timely delivery, and monitors quality and outcomes (DH, 2011a).

Staff working in the agencies involved – education, children's services, adult services and transition services – must work at improving their communication throughout the process.

If we are going to address the challenge of poor coordination, the players from different agencies need to be clear about their own role, and the specific roles of the wide range of other professionals who might be involved, and who might need to be increasingly person-centred in their methods and their outcomes.

Using the positive experiences of young people and their families. One very productive and low-cost approach that can be tried is to set up mentoring arrangements in which young people and their families who have gone through transition provide support to new families. This can have the positive effect of raising expectations among professionals with limited experience of supporting young people with learning difficulties through the process of transition.

Extending the life experiences of young people with learning difficulties before leaving school. This can be as simple as encouraging younger people with learning difficulties to try for Saturday jobs, and for schools and other support agencies to help young people avail themselves of good work experience placements and volunteering opportunities.

Learning from what works well – using outcomes-based evidence. There is a growing body of evidence on the effectiveness of person-centred planning. The flexible use of the tools and techniques that have been developed improve the chances of delivering transition plans that really are based on what the young person wants, and of monitoring the achievement of the outcomes they and their family desire. At present there are few, if any, agreed structures for monitoring the quality and delivery of transition plans (DH, 2011a).

The task of introducing person-centred transition plans needs to address the fact that staff in children's services have little knowledge about what people with learning disabilities can achieve, and about some of the creative options that might be available.

Remembering that there are other transitions in the future. The process and activities of transition must allow and support young people to develop skills and interests that they can continue and further develop after leaving school. Post-school educational or vocational options must allow young people to build careers.

Addressing the ten challenges at organisational and policy level

How can a social worker and their managers improve transition practice and change the system at organisational and policy level?

Being fully person-centred. Concern is sometimes expressed that schools may not be as committed to person-centred planning as they could be because they do not have a long-term stake in the outcomes of the planning (DH, 2011a). It is important for there to be visible and explicit 'buy-in' for the full-scale adoption of person-centred planning within local transition at agency or authority level, and that this incorporates a commitment to the involvement from agencies beyond the statutory sector in facilitating transition plans.

The agreements should be consolidated by including a commitment to the provision of training and support for staff, from all the agencies involved, young people, their families and others.

Giving the young person a voice. Agencies can commit to supporting independent self-advocacy and citizen advocacy programmes, and to citizen leadership initiatives that support young people with additional support needs to be more present, more involved and more influential in their local communities.

Starting planning early. For transition to be most effective, it should always start well in advance of school leaving. Only then will it be possible to do good enough preparation and planning with the person, their family and the agencies involved in their future support. Commitment of time is necessary so that the young person's needs and aspirations are properly discussed, evaluated and developed.

It is vital that key services are involved as early as possible in transition planning, and especially as supports are being designed for people.

Providing good information to the young person and their family. Before and during transition planning, young people, their families and professionals need access to good, accessible information about what is possible and what support is available (DH, 2011a). Lack of such information about planning, services and budgets places obstacles in the way of achieving individually tailored, creative transition plans.

Service staff need to be supported to provide and share information on examples of best practice from elsewhere, ideas about creative alternatives, and not just the standard service options currently provided locally.

Offering real options, real choices and real budgets. Some young people and their families still don't have access to personal budgets. Personalisation and self-directed support arrangements (including RAS and provider development) are not consistent across different localities. Managers need to ensure that clear information and support is made available to families to take advantage of this route. Some groups will, in fact, need focused extra support to take up personal budgets. This was exemplified earlier in this chapter in the case study of the Grapevine All Means All project supporting people in transition from BME communities in Coventry.

Making sure services and supports are well coordinated. As already noted above, transition support often fails to bridge the gulf between children and adult services, with no single agency or worker taking responsibility for creating good practical future plans for individuals, and then making sure that these are properly implemented. Transition activity really must be coordinated between all key agencies and professionals, to avoid confusion, duplication and overlap for young people and their families.

To address the challenge of poor coordination, joint or integrated transition has been created in an attempt to improve cohesion between agencies. There are many varieties of transition team with different degrees of formal inter-organisational collaboration – for example, there are single or joint agency teams that span children and adult services, and joint teams within either children or adult services (Hudson, 2006). What they should all share is an acceptance and belief that there is a need to use professional time and resources more effectively during the transition period.

Another approach is to appoint transition coordinators whose role is to improve overall coherence. These may have a role across agency boundaries or a role within each key agency. Transition coordinators operate at practitioner level or at a senior level in agencies, where they work to enhance the coherence of efforts and to improve working links between agencies in transition work.

In some areas, communication problems have been addressed at inter-organisational level through the creation of shared protocols. However, in many areas, collaboration remains limited, and is not yet working to fully integrate self-directed support, personalisation and personal budgets into the process.

Hudson (2006) points out that in addition to such technical efforts to improve communication, it is important to recognise the importance of measures that are designed to improve knowledge across agencies, and also approaches to improving relationships between professionals that can be instrumental in improving the efficacy of joint working.

Using the positive experiences of young people and their families. Agencies can easily incorporate stories of the educational, entrepreneurial and social/recreational achievement of young people with learning difficulties in multi-agency training programmes, and in information leaflets and resource materials about transition provided to each new generation of young people and families as they reach and work their way through the transition process.

Extending the life experiences of young people with learning difficulties before leaving school. Schools and families can seek to improve the ability of young people to make independent choices by widening their repertoire of social and cultural experiences.

Learning from what works well – using outcomes-based evidence. We know from hard evidence that person-centred planning is effective (Robertson et al,

2005). Yet it is still the case that training for support staff across the agencies involved in transition support is patchy, or even non-existent. Inter-agency commitment to person-centred working, backed up by a commitment to training, can and will help address this situation. Agencies, the government and researchers need to back this up by developing ways of monitoring the impact and effectiveness of person-centred planning.

Agencies also need to get better at educating staff and families about how a personal budget would work, and at committing to working with people on how to complement service support with natural and unpaid support. In this regard, circles of support, community circles and neighbourhood networks are crucial.

Remembering that there are other transitions in the future. At organisational and inter-organisational level it is all too easy to forget that a decent experience of transition will enable young people to develop skills and interests that they can maintain and develop after they leave school. These skills and experiences can be supported and acknowledged in later transitions, such as when the young person leaves home to live in their own place, or leaves college to go to a job.

Conclusion

To support young people with learning difficulties to navigate the path to adult life, it is essential to focus on outcomes and activities rather than on services. It is important that there is action to make plans happen, not just reflection on what a 'good enough' future might look like. If social workers and their partner professionals in the other agencies concentrate on what needs to happen, rather than focusing on service structures, it is more likely that the transition will be characterised by all of those with a stake in the young person's future coming up with creative proposals for delivering support for a 'good life' – even a great one – through working on relationships, employment, and when appropriate, an independent home life.

In this spirit, the following chapters address the issues of setting up a home, getting a job and having a family.

5 Setting up home

In view of the dissolution of the traditional, often Victorian, institutions in favour of community living, this chapter considers what differentiates a 'house' from a 'home', and why this is important in the lives of people with learning difficulties. Community living, in its various forms, is discussed, and its characteristics set out, together with case studies that also reflect on the challenges for social workers and families. The chapter concludes with a reminder that having a house is only the starting point to creating a better life, and that in order to do this, individuals require support to move beyond community living towards fostering community connections.

Leaving home and setting up house

Leaving home is one of the biggest life changes that a person with learning disabilities will make, so it's important to spend time considering what they would like, and what kind of life their family carers envisage for them.

Many people with learning disabilities are able to express clear views of their own, and it's important that those involved talk to and involve them in planning for them to leave home. In addition to parents, there may also be other people, such as grandparents, school teachers and others, who know the person well and who can be helpfully involved in the consultation.

Some parents may always have envisaged their son or daughter leaving home when they became an adult; others may have planned to continue caring until ageing, illness or other difficulties make it impossible for them to continue in their primary caring role. Whichever is the case, for most parents, being a carer has been a positive choice and an enjoyable experience, and they may be reluctant to start even thinking about change. All parents tend to feel anxious when their children leave home, and change can feel daunting, even when it's likely to benefit everyone in the long run.

By engaging in planning and preparing for a move it is more likely that the person with learning disabilities will get the right kind of housing and support. It can take a long time, even several years, to find the right home and the right support. What is clear is that waiting until serious illness or some other family crisis forces parents to act quickly will almost certainly mean that there will be fewer choices and less time for everyone to get used to the idea.

Making a house a home

Etmanski et al (2015: forthcoming) point out that parents the world over rate as one of their highest priorities for their sons and daughters to have a stable and hospitable living environment. They also state that a house, however, doesn't become a home automatically. It requires thoughtfulness and care.

What does 'home' mean to the person with learning disabilities? What are they used to? How might that be re-created? How can you ensure that their life will be lived to the fullest there?

Etmanski et al are clear that:

> You can create a sense of home wherever you live and regardless of who owns or manages the building, house, or flat. The key to creating a home is to:
>
> • have control over the home environment
> • make sure it reflects your family member's personality
> • ensure that your family member chooses who, if anyone, they live with. (Etmanski et al, 2015: forthcoming, p 67)

No matter where the person lives, it is important for them to have a choice in the matter. Of course some people will want to live on their own, whereas others will want to share with people they know and like. Some will live quite independently; others will need intensive staff support.

Nowadays there are many high-quality providers that are responsive and genuinely sensitive to helping the people they support have a good home life. But families still worry. What if there is a change of staff or service manager? What if there is a change in the leadership of the agency? What will happen if there are funding cutbacks?

Although there are now many excellent supported living options, many families we work with remain cautious, and express concerns that:

■ someone else may ultimately decide where their family member lives and with whom;
■ in some services the 'atmosphere' is shaped not by those who live there, but by the people who work there;
■ in group settings, an individual's needs and aspirations can sometimes become secondary to those of the other tenants;
■ people in individual tenancies can become isolated and lonely;
■ not all services welcome the active involvement of family and friends;
■ in services with high staff turnover, the loss of caring and understanding staff can have an immediate impact on individuals.

As a result of these kinds of concerns, more and more families are looking for alternatives that provide flexibility, continuity and greater control. One such option is self-directed support.

Think spot

What makes a home a home?

Take two minutes to think about what makes a house a home for you, and jot these down. It might help to contrast this with a time when you lived somewhere that you didn't consider home, and note why.

> Did you choose where to live, and who lives with you?
> Do you have a key?
> Do you control who has access?
> Do you have to ask permission to decorate?
> Do you have security of tenure?
> Do you like spending time there?
> Does the house reflect your taste and style?

Compare your answers with those you imagine would be given by someone you know with a learning difficulty. Where are the overlaps? What are the differences? Why is this the case?

Why having a home life is important

Without a decent place to live and without a secure base, it is difficult to participate in society, to be included, and to contribute. And having a home of one's own is not something people with learning difficulties take for granted. The majority of those not living with their families do not control or own their living space, and probably don't even have security of tenure. Whereas 75 per cent of people are homeowners, only 12 per cent of people with learning difficulties rent or own their own home (Fitzpatrick, 2006b). Even those who have always lived at home are vulnerable to 'crisis resettlement' in the event of their carer's death or illness. Not only do nearly 50 per cent of people with learning difficulties live with their families, but 29,000 live with parents who are over 70 years old (Mencap, 2001). For these reasons, social workers should have an acute interest in the housing field, despite its structural and legal 'separateness'. To make a difference in people's lives, social work must engage with housing matters, and re-think assumptions based on individual incapacity and family dedication that have characterised professional design for living options for people with learning difficulties.

Evolution of different approaches

This 'domination' of service development by the trend for 'deinstitutionalisation' over the last 40 years (Emerson and Hatton, 2005) can be seen as a continuum or evolution from total institutions accommodating thousands in the heyday of 'mental handicap' hospitals, to residential care and hostels in the community (congregating 25-30 people), to small group homes (6-8 people initially, or 2-6 later), to supported living, individual tenancies and home ownership. Research findings broadly support the idea that 'small is beautiful', with such community-based models scoring better on quality of care and life than congregate settings.

Challenge of community living

By the early years of the 21st century, most learning disability hospitals had already closed, or closure was imminent (Scottish Government, 2000; DH, 2001a). We have also now become more sophisticated in our understanding of the dangers of assuming that deinstitutionalisation is about disposing of large buildings alone. Experience of developing community resources over the past 30 years has taught us about the pitfall of 'mini-institutions' in the community (Collins, 1995; Ager et al, 2001). As Kinsella crisply reminds us, institutions are a 'state of mind', and that while size and the nature of the support practices are important, it is 'changing the balance of power (in favour of service users) that is the real key to deinstitutionalisation' (2005, p 41).

A parallel conceptual point was made by Michael Bayley (1973) in the early years of the development of community services – namely, that a distinction should be drawn between 'care in the community' and 'care by the community'. In other words, 'community presence', to use the language of the five frameworks for accomplishment (O'Brien, 1987), doesn't guarantee integration in and belonging to that community. The challenge of community living initiatives is to get people who use services to become 'connected' with other people, as well as being 'present' in the places where everyone else lives, works and plays, and to ensure their centrality to the decision making in how that is achieved.

Community living is where formal services and unpaid supports are arranged in such a way that people are able to live in their own homes and are part of their own local community. In other words, this approach aspires to respond to individual needs to live in a home, not simply a 'home-like setting', a place where an individual has been involved in the choice of home and the people who support them. The service is built around the individual rather than the individual being fitted into a service or filling a recent 'void'. Traditional services (such as in residential care) usually consist of buildings and staff who exist independently of any particular service user's presence or particular configuration of needs and wants. Individuals are in the position of applicants for any service whose staff then decide on suitability; the individual is not the commissioner of the service. The service offered is likely to have general relevance to needs, but is unlikely to be tailored to meet precise ones.

The ability to construct/conceive of individualised services has been promoted by recent legislation and guidance (Community Care Acts, Supporting People, and in particular, individualised funding and most recently the In Control initiative,[1] *Putting People First* [HM Government, 2007] and in Scotland, the introduction of new national guidance on the introduction of self-directed support [Scottish Executive, 2007]), as well as by the aspirations of people who use services and their families. This has also had implications for how services, statutory and voluntary, are managed, and how individual social workers operate (more on this later).

There is a range of terminology in the literature by which this concept of community living is described – in particular, 'supported living', 'supported housing', 'independent living' and 'ordinary life'. The terms are often used in the context of hospital resettlement and the re-provisioning of community-based residential services, but can be equally applied to building support around someone in situ, for example, following the death of a parent or other change in circumstances. It is also relevant to more recent developments in the field of 'home ownership' and people with learning difficulties (Fitzpatrick, 2006b).

Earlier influential concepts, important in creating a culture of community care, such as 'an ordinary life' developed by the King's Fund (1980), and 'supported accommodation', certainly have overlaps with the concept of community or supported living, but may not reflect all the criteria encompassed within it.

It might help to spell out how community living differs from the continuum of care (residential care and group homes) familiar to most practitioners. It does require a different way of thinking and acting. The characteristics of community living are set out below:

■ *Support for the individual, not their 'readiness'*. This is the guiding service principle. In other words, eligibility does not depend on capacity, but on the right to have a home and to live in the community alongside everyone else. In person-centred planning, this is sometimes referred to as the 'gifts' model rather than the 'deficit' model (Snow, 1992), and is based on rights or citizenship rather than welfare.

■ *Person-centredness.* Being person-centred means engaging with the worldview of the individual requiring support. Here, support is tailored to individual requirements rather the availability of service providers or simply patching people into 'voids' in existing resources. Staff are *accountable to users*, not only agencies, and may even be direct employees. This point is essentially about where the power is located – with the user, or with the service? Direct payments, the ILF, the In Control initiative and self-directed support effectively make the service user the employer, and therefore well able to recruit and manage staff in a way that reflects this locus of control.

■ *Assumption of competence.* Related to the idea of gifts is that of competence. This requires support to start from the assumption that not only do individuals have something to offer, but that with support they will be able to participate, to manage, to make decisions. It means that if one arrangement doesn't work, that staff need to see this as an insufficiency in their input rather than seeing the individual as 'too disabled'.

■ *Inclusion.* The purpose of inclusion is not simply to be present in the community, but to 'belong'. The concept of 'getting a life rather than getting a service' has become influential for those promoting this approach to community living. All this is related to the support and citizenship model. It means that staff need to conceive their task as one of a 'community facilitator' or 'connector' rather than as a care worker within four walls (Rowley et al, 2009). This is a major change in worldview that is very difficult to achieve, especially as regulation and registration increasingly pull services in opposite, risk-averse ways.

■ *Control.* Aligned with the importance of having some control over who, if anyone, people live with, is that it should be services that move and not people. The classic example is when an elderly parent dies and the remaining son or daughter is moved into residential care in response to the crisis, without consideration of whether they might be supported in situ or nearby.

■ *All means all.* When the support model is truly embedded, services will be supporting individuals irrespective of disability, and not using the disability as an eligibility criterion.

Taking into account what people with learning difficulties say about their preference for independent living if they can't be at home with family (McConkey, 2005), as well as the looming housing crisis for the large numbers of people still living at home when parents die (Mencap, 2002), supported living models represent an important way forward.

Independent living may be a difficult concept for some BME families to comprehend. In such circumstances, work with local communities may be necessary in considering possible options. 'Independence within the family' may be an alternative to traditional options (Foundation for People with Learning Disabilities, 2012).

Fiona's story

Fiona is in her mid-thirties, and has always lived with her parents and her younger brother, until he married. Fiona went to special school, has limited speech, but can make herself understood by people who know her well; she has strong preferences. She attends a day centre reluctantly, but enjoys the two days a week helping in a local charity shop.

When Fiona's mother suddenly died from a pernicious leukaemia, the whole family was thrown into disarray and her father was increasingly unable to cope with Fiona's distress that manifested itself in her refusal to go to the day centre, her inability to sleep and her increasingly poor control of her epilepsy. Fiona's father's employer has been 'understanding', but six months on is beginning to lose patience with his absences.

One day, after her father lost his temper at her refusal to go to the day centre and shouted at her, Fiona arrived on her brother's doorstep saying she was moving in with him. He called social services.

What is the social work response?
A place in a group home, about 20 miles away, with five other people in it and 24-hour staff support. Increasingly distressed behaviour, deteriorating health and pushing over another resident who banged her head led to an admission to an assessment unit in a former long-stay 'mental handicap' hospital. During the next three years living on a ward during the week and at home over the weekends, no one came up with alternatives.

What might be the alternatives?
Starting afresh and working back from the ideal – a house in her old neighbourhood, near her father, no one to interfere with her possessions, near the charity shop and a very supportive GP. A specialist supported housing broker helped Fiona get a grant form the Health Board and Communities Scotland for a deposit, established that Fiona had capacity, although limited communication, so her father took power of attorney; raised a mortgage with a bank; and applied for extra Income Support to pay for her mortgage

interest and direct payment for a support worker chosen by Fiona, who lives with her as a flat-mate.

What this story demonstrates is the vulnerability of individuals and the programmed response of services in a crisis to seek an institutional solution. The flip-side of this is the widespread lack of forward planning, and indeed, reluctance to plan even among elderly parents (McConkey et al, 2006). This same study (McConkey et al, 2006) also showed that professionals had not approached families about future provision for their disabled son or daughter, and ignorance of possible options was widespread.

Joe and Marie's story

Joe's mum, Marie, is 70 years old, but increasingly frail from rheumatism and arthritis. She knows from the experience of Joe's friend at the day centre that the council won't let him stay in the house when she dies, because "mentally handicapped people can't understand a tenancy agreement." The parish priest suggests she look into the Right to Buy scheme, and maybe Joe could inherit the house. The house is ideal for Joe, who has significant mobility problems, because it is adapted and has space for his various aids. Marie had never owned a house and worried about the upkeep, even for herself. So the priest suggests consulting the social worker.

What is the social work response?
The social worker is sympathetic, and gives Marie and Joe information about a specialist housing association with accommodation for small groups of people around Joe's age in ordinary houses supported by staff. They like this suggestion, but there are long waiting lists. Another option is that a local nursing home has regular vacancies (people die!), and the social worker suggests a trial visit for a weekend. It goes well, but Joe is very quiet on his return, and from his suitcase, it seems he hasn't changed his clothes while there. The second time he refuses to go, saying he was hungry and there was nothing to do. Marie stops sleeping because of the worry, and the GP says he'll ring the social worker. She says her hands are tied with the current budget cuts, but suggests an independent advocacy organisation.

What are the options?
Joe has an adapted house that meets his needs well, and he likes the street, which isn't too busy for him to get across the road to the shops. He has two friends down the road and in the local church. It is likely that Marie could buy the house and manage the upkeep, but the thought of it worries her too much, and so the advocate concentrates on challenging the council's presumptive

view that Joe couldn't agree to the tenancy. No one in housing has seen him or asked for an expert view. Marie gets specialist legal housing advice to the effect that the decision to refuse to assign the lease to Joe could be challenged in court where the council would have to prove he couldn't understand the tenancy, *even with support*. Marie, the advocate who is familiar with person-centred planning, and the priest have begun to build a network of local friends and a plan for the future, including an application for a direct payment and information at the ready from Income Support to meet the rent costs. The social worker has subsequently moved on.

This is a typical story of presumptions about capacity on the part of housing, attempts by the social worker to secure a more forward-looking option within the standard range of options, but being beaten by resource and budgetary constraints, and discontinuity in professional support. What may be less atypical is an older parent who is attempting to plan ahead, a social worker who recognises the importance of independent advocacy, and an advocate prepared to invest time in challenging the system. What is crucial here is the concept of understanding 'with support', and the existence of a network of people who are around for the long term and not just until the next job, to make that support a reality.

Expanding the range of options

Quite apart from perceptions and ingrained professional conventions around accommodating people with learning difficulties, there is a knowledge gap in expanding the range of options available to people with learning difficulties. Professionals do not often realise that even if someone relies on benefits, they can still get a mortgage; that benefits can be used to support mortgage payments; that the path through the legal complexities of questions of 'capacity' can be smoothed by the creation of trusts, the use of Power of Attorney and the promotion in the Adults with Incapacity (Scotland) Act 2001 and the Mental Capacity Act 2005 that introduced a modernised concept of capacity as multi-faceted rather than an 'all-or-nothing' one.

It is a tough path for a busy professional to take because there are conventional options that are more available and more accessible funding routes. It is likely that statutory social workers will be under pressure to 'move on to the next case' once plans are in place, and are therefore unable to develop relationships of sufficient trust to consult and support families over the length of time required to put these arrangements in place. It is important for workers to ally themselves with like-minded colleagues, and with organisations such as the housing brokerage service and the independent advocacy organisation featured in the above example, which can do this.

While social workers are not housing officers, and are typically not well informed on complex housing matters, they need to make this their business as it raises important issues of equality, personalisation and inclusion (Pannell and Harker, 2010). It is important to advocate that the needs of people with learning difficulties, including those from BME communities, are included in local authority housing strategies.

Being competent and knowledgeable in this area also presents challenges in supporting families, individuals and services to invest time and energy dealing with the complexities. Social workers have skills in all these domains.

Beyond supported living – fostering community connections

For our purposes, it is the idea of mutual support and community connections that is important. Both were initially greeted with suspicion by professionals and commissioners of services. A service built on mutual support was seen not only as unrealistic, but also, from a normalisation perspective, as stigmatising, by 'forcing people with learning difficulties together' (Poll, 2007, p 53). There is a classic story of staff resisting the idea of a KeyRing t-shirt as stigmatising, but as an evaluation pointed out, this missed the point that KeyRing was an association, a club of which members were intensely proud, and not a service. This also misses the point that people have skills and 'gifts' to offer, not just problems and deficits to be made good; they have resources that can be pumped into the community, as well as supporting fellow members.

People with learning difficulties and their families' views of their options

We know relatively little about what families and individuals with learning difficulties think of these models of community living, not only because they are new, but also because the majority of people with learning difficulties have always lived at home with their family (Braddock et al, 2001). Models for community living have emerged out of the experience of closing institutions, specifically the long-stay 'mental handicap' hospitals, but have informed the re-provisioning of traditional residential homes and hostels in the community.

Two studies in Northern Ireland (McConkey, 2005; McConkey et al, 2006) produced some interesting insights from both people with learning difficulties and their parents. They agreed about two things. First, participation in the research was the first time that they felt their views and preferences had been explicitly sought. Second, the preferred option for everyone was living with their family.

It is at the point that family living is not possible that divergences begin to occur. People with learning difficulties had a preference for independent living rather than group homes, despite the experience of some harassment in some neighbourhoods. Those aspects of their living situation that were most important to them were their own bedroom, playing a part in the running of the home, ready access to activities that were community-based, and contact with family and friends. This was true irrespective of where they lived. Their preference for independent living was at odds with parental preference for residential or nursing home placements. In a crisis, and combined with professional views, a tendency for this preference to prevail was identified (McConkey et al, 2004).

It also emerged that not only were most parents reluctant to consider future living arrangements for their son or daughter living at home, but they were also poorly informed about the range of options available and their differential benefits, they lacked ongoing support from social services to tackle these difficult issues, and relatives were relatively 'home-bound', apart from attendance at day centres. There was a degree of what McConkey calls 'separateness' rather than partnership between professionals and families. There is clearly a way to go before professional practice reflects the views of service users, and engages with the conflicts between them.

However, as services become more personalised and choice is a key factor in empowerment and control, it is important that one monolithic form of service provision – institutional living – is not simply replaced on a 'take-it-or-leave-it' basis by another – independent living. What seems important is that there is no default position, no Hobson's choice; we need to be able to support people to make a range of choices – some may opt for intentional communities, and others to become homeowners. Some may choose to live on their own or with a friend as part of a mutually supportive network, such as KeyRing; others may choose to employ a flat-mate.

The increasing provision of direct funding, in which control for commissioning a service passes from professionals to people with disabilities, whether in the form of direct payments or through the In Control initiative and individual budgets, will support diversity in the social care system. However, this change in the social care system needs to be matched by a comparable culture shift in professional practice.

Housing Options Scotland offers these helpful suggestions about how to plan for, and find, the right house in the right place:

■   It is easier to think about where someone wants to live, and then about the type of house and the type of support they might want, once it's clearer what type of life they want, and what they want to do.
■   Think about what type of support this person wants, and then look at which support services can provide this.
■   Start planning early, as it can take a while to get the right house in the right place, especially if someone needs a special type of house.
■   Think of a house and support for someone as a way of helping them have the type of life they want, rather than letting the house determine everything else.

Conclusion

In answer to the question 'What makes a house a home?', three main areas come to mind: control over the home environment; ensuring that it reflects the personality of the person who lives there; and choice over who else lives there, if anyone. Many forms of community living have emerged in the wake of the closure of institutions, although few offer people with learning disabilities security of tenure. Homeownership, in particular, is underdeveloped, and we have seen examples here illustrating how this can be achieved. Without a decent home and a secure base, it is difficult to participate in community living. As Kinsella (2005) points out, institutional living is a state of mind as much as bricks and mortar. Kinsella also explores how easy it can be for an institutional mindset to re-assert itself in the face of a crisis such as the current austerity measures facing many local authorities.

For hard-pressed social workers without like-minded colleagues, and without support from organisations such as housing brokerage services and independent advocacy resources, it is difficult to sustain individualised, inclusive and support-led planning; conventional options and standard solutions based on competence and 'readiness' models may seem more appealing. The challenge for social workers is to recognise that having a house and a home is not an end in itself; it is a means and a starting point for building the kind of life the service user wants.

Note
[1] See www.in-control.org.uk

6 Getting a job: from occupation to employment

In this chapter we focus on the ongoing debates about:

■ the place and value of work in the lives of people with learning difficulties;
■ supported employment, personalisation and co-production;
■ whether there is still a place for day centres;
■ the role and contribution of social work in this rapidly changing area of practice.

We explore how day services, despite their greater proximity and susceptibility to outside influences, initially evolved in common with hospital and residential services within the dominant 'serviceland' paradigm; in other words, only those individuals who were 'ready' for work, college or independent living moved outwith the service ambit. The chapter concludes with a discussion of how the application of the concepts of 'support' can breach these confines, with particular reference to 'supported' employment, person-centredness and co-production. The questions of how social work can contribute to making a difference in people's lives, and of how to ensure that social workers, as professionals, continue to listen, rather than applying another 'set' solution, are addressed.

Why the f★★k would I want to go there [ATC]? We were treated like weans and the staff called the shots. We had to call the centre manager Mrs Smith while she called us by our first names. We did the same old things every day. Boring. What was the point of them? Now they have a resource centre and everybody goes out in the community. I see them walking up and down the shopping mall. Guess what? They are even more bored now. (Heartfelt associate, 2012, personal communication)

I liked going to my centre in Glasgow. I felt respected, and that was where my friends went. Had gone there for years and the next thing, the council closed it down. No more centres they said, but no one asked the people who went there what they thought. No one helped us stay in touch and I lost most of my friends. Did they think that having friends who had a learning disability wasn't a good thing? (Heartfelt associate, quoted by Hunter, 2012, personal communication)

What are we to make of these two quotes? The speakers are talking about day centres which, until very recently, were the main option for daytime activity for people with learning difficulties. In fact, attendance at a day centre, from leaving school until 'retirement', could be the only service on offer, apart from no service. What these quotes tell us is that for some, attendance at day centres was 'boring', but that it could be equally boring spending time wandering around shopping centres in the name of 'community care and inclusion'. For others, the closure of centres has resulted in loss of friendships, often long-standing, and loss of identity and respect derived from these connections. The second quote also contains the serious challenge that the emphasis by service providers and commissioners on the importance and superiority in a post-day centre world of mixing with non-disabled people has, for many people with learning difficulties, undermined their self-esteem by putting a lesser value on people with learning difficulties as friends.

There is a cautionary message here for social workers, that replacing one monolithic approach to service delivery with another may lead to no better experience from the user perspective, and indeed, might undermine important relationships in the process. If we fail to listen to people, we may fail them on a broader front, however inclusive and 'modernising' our intentions are in terms of current policy documents. In this context, a person-centred approach and co-production in assessment and planning are central to positive outcomes, especially at transition points, such as that from school to the adult world. We must remind ourselves that the question is what is important 'to' the person, and not what we think is important 'for' them.

What the quotes don't convey is anything about the importance of work in the aspirations of people with learning difficulties. We know that most people with learning difficulties aspire to paid jobs, but only 10 per cent ever realise this ambition, despite the knowledge and technology to deliver 'real jobs' for disabled people, including people with complex needs (Gold, 1980; Emerson and Hatton, 2005; Beyer and Robinson, 2009). We also know that central government policy to promote 'real jobs' has both philosophical and pragmatic drivers to achieve positive gains for individuals with difficulties, for wider society, and for the economy (DH, 2009a). The government made clear its belief that all people with learning difficulties should share equally in the aspiration set out in the 'life chances' report that 'any disabled person who wants a job, and needs support to get a job, should be able to do so' by 2025 (PMSU et al, 2005, p 17).

The Foundation for People with Learning Disabilities report, *Learning Difficulties and Ethnicity: Updating a framework for action* (2012), notes that 'It is difficult for some communities to accept the idea of paid work for people with learning difficulties because of how learning difficulty is understood and perceived in certain cultures. This sort of stigmatisation can lead to people being hidden away from the rest of society....' (pp 16-17).

The report also notes that people with learning difficulties from BME and newly arrived groups may experience language barriers as well as issues of cultural insensitivity when they are seeking work.

Evolution of day services – from institutions to supported employment

Given the dominance of the 'mental handicap' hospital closure programme and deinstitutionalisation outlined earlier in Chapter Two, it is easy to forget that most people with learning difficulties have always lived in the community, and mostly with their families (Mencap, 2014).

Services to support them and their families have evolved slowly, through a range of different, often co-existing and competing models, focusing on occupation, training, social education, respite, and eventually, in more recent times, supported employment.

Occupation

The evolution of day services since the Mental Deficiency Act 1913 has been 'piecemeal', reflecting gradual acceptance by the government of responsibility for the welfare of vulnerable groups, and society's increasing awareness and knowledge of their needs (National Development Group, 1977). This evolution can be seen in the constantly changing names and functions, from occupation, to adult training, to social education and resource centres. For this reason, perhaps together with a lack of scandals, low political visibility, but proactive parental support, day services have proved more resistant to closure than learning disability 'mental handicap' hospitals. Nonetheless, the 1913 legislation was custodial in intent, and sealed the trend for segregation and containment in day services for people with learning difficulties just as certainly as in the institutions.

While the 1913 Act introduced the possibility of compulsory detention in hospital on the grounds of disability, it also enabled local authorities to develop resources for 'occupation, training and supervision' for 'defectives' living in the community. The development of occupation centres was slowed by the First World War and, on the run-up to the next, there were 4,000 places in England and Wales (National Development Group, 1977). This was the era when few people with severe disabilities survived long into childhood, let alone into adulthood, and so those who did survive were relatively fit, and being 'occupied' meant contract work or repetitive assembly work. Occupation centres essentially operated as sheltered workshops; other people simply stayed at home with their families. The element of containment in these arrangements is clearly visible.

Following the Second World War and the accompanying changing climate of social expectations that influenced so many aspects of British society, culminating in the creation of the welfare state, the National Health Service, affordable public housing to name but a few, there was a steady but significant expansion in day centre places. This increase was driven by several factors including: the shift away from institutional living and towards community-based provision, discernible in government documents such as the *Royal Commission on the law relating to mental illness and mental deficiency* (HMSO, 1957); by advances in professional knowledge and practice about the potential for people with learning difficulties to learn; and by the parents of people with learning difficulties who began to mobilise and campaign for support services.

Training

Enabling powers with regard to residential accommodation, training and support in the 1913 Act were converted into duties on local authorities. In relation to 'mental handicap', most local authorities had developed ATCs by the 1970s; the White Paper *Better services for the mentally handicapped* (DH, 1971) had set targets for service development in the community over the following 20 years; and a model of good practice in ATCs was published by the-then Ministry of Health (1968, cited in Thatcher, 1971). This provided explicit guidance that the main function of the centres was to train people to move out of them into outside employment – a process that would now be called 'train and place'. However, in the absence of a strategy to achieve this, train-and-place objectives remained at an aspirational level; the majority of individuals became life-long 'trainees' and remained 'stuck' in centres where occupation continued to be provided for those who did not move on.

Attention also turned to the other recommendation in the White Paper, to undertake explicit assessment of users' needs. The question 'assessment for what?' is a good one. It seems that it was assessment for graduating through an internal tiered system ranked by increasing levels of skill. Ultimately some detailed systems were developed, resulting in a stratification of users based on degree of disability and on centres depending on function. Despite explicit guidance to train people for work so that they could move out of the centres, the robustness of the philosophy of containment is evident, and individuals continued to spend time in what we now call 'serviceland'.

Social education

The influential National Development Group pamphlet (1977) recommended that the role of the ATC be broadened even further to encompass education, leisure and independent living skills, and that they be renamed social education centres (SECs).

Clearly the ATCs/SECs were to be central planks in the drive towards community care, but it wasn't just about numbers. As the numbers of users of day services increased, so did the staff, but importantly, together with a push for professional training. In 1964 a national body for training staff working in centres, the Training Council for Teachers of the Mentally Handicapped, was created. The association with education and learning was apt, and reflected both a philosophical re-orientation towards prospects for learning and development, an assertion of professionalism, and an investment in staff development by the government. This body was ultimately absorbed into the social work training body, the Central Council for Education and Training in Social Work (CCETSW).

Respite

Parents of people with learning difficulties began to mobilise and campaign in the post-war period. This was also an international phenomenon (Perske, 1972), and reflected the growing confidence of citizens to lobby for entitlement to community-based provision. Unlike parents of non-disabled children who could look forward to diminishing responsibility over time, these parents continued to care, but sought in return services that provided an opportunity for their sons and daughters and daytime respite for themselves. In relation to day services, the potential divergence of interest and concern between users and parents is stark. It is one that is not resolved but requires re-visiting, re-shaping and re-negotiating as each generation of model emerges, and one type of service or option morphs into another. The legitimacy of the parents' position in the face of modernising services is well argued by Dowson (1998), and has resurfaced recently in *Valuing People Now* (HM Government, 2009), with the emergence of a significant gap between family and both users and professional perceptions on the closure and centrality of traditional day care services, especially for people with complex needs.

All things to all people – the struggle for clarity and consensus on purpose

By the time Seed (1987) in Scotland and Beyer et al (1994) in Wales undertook their surveys of day centres, the numbers of those attending had expanded in just over a decade, from 24,537 to 47,464 (Taylor and Taylor, 1986). The centres had become 'catch-all' operations, with a shift away from a sheltered workshop model to a social educational one, but also offering a broad range of activities, including some work-related ones, and daytime respite for carers. Inevitably, as reported by Stalker (2001), the centres were pursuing not only multiple objectives, but also sometimes conflicting ones. Overall there was a lack of focus, and what Wolfensberger termed 'model coherency', with the centres trying to be everything to everyone – social contact and some 'occupation' for users, safe respite for families, and manageability for staff.

Seed's research demonstrates just how diverse and indeed 'confusing' day care had become by identifying seven models – work, social care, further education, assessment and throughput, recreational, shared living and resource centre – which he then reduced to three recommended types of resource development – the 'work' resource centre, the 'further education' resource centre and the 'community resource' centre.

Think spot

A good illustration of the 'problem' and the struggle for coherency is to be found in a day services review from Glasgow of Strathclyde day services (Strathclyde Regional Council, 1993), at a time when the community care legislation was several years old. Consider the following service produced in the course of the audit.

People using the service

> A total of 3,500 adults with learning difficulties.
> Ranging in age from 16 to 85.
> A total of 120 people in each location.

Resources deployed to provide the service

> Fifty-one buildings.
> A total of 120 mainly qualified staff.
> A budget of £15 million.
> Eighty-four per cent absorbed by staffing and transport.

Service activities

> Education, personal development, leisure, employment, sport.

From the information provided, what initial conclusions can you draw about the nature of the service on offer?

Closer examination reveals the following further information:

> Sixty per cent of the people supported have spent 6-20 years in the service.
> Seventy per cent of the people had no additional disabilities requiring intensive support.
> Seventy-five per cent of people attending spent 4-5 days a week in the service buildings.
> Seventy-nine per cent had no further education input.
> Ninety-seven per cent had no involvement in work experience.

What is the likely experience of service users in this service? How does this match the aspirations of a 'good life' set out earlier in Chapter One?

Along with the authors of the review, you might conclude that far from fulfilling the policy objectives of an 'ordinary life', the service remained a segregated service for all but a tiny number, perpetuating social exclusion rather than promoting inclusion. Despite the explicit commitment of this service and its staff to personalised support, the extensive remit and activities of the organisation undermined its capacity to realise this.

The review went on to make a series of recommendations to make a reality of what it called 'full social integration'. In order to do this, it was decided to break the service down into three chunks – employment, leisure and education. While this is reminiscent of Seed's study (1987), there is a greater emphasis on the use of generic resources. So all the activities would move away from being centre-based towards integration into mainstream resources or buildings. In other words, leisure opportunities would be developed in community sports and cultural centres, education in mainstream colleges, and employment in business units. A 'growth' or developmental model would be initiated, but importantly, the 'readiness' model would be replaced with a 'support' one. Drawing on the Changeover Programme developed by Scottish Human Services (1995), the approach was conceived as a 'bottom–up' strategy that worked on a participative basis with users, carers/families and professional/service staff in what today would be termed 'co-production'. The other main example of this approach can be found the Changing Days Programme subsequently developed by the National Development Team (Wertheimer, 1996).

Resilience of the day centre model

Despite a greater appearance of focus on quality of life, skill development and community integration, day centres developed 'in the community' were, and continue to be, overwhelmed by the struggle to become 'of the community' (Bayley, 1973). A gap has developed between aspirations and reality, so that service users made 'excursions into the community', but have neither been supported to engage with it, nor developed skills to find an individual niche, identity and contribution (Ritchie et al, no date).

We now face a paradoxical situation in which few people with learning difficulties live in institutions, yet for large tracts of the day, they are transported back into 'serviceland', where they become stranded. Even if they undertake dispersed activities during the day, these tend to be filtered through paid staff, with few community connections bring made. Few people have moved out of 'serviceland', and despite the best intentions of the day care service, many users have expressed dissatisfaction and boredom (Strathclyde Regional Council, 1993). It is clear that people relying on day centres have become isolated in their own communities; only a few have overcome their 'deficits' and been considered 'ready' to move out. Increasing refinements of user groupings by degree of disability and diversification of activities has done nothing to realise the ambitions of community care nor the people who use the services, 65 per cent of whom said they wanted jobs (Glenn and Lyons, 1996). People have remained segregated and congregated, but with greater degrees of refinement.

So why has the pace of change in day services been so slow? Why has it proved so difficult to achieve comparable systemic change in day service provision? Why has the white elephant of day centres proved so resilient?

In contrast to the success of the 'mental handicap' hospital closure programmes, significant re-provisioning of day services from the traditional building-based ones has proved elusive. The reasons for this are not hard to identify. There has been no external impetus for change within day services comparable to that generated by the hospital scandals of the 1960s and 1970s

(Martin, 1984), or by the financial liability of replacing dilapidated Victorian buildings. There has been no national initiative at central government level comparable to the hospital resettlement programme that made central government monies (bridging finance) available to local authorities to allow a period of double funding while new, non-institutional services were established. Notwithstanding innovations such as supported employment, there has been no national consensus as to how day services should be re-provisioned, nor have any well-developed theoretical perspectives merged to underpin any modernising programme. Family carers have had legitimate concerns about the withdrawal of a resource that provides activities outside the home for a family member with learning difficulties and that allows other family members opportunities for work and respite (Dowson, 1998). And staff committed to promoting change within day services have been attracted into the supported employment schemes that began to take root in the UK in the 1980s (Beyer and Kilsby, 1996).

These changes have been incremental without producing the 'transformational change', that is to say, a change in the belief system, culture and structures. However, since the 1980s, we do have one exemplar of such transformational change, and that can be found in the concept of supported employment. This also sits well within current policy agendas of personalisation and co-production.

Supported employment

> Before starting her first job, Karen attended a day centre 5 days a week, for 20 years. Karen now works full time at Blackpool Council and says: "I am very happy that I have my job. I am proud of myself and I am much more confident". (HM Government, 2009, p 38)

In the context of this mismatch between outcomes and best intentions in day services, such that only one per cent of 'trainees' ever moved out of day centres into jobs, that users of the centres consistently reported being bored there even though they enjoyed the social contact with each other (Beyer and Kilsby, 1996), that little individual choice was available (Stalker, 1998) and what people really wanted was proper jobs (Flynn and Hirst, 1992), supported employment began to take root in the UK in the 1980s. It often operated alongside existing activities within day centres; for example, one survey showed that local authorities provided 51 per cent of supported employment projects (NDT, 1992). By the 1990s it had emerged as a serious alternative to traditional day services, with a couple of authorities adopting supported employment as their prime activity, and with an increasing number of independent, often voluntary sector, providers.

Origins of supported employment

Supported employment, as it eventually became known, was developed in the 1960s by a Californian psychologist, Marc Gold (1980), who believed people with severe disabilities could be helped to learn in order to undertake jobs in the competitive workplace. Essentially he developed a supportive learning technology based on task analysis that is now known as training in systematic instruction (TSI). This is a very structured approach, and is still used as one of the foundation techniques, along with vocational profiling (the Virginia protocol is described by Mank, 1994), in supported employment projects.

At the same time as Gold (1980), Bellamy et al (1980) and others were developing the TSI, Wolfensberger was elaborating his principles of normalisation/SRV in which employment was emphasised as a highly valued social role. A strong association developed between the two sets of ideas that is still evident today. (Some supporters of the social model of disability and indeed, person-centred service development, have raised concerns about the resulting pre-eminence of the idea of culturally valued roles to which we shall return later; see Wilson, 2003.) In addition, Ridley (2001) provides an overview of the reported significance and importance of supported employment in its potential for delivering social integration in ordinary settings. In other words, a job is important because it confers status in our society, but for people with learning difficulties, whose social networks tend to be restricted, it might also offer a means of expanding these. Finally, it is an effective way of meeting the aspirations of people with learning difficulties to have a job (Steele, 1991), an income, and to be a contributor to society rather than a burden on it.

So what is supported employment? How do its underpinning ideas and practices illustrate personalisation and co-production? And how can social workers harness these developments to make a difference in people's lives?

Given the range of beliefs about people's capacity to learn, about the importance of socially valued roles and the potential for social integration, it is not surprising that supported employment gets variously defined, and this has been a source of contention among specialists. Various offerings have been made.

The National Development Team proposed that 'real work' is in an integrated setting with ongoing support provided by a social services agency (Wertheimer, 1992).

> … people with learning disabilities work in real jobs in real workplaces alongside people who are not disabled and receive the usual wage for the job. (Corden, 1997, p 2)

A more recent quote from the European Union of Supported Employment (EUSE) reads:

> ... providing support to people with disabilities or other disadvantaged groups to secure and maintain paid employment in the open labour market. (EUSE, 2006, p 13)

And again, from Hunter and Ridley (2007):

> Supported employment is real work for 16hrs or more per week in an integrated setting with ongoing support. (Hunter and Ridley, 2007, p 6)

The sources of contention centre on the specification of a job as one that a non-disabled worker would do, of setting a target of at least 16 hours' a week employment, and the claims for social integration outcomes. Notwithstanding this, there are common threads running through these definitions. Most supported employment projects would subscribe to the following ideas and objectives.

First is the belief that people with learning disabilities are capable of employment, and acceptance that this is a valid aspiration; related to this is the 'presumption of employability for everyone' (Hagner and Dileo, 1993).

Second, learning 'how to do the job has to be done *on* the job' (Ritchie et al, undated); in other words, the model of onsite support has supplanted the readiness model characteristic of sheltered workshops. Instead of 'training and then placing', supported employment projects 'place and then train' people on the job.

Third, the support and assistance required is based on structured teaching and support technology, such as TSI.

Fourth, the task of the job coach goes beyond job matching and training to providing support on an ongoing basis, as opposed what EUSE calls the 'place and pray' approach.

Fifth, the jobs should be real jobs for real pay, in ordinary (integrated) work settings; in other words, employees working alongside non-disabled workmates (not in sheltered workshops or 'enclaves') for equivalent wages.

In practical terms, this usually means that a 'job coach' (employed by the supported employment agency) will meet with someone wanting to work to create an individualised vocational profile, which is then matched to available jobs on the market or through direct contact with employers. The job coach will then undertake a job analysis, provide job support on site to both the employee and employer (ongoing as necessary), and help in career development. The support may 'fade' or be complemented by 'natural support' from workmates, but it will be made available as required.

Supported employment in action

Delroy has severe learning difficulties and needs intensive two-to-one support. He has been living in residential care for most of his life. Delroy's support workers from the Brandon Trust noticed that he liked to crush plastic bottles. He also loved walking outdoors. Drawing on these interests, he was supported to start a small local business, collecting plastic bottles, and taking them to be recycled – a much-needed local service. With his first profits, he took a trip to London and travelled by open-top bus. He was back at work the next day. Delroy works within the Permitted Work rules on a self-employed basis. With support from his partners, he will be in a position to grow his business over time. An account of Delroy's story can be found in *Valuing Employment Now* (HM Government, 2009).

Opportunities and obstacles

There has been a steady growth in the numbers of people with learning difficulties and agencies offering employment opportunities in the last 20 years in the UK, and indeed, in dedicated supported employment agencies, which increased from 5 in 1986 to 210 (5,000 people) in 1995 (Beyer and Kilsby, 1996). In principle and practice we now have evidence that people with learning difficulties want to have jobs and be gainfully employed; that supported employment offers an effective approach to getting and maintaining people with learning difficulties in paid employment, including people with severe disabilities (Weston, 2001); that employers value people with learning difficulties as 'reliable and motivated employees' (Ridley, 2001; Freud, 2007); and that it is possible for people with learning difficulties (and their families) to benefit financially and socially.

However, a survey in Scotland (Ridley et al, 2005) showed that while 3,000 people were described as being supported in employment, the majority were being offered 'work experience' or 'volunteering'; half those in paid jobs worked for under 16 hours a week, thereby limiting the likelihood of making good connections with fellow workers and of being better off through eligibility for tax credit; and people with severe disabilities and women were under-represented. Although opportunities have been created in the UK for employing people with high support needs (Bass and Drewett, 1996; Weston, 2001), it is those with relatively few support needs who have benefited (Beyer and Kilsby, 1996). This is disappointing, but there is an opportunity to be grasped in the shape of recent and favourable policy initiatives geared towards 'employability' and enabling those 'furthest from the labour market' (Beattie, 1999; Freud, 2007) to gain sustainable employment. Now is the time to capitalise on this in order to reinvigorate and reverse what two decades ago Mank called the 'underachievement' or unfulfilled promise of supported employment (Mank, 1994).

While employment is not a new idea in services for people with learning difficulties, open employment certainly is. Add to this the idea that no 'passport' into employment has to be earned, and that demonstration of advance competence is replaced by onsite training, and the mould is broken. In this approach, the support and skill of the job coach and supported employment project come under scrutiny as much as the capacity or 'the 'label' of the prospective employee.

The idea, implicit or explicit, that supported employment is for the most able people has a companion idea from two decades ago that only the most able people could move out of institutions, and that there would always be a 'hospital-dependent' population. History may be repeating itself in day services, with the result that people with severe disabilities are overlooked or not considered eligible. This is ironic, as supported employment was originally developed to meet the needs of people with high support needs. Stalker (2001) sets out a number of reasons for this, including the greater ease of finding jobs and meeting the target numbers of commissioners, to which could be added anxiety about loss of benefits, respite for carers (especially family carers), and the requirement for high levels of investment in job coach skill and continuing, possible permanent, presence on the job. It is one of a number of challenges that confront supported employment as we move into the 21st century.

The *Learning difficulties and ethnicity update* report (Foundation for People with Learning Disabilities, 2012) makes the clear point that most of the key changes recommended by *Valuing Employment Now* (HM Government, 2009) are especially relevant for people from BME communities:

- more effort to show that people with learning difficulties can hold down paid jobs;
- statutory, voluntary and private sector agencies should work together to develop clear employment pathways based on individual (person-centred) approaches;
- schools, colleges and adult learning should improve their job preparation content;
- more use should be made of personal budgets;
- high-quality job coaching should be increased;
- self-employment should be promoted;
- employers should be persuaded of the business case of employing people with learning difficulties;
- local transport to work arrangements should be improved;

- the barriers to work for people in particular types of residence should be removed;
- particular attention should be paid to the support for people who are presently the most excluded from jobs;
- there should be more emphasis on gathering better data and performance management for increasing employment opportunities;
- people with learning difficulties and their families should be leading the way.

Source: Foundation for People with Learning Disabilities (2012, p 17)

The shift has been one of gradual reform rather than radical change. However, supported employment is just that. It is assumed that everyone should have the option of employment – although they should not be coerced into it. Supported employment should be the default position, not day care. However, without the central strategic leadership and additional transitional funding allocated to hospital closures, it may remain an option for only the few. A number of these features are reflected in Gary's story below, which has the additional interest of being an example of a 'micro enterprise', self-employment and entrepreneurship.

Gary's Eggs[1]

Gary is a 22-year-old young man who, three years on from leaving college, is running his own fresh egg business called Gary's Eggs. What is unusual about this start-up, apart from his age, is that Gary spent his school years in special school, and has a particularly complex and deteriorating form of epilepsy, with frequent daily seizures that 'wipe' his memory.

How he became a successful entrepreneur is a story of building on his interests, as someone whose family farming background gave him confidence and some land where his project could be developed; a mother who had heard about person-centred planning; a job coach from a supported employment agency able to undertake some vocational profiling with him; a grant from the Prince's Trust; a direct payment and support package with support workers managed by the family; and a supportive social worker in a local authority with a corporate strategic plan that viewed the offer of support to get employment as a central plank for 'modernising' its day service provision.

Within three years Gary's business base has grown from 15 to 250 chickens. It can be isolating work, but he sells eggs to regular customers at local coffee mornings. The development of a marketing strategy is now high on the agenda. People in his person-centred planning group will help with this. Gary now works on his business four days a week in order to manage his health safely, and to have some support to do other leisure activities. His mother says that Gary is getting more independent, and might soon be thinking about getting his own place to live.

While Gary's story has some fortunate features in it, such as his family's background and support, it has not been plain sailing. His early efforts to get jobs were hampered by the severity of his epilepsy; he does not work full time, and has support for other leisure activities, but it has taken time and effort to establish a group of local young men who share his interests as his support team, and it helps that one of them has a 'bit of farming' background. He does not get a wage, but the business is now covering its costs, with the help of the start-up grant, but marketing and expanding the customer base is the next stage. The direct payments cover exclusively his support and not his business costs.

Influence of person-centred approaches

Person-centred approaches and individualised funding are seen as a central plank for realising the aspirations of both *Valuing People* and *The same as you?*. In other words, there is reason for optimism that current policies of personalisation will provide the driver for change, and an antidote to the stigmatisation and block planning that has characterised so much development of services for people with learning difficulties in the past. Seeing the person as an individual rather than as a label is a core social work value, but this genuinely held belief within the profession has not prevailed against the development of monolithic day centres.

Much of the traditional methodology underpinning supported employment is grounded in a person-centred approach, from creating a picture of the individual's employment aspirations and assets (in technical jargon, a vocational profile), to careful matching between the individual and job description as opposed to slotting people in where there is a vacancy, to the provision of individualised support and training through TSI. The establishing of person-centred planning as a widely used or recommended tool for lifestyle planning in services for people with learning difficulties reinforces the relevance of supported employment approaches.

From this attention to person-centredness, it should be a logical step to viewing supported employment as a user-led activity. However, the predominance of entry-level jobs among those secured through supported employment projects suggests the lack of career development once people had secured a job, which seems to reflect the ongoing influence of stereotyping rather than personalisation. Again, this underlines the importance of the value base. One promising development in this context is the occasional example of self-employment and entrepreneurship in which an individual is supported to develop an interest or hobby into a business using direct payment funding or start-up monies through the likes of the Prince's Trust. In such examples we see the confluence of individual planning, a focus on capacity rather than incapacity, choice, and the key role of support rather than eligibility.

Partnership and co-production

Person-centred employment planning

The introduction of personal budgets gives support staff an important role in helping to change the work expectations of unemployed adults with learning difficulties, and to identify a pathway into employment.

Social care services should use person-centred planning to help individuals to explore their interests and aspirations, and specifically, to think about the implications of these for work. Getting a job should be a priority for all working-age adults. The individual's support plan should then indicate what action will be taken, and how the available resources will be used, including an employment plan. This should contain action to connect people to employment services and organisations that can offer benefits advice and start the jobseeking process. The plan should also indicate how the person's personal budget could be used to support job coaching and support.

Source: Adapted from DH (2010a)

The potential of supported employment to realise individual aspirations for employment, earning a living, being part of the community and utilising one's preferences and strengths as the basis for building a positive lifestyle, are evident. The potential for partnership and co-production may be less obvious but equally important.

Using people's aspirations as a starting point for planning via the tools of person-centred planning and vocational profiling has become axiomatic in supported employment, but to avoid failure down the line through poor job matching (Hagner and Dileo, 1993) and under-resourcing, employer and worker support requires attention to partnership and co-production. Projects and their workers need to approach the supported employment venture in the spirit of clear partnership with people with learning difficulties, as evidenced in career development or even simple job changes of choice. This means using professional judgement and the technical tools of the trade to achieve user ends as far as possible, rather than exercising them as an end in themselves.

Equally crucial is the achievement of partnership with employers. Research has shown that employers can be great 'champions' of people with learning difficulties, both in terms of being prepared to offer employment and to promote the idea with their associates (Ridley et al, 2005). Crucially this promotion is based on the business case for supported employment rather than the welfare one. In other words, people with learning difficulties (well matched to the job) prove to be 'good employees' – reliable, motivated and hard working. This is enormously valuing for people who are used to being devalued and marginalised. The same research also confirms that availability and responsiveness of the job coaches/supported employment projects is valued by employers, and the support offered is an important ingredient in the initial success of placements.

Finally, direct and indirect partnership with parents and formal carers is a further requirement for success. As discussed in Values Into Action's document (Dowson, 1998), parents have a legitimate concern for the safety of their sons and daughters, as well as a vested interest in the respite offered to enable their own lives to continue well. Paid carers in services, such as day centres or accommodation services, may have limited expectations and be sceptical of the possibilities for change based on ingrained attitudes within these services rather than mal-intent.

This adds up to co-production in the sense of stakeholders being an active part of the problem-solving process, but also 'expert' in their own problems (Hunter and Ritchie, 2007), rather than simply 'assets' to the service delivery process (Boyle et al, 2006). Earlier studies have identified a 'cost benefit' effect to supported employment in the sense of savings to other welfare systems (Beyer, 1996), but as part of a raft of arguments in favour of supported employment. From a social work values perspective, the value of supported employment goes beyond economics and assets, and lies in the opportunity it offers for self-determination, choice and self-respect to vulnerable individuals.

What role for day centres?

Or, to put the question differently, should everyone with learning difficulties be doing supported employment? In terms of the philosophy of ordinary living, it makes sense to start with the idea that it is reasonable for school leavers to be considered for employment. Similarly, it is logical that we should take seriously the request for employment by any adult currently in day services, given that we now have the evidence not only of the value of this to both the prospective employees and potential employers, but also the technology to support this activity.

However, the point of this discussion has not been to replace the fixed diet of the day centre with that of supported employment. What is required is an approach based on person-centred planning, in line with the policy drive for individualised services. It is then likely that support will become truly person-centred rather than service or centre-based, and that this support will make greater use of generic resources and make greater demands for these facilities to be fully accessible.

Making a difference

Where does or should social work sit in all this? How can the interventions of social workers make a difference? Today's challenges are about re-thinking how people with learning difficulties can be supported in 'ordinary lives', in how they spend their time as well as where they live. If person-centredness, inclusion and personalisation are central considerations, then it is likely that any planning for individual futures will include the possibility of work.

The challenges for social work are at both systemic and direct practice levels. Practitioners are likely to be supporting individual networks of support around vulnerable individuals, not delivering readymade services and packages of care.

Traditionally, in day services, social workers assessed school leavers for a place in a centre, and the process was about fitting individuals into the service available, and not tailoring the services to individuals. They were not involved in direct service delivery in centres, and neither were they in the world of modernised services. Social workers do not have the skills of job coaches or PAs.

As Gary's story reveals, the social worker was actively involved initially in facilitating Gary's college placement, and a direct payment was used for a small amount of social support. The social worker subsequently undertook an assessment for a direct payment and funding for a support package, both critical elements in the realisation of Gary's aspirations, or, in the current jargon, his service outcomes. The social work role thereafter has been supportive and facilitating for Gary and his family. It can be seen here that the social worker has moved from assessing for a service to assessing for personalised support. Person-centred planning is an ideal tool for this, but a knowledgeable family member is able to lead on this, reinforcing partnership and co-production. If the social worker is familiar with this technique (and not all are), it is not their place to be the 'expert' and lead, but to support family and friends, as invited. Building alliances has to go beyond the family, and includes community health staff able to keep a close eye on controlling Gary's epilepsy. Community connecting was taken on board by the family, and locally based young male support workers selected by Gary and his family.

Strategic intervention on a number of fronts, in concert with other universal providers such as education, leisure and recreation and employment services, is likely to be required. Specifically:

- ensuring that all school leavers are routinely presented with the possibility of college and/or employment. As for other young people, there should be a presumption that further education and employment will be a routine consideration, and not an exceptional one. Gary was fortunate to live in an authority that had taken a corporate strategic decision to initiate restructuring its day services by ensuring that all school leavers were assessed and offered a college placement and/or referral to a supported employment agency;
- person-centred planning should be used to explore the possibilities of accessing ordinary community services with the support of neighbourhood workers such as in LAC (Bartnik and Chalmers, 2007);
- provision of drop-in facilities, but not in the day centre style or scale. This will enable socialising and the maintenance of existing friendships and be particularly supportive (at least transitionally) for people with complex needs, as generic buildings are modified and activities made more inclusive;
- providing staff, and not buildings, with the consequent restructuring of budgets; the promotion of individualised funding through direct payments, the In Control initiative and so on; training for staff that addresses the shift from readiness to support; and management of dispersed rather than congregated staff;
- systematic engagement with parents and families to explore how their concerns about respite, safety and reliability can be met.

Such a strategy, currently being developed by many authorities, will allow transformational change rather than mere reform; create changing expectations among service users and their families; and just as critically, re-focus working practices and cultures in those providing the service.

North Lanarkshire Council in Scotland has illustrated the business case for this kind of approach. With partners, since 1999 it has supported over 130 adults with moderate and severe learning difficulties into paid work. These individuals work on average 24 hours a week, and their income has almost doubled from when they were not in work. The council invests £783,000 a year on the supported employment service, which provides a service to 220 individuals, and is considered a cost-effective alternative to day services. The cost per job is half as much as a day service place. An independent evaluation also indicated wider savings to the taxpayer. The service is based on the models of supported and customised employment developed in the US. Welfare rights advice and early engagement with families are also essential components. The service has now grown to 18 job coaches, and includes people with mental health conditions and acquired brain injury.

Customised employment, 'even' for Marcie

Marcie doesn't speak, and had been described as functioning as a seven-month-old infant, but her parents wanted her to experience a typical life, and especially a job.

Marcie rarely interacts physically, but through 'discovery' it was learned that she does have some control over her right arm and seems to enjoy music. This led to a way for her to control her environment: Marcie could be assisted to turn on music with a tape player, and after 20 seconds, the tape would rewind automatically.

This single idea was the basis for Marcie's job, using customised employment, as a 'specialty stapler' at a newspaper in Texas. The switch that Marcie turned on, initially to hear the music she liked, operates the stapler. Within a couple of months, the music was no longer needed.

Marcie receives commensurate pay for her work, and assistance from a job coach funded by the state. Since starting work, Marcie has routinely made more money per hour than her support staff. During the first year, shredding personnel documents was added to her responsibilities.

Marcie has now been employed for over 10 years.

Source: Callahan (2002)

Social work has a particular interest in seeing the agenda of day service development taken forward. Social workers are in the paradoxical position of being members of the profession that has responded most actively to the aspirations of its users, but are not equipped with the business skills and expertise to ensure that supported employment becomes widely developed. In the consultation on *Valuing People Now* (HM Government, 2009), 90 per cent of people with learning difficulties who responded agreed that employment should be a priority. Evidence shows that, with the right support, people with learning difficulties – including moderate and severe learning difficulties – can not only work, but can do an excellent job that they and their employers value highly.

We now need a concerted strategic and practice effort, both to exploit the government's employability agenda to reinforce the provision of supported employment for individuals, and to harness the personalisation agenda and individualised funding to support individuals to develop lifestyles in their communities and neighbourhoods that enhance their self-esteem and control over their lives. The move to personal budgets (which can be taken as direct payments) provides an important opportunity to support adults with learning difficulties into work. Personal budgets can and should be used for this. Learning Disability Partnership Boards have been encouraged to review day service modernisation plans, to ensure that they have employment at their heart. And social workers need to understand how to support individuals who choose this route.

Conclusion

This chapter has identified the contradiction arising from the deinstitutionalisation of long-stay care in 'mental handicap' hospitals, whereby most people with learning difficulties moved to live in the community, but were transported back into 'serviceland' for their daytime activities within segregated day centres. A range of explanations has been given for the lag in systemic change in day services, including the lack of pressure from government or public opinion in the absence of the scandals that characterised hospital services; initial lack of double funding to support new services; a lack of model coherency in a service that attempted to be all things to all people; and the understandable concerns of families about the withdrawal of an important resource that offered daytime respite for them.

Three possible vehicles for transformational change – supported employment, person-centred planning and co-production – have been discussed, and examples provided that additionally illustrate the role of the social worker who is not an employment expert, but who has skills in building alliances with important services such as education, in community connecting, negotiating with families and ensuring a person-centred approach when young people leave school and beyond.

As expectations of a 'life like any other' begin to take root in the aspirations of people with learning difficulties, as expressed in the wish to have a home of their own and a 'real job for real pay', so some people will want to have intimate relationships and become parents. The next chapter explores this issue, and where and how support can be offered.

Note

[1] With thanks to Gary and his family for permission to tell his story. A full version can be found in the Values Into Action Scotland Newsletter, Summer 2013.

7 Becoming a parent

We start this chapter by noting the definitional and epidemiological uncertainties in our knowledge of adults with learning difficulties who become parents. We set out what we know about their experience of service systems, and the disadvantages and prejudice they face. Relevant research findings about the process of court proceedings, children's hearings in Scotland, broad child care and protection interventions are discussed, and the contentious question as to whether adults with learning difficulties can be 'good enough' parents is addressed. Attention is drawn to recent good practice guidance and the strengths of a person-centred, multi-disciplinary approach that is embedded in the social networks of the individuals. A case study is presented to illustrate the challenges social work and social workers face in offering an holistic and responsive service. The discussion is set in the context of equalities and human rights legislation.

We do not know how many adults with learning difficulties are also parents. Estimates are variable due to lack of consistent definitions of learning disabilities, and uncertainty about numbers of adults not known to services, although one study (Emerson and Hatton, 2005) found that in their large sample, 7 per cent, or 1 in 15 adults, were parents.

The emerging profile of parents with learning difficulties in the literature is a recent phenomenon. As community living has replaced institutions, expectations have changed, and individuals have aspired to be parents as well as householders and employees.

Experience of the service system

We know that parents with learning difficulties are disadvantaged when they come into contact with the public child care system (McConnell et al, 2002; Swain and Cameron, 2003; Elvish et al, 2006). Booth and Booth have claimed that presumptions of incompetence result in decisions to remove a disproportionately high number of children from parents with learning difficulties (Booth and Booth, 2003). They are also more likely to lose their children to state care, and despite the policy emphasis on kinship care, their children are less likely to be placed with extended family members (Booth et al, 2005).

- Internationally, 30-40 per cent of parents with learning difficulties have their children taken into public care.
- In the UK, between 40 and 60 per cent of their children are removed.
- Mothers with learning difficulties living on their own are more likely to be without their children than if living with other relatives.
- Only 10 per cent of children removed from a mother with learning difficulties were returned.
- Most parents with learning difficulties live in difficult circumstances with high levels of poverty, poor housing, unemployment and harassment.

Source: Tarleton et al (2006); Booth and Booth (2007); DH and DfES (2007); Ward (2008)

We also know that service silos separating children and families' teams from adult services teams mean that parents are unlikely to get support in their own right from workers experienced in adult disability services, but much attention from child care and indeed child protection workers inexperienced in working with disability. The gaps between maternity, health and children's services further fragment support. The importance of early and appropriate support is therefore crucial to safeguarding the wellbeing of children and protecting the rights of parents under the Human Rights Act 1998 and disability discrimination legislation.

Partnership for good support

Partnership between health and social services lies at the heart of providing effective support to adults with learning difficulties as they make the transition to parenthood. Good practice guidelines (DH and DfES, 2007; SCLD, 2009) set out some of the dilemmas for professionals in this area.

> 'I am proud of what Nina [daughter] has achieved but sometimes I think it is in spite of services and not because of them. Often, professionals and social workers in particular, have assumed that they know best and those parents are always against change ... as if we have some agenda against seeing our sons and daughters living full and real lives. I want for Nina the same things virtually any mum would want for her daughter. I want to see social workers as agents of change, people who can make good things happen. Is that asking too much? For some, it seems like one big power-trip – they need to remember it is their career but my daughter.' (Parent, quoted in Hunter, 2012, personal communication)

'My name is John…. I have five children. I have learning difficulties
and so do two of my children. We don't have any support at home to
help us. My wife won't allow it. She's terrified of social workers. She
won't go and ask them for help even if we need it. She is terrified
that they will judge us for needing help, and decide to take our
kids away.' (People First member/parent, quoted in Hunter, 2012,
personal communication)

The above quotes, one from a mother of a child with disability and the other
from a parent with a disability, make discouraging reading for professionals,
pointing, as they do, to negative attitudes, lack of help, and even fear. This is
challenging for a profession that sees itself as fighting prejudice and assisting
people to make positive change in their lives. It jars with the caring mission
of the social work profession.

Why might this be so? It might be explained in part by negative press
coverage of tragic child deaths, and the duty to protect that lies with social
workers. Then there is the stigma that goes with seeking help from a
profession associated in the public mind with those unwilling or unable to
help themselves. Furthermore, in relation to disability, social workers are
also hampered by the tendency of much research up to now to 'pathologise'
children and their families where disability is present (Connors and Stalker,
2002, p 1). In other words, the focus tends to fall on the 'impairment' and
deficits of both children and their families at the expense of the whole
person, of which any disability is one aspect, and of their capacities, and
what in the literature are sometimes termed their 'gifts'.

There are limits to what individual social workers can achieve in changing
public attitudes quickly, but they can rise to the challenge of recognising
and promoting individual strengths, whether in children or in adults. Social
workers can make sure that their practice assumptions treat children as
'children first' who have similar needs to all children, but who also happen
to have a disability that requires specific consideration at specific times.
They can also question presumptions of incompetence in parents with a
learning difficulty based solely on the presence of that disability, and adjust
their practice to take account of particular support needs. In this context, a
person-centred and community-based approach has much to offer in terms
of bringing together a network of resources that can support individuals
and families in a manner that explores their strengths.

Think spot

Does anyone have the right to be a parent?

The alternate argument is posed as a matter of rights – is the wish to become a parent a natural extension, and indeed, a rightful natural extension, of inclusion, participation and citizenship? Are parents with learning difficulties discriminated against in their wish to become parents purely on the basis of their label? To what extent should one group of parents be expected to earn the right and to be required to demonstrate competence to become parents when other groups of adults, at risk or otherwise, do not?

Imagine we live in a society with a government agency, the Parenthood, Parenting and Childcare Agency (PPCA), charged with regulating parenting matters in relation to all its citizens.

PPCA's remit is to improve the quality of life of all children through the inclusion of compulsory parenting skills as part of the 10-14 national curriculum; to implement vetting and 'quality assurance' procedures measuring acceptable attitudes and motivation in applicants wishing to become parents; to grant 'licences to procreate' to those who are successful; and to impose severe legal penalties on those by-passing the system.

Do you find the idea of the PPCA reasonable? Tolerable?

Would it make any difference to your answer if you knew that there was also a provision to implant fertility inhibitors in all young people at the point of puberty in order to ensure the success of this policy to protect children? It would be removed on adulthood, and on presentation of the appropriate licence.

What do you think of this process for ensuring that children are only born to parents who have passed some such test of 'adequacy' or 'good enough' parenting competence?

Source: From an idea by Gavin Fairbairn

Most of us would probably reject the idea of having to apply for permission to procreate. For most of us, becoming a parent is a probable next step from having a home, an income and a supportive, intimate relationship. Becoming a parent is a socially valued role, and a particular mark of adult status that for many people in our society is a matter of personal choice and private concern. We tend to assume that if we want to have children, we have the right to do so, as and when we please.

The view that we should try as hard as we can to avoid people with learning difficulties becoming parents is reinforced by the fear that if they do become parents, they will fail at the task, with bad outcomes for the child or children. Furthermore, it is seen as almost inevitable that others, whether relatives or the state, will, in the end, have to take responsibility for the care of their children.

An entitlement to be parents

A measure of changing attitudes in general is highlighted in a study (Tarleton et al, 2006) citing the *Daily Mail* coverage of the removal for adoption of children from parents with a learning difficulty. The article raises questions about lack of support to these parents rather than querying their right to be parents. This is a sea-change from reports of routine sterilisation practices in Sweden and France as recently as the 1970s (Brober and Roll-Hansen, 1996). We are also seeing 'dating agencies', supported both by health monies and the voluntary sector (for example, Stars in the Sky in England, Dates'n'Mates and Get2Gether in Scotland) that provide further evidence of this attitudinal change.

In relation to legislation concerning parenting with learning difficulties, Section 8 of the Human Rights Act 1998 makes it clear that children and their parents, including parents with a learning disability, have the right to have a family life; to support to stay together; and that any intervention must be 'proportionate' to the problem. The European Court of Human Rights recently ruled that a German family's right to family life had been breached when its two children were removed and ultimately fostered in the absence of evidence of ill treatment by the parents, or the provision of educational and financial support by the state. The official action was deemed not 'proportionate'. Article 6 requires a fair hearing in court with due regard for the need for adjustments to procedures and additional supports; this is clearly of benefit to parents with learning difficulties, but not evident in the studies reported by Booth et al (2004).

In the UK, there is general legislation to support the rights of people with disabilities to equal treatment. For example, the Disability Discrimination Acts (1995 and 2002) refer to 'reasonable adjustments' including provision of services to ensure comparable service to that of non-disabled people, and the Disability Equality Duty (2005) requires public bodies to promote equality of opportunity for all disabled people, including favourable treatment if necessary.

There is also specific adult welfare legislation relevant to parents with a learning difficulty. For example, the Fair Access to Care Services guidance (DH, 2003, para 28), and the later, 2010, Putting People First guidance (DH, 2010c, Executive Summary, para 1) draw attention to the need to carry out assessments on an individual basis to support an independent life in a manner that is fair and proportionate in terms of impact on individuals and the wider community.

Community care assessments were expected to take into account the person's needs as a parent and, in addition, both *Valuing People* (DH, 2001a) and *The same as you?* (Scottish Executive, 2000) were clear that local authorities and NHS Trusts should 'make sure' that the needs of parents with learning difficulties were met, and that they were supported in this role.

Furthermore, the Children (Scotland) Act 1995 places duties on local authorities to provide a range of services to 'safeguard and promote the welfare of children in their area who are in need' and to 'promote the upbringing of such children by their families' (Section 22(1) Children (Scotland) Act 1995); this applies if the disability of a family member is having an adverse effect on the child (Section 93(4)(a) Children (Scotland) Act 1995). The Children Act 2004 recommends that parental disability should not inevitably trigger concerns about the welfare of their children, but that where support is required, both the children and adult legislation can be drawn on.

Notwithstanding this, families with parents who have learning difficulties probably constitute 1 per cent of the population, but one in six child protection court hearings involve parents from this group (Booth, Booth and McConnell, 2004). We know from findings in both the English and Australian literature that judgments about parenting capacity are not confined to, or substantiated by, evidence of risk (McConnell et al, 2002); most court proceedings against parents with learning difficulties are brought on the grounds of neglect rather than abuse (McGaw et al, 2007; Booth, 2000). Crucially, there is evidence that the best predictor of neglect is the lack of social support rather than the presence of disability (Tymchuk and Andron, 1990; McGaw and Newman, 2005; Aunos et al, 2008).

Being 'good enough' parents

There has been a burgeoning of literature to inform social work practice in this area since 2000 in universities, such as Bristol (Norah Fry Centre) and Sheffield (Tim Booth and Wendy Booth), the voluntary sector, such as Barnardo's (McGaw and Newman), and government departments, such as the Department of Health. This body of work draws on earlier seminal work in the UK by the Booths (1997 and 1998), and on a wider international literature that underlines the emergence of parenting by adults with learning difficulties as a professional practice issue.

Such writing offers a counter-narrative to the explanations that are rooted exclusively in the label of disability, and that fail to take account of the evidence of capacity to learn when properly supported, not to mention the additional problems of poverty, harassment, poor health and poor housing, as described by a number of commentators, and summarised by Ward (2008).

Here are some of the arguments discussed by these authors setting out the evidence and implications on good enough parenting. The following discussion draws on the work of the Booths, with the arguments organised along five dimensions:

- *Services and practice that presume 'incompetence'.* Not only is there a widely held belief that IQ scores determine parenting skills, but also that any shortfall is irremediable, and skills cannot be improved (McGaw and Newman, 2005). Worryingly, it would seem that not only do the general public and some professionals hold such stereotypical views, but that even some expert witnesses show a lack of awareness of research to the contrary (Feldman et al, 2012). The work of authors such as McGaw and Newman (2005) and the Booths (1997, 1998) demonstrate that parents can learn, and with support, provide a caring family context for their children. McGaw in particular provides detailed and empirically validated accounts of the effectiveness of a range of supports while drawing attention to the complexities of 'learning to parent' through the filter of learning difficulties. She concludes that learning difficulty alone is not a sufficient or even main indicator of parenting ability, but that 'the main predictor of competent parenting is an adequate structure of professional and informal support' (McGaw and Newman, 2005, p 24).

- *Services and practice that focus on deficiencies.* Exclusive reliance on IQ scores as a predictor of 'parental adequacy' is now queried, although it should be noted that there is evidence of less competence where parental IQ scores fall under 60 *and parents are unsupported* (McGaw and Newman, 2005, p 27). This historical reliance on assessment of cognitive abilities, such as IQ scores, is reflected in typical professional practices and assessments that focus on what people cannot do rather than on their strengths. This has resulted in failure to make use of assessment tools tailored to the needs and learning styles of people with difficulties (McGaw and Newman, 2005). Functional assessment tools are now available to assist in assessing parenting skills, but until recently, few have been standardised for people with learning difficulties. Those designed for working with people with learning difficulties that are easily available and accessible to a range of practitioners include First Steps to Parenthood (Young and Strouthos, 1997) and You and Your Baby (CHANGE, 2012).

Additionally, recruiting support from relatives or friends to share parenting tasks is often taken by social workers as further evidence of parenting weakness rather than evidence of resourcefulness and mature problem solving. It is as important for people with learning difficulties as other groups in the population that 'resilience' as well as risk factors are taken into account in assessment practices and protocols. In the children and families literature, this is often referred to as holistic planning. While this has commonalities with person–centred planning, service user involvement and a focus on 'gifts' is less explicit. Person–centred planning, long familiar to practitioners in the learning disability field, is beginning to have an impact in practice generally, although it is unlikely to be as familiar to children and families workers.

■ *Services that are ill equipped.* Many of the established parenting training programmes were designed for the general population of parents seeking support, and usually for delivery outside the home. There has been a lack of available support tailored to the needs of parents with learning difficulties and their learning styles. However, this is changing so that not only can relevant skills training programmes be accessed, but also programmes providing a mix of individual home-based support and group work using cognitive behavioural methods to explore managing relationships, emotions, etc. Such groups have been seen to improve self-esteem compared with those individuals who did not attend the groups, with the added bonus of extending people's social networks, a factor we now know to be associated with good parenting outcomes (McGaw and Newman, 2005).

The Social Services Inspectorate (SSI) report, *A jigsaw of services* (Goodinge, 2000), notes that assessments conducted by children and family workers with little knowledge of adults with disability result in narrowly, child-focused accounts rather than family-focused assessments that take account of the 'ecology' of the family situation. Many parents live with a relative or have active supports. These are key considerations in any assessment; assessment of resilience factors does not get the prominence given to risk factors.

■ *Services and professionals that don't speak to each other.* Parents with learning difficulties may require services from children's workers in their role as parents and from adult services in relation to their disability. If children's workers are lacking in knowledge and expertise around the impact of disability, and adult workers are out of date in child care, the requisite appropriate support and cross-sector coordination cannot be guaranteed. Indeed, Glennie (cited in Booth, 2000, p 6) comments how parents presenting 'grave concerns to children's services because of child neglect, did not meet the threshold for adult service'. It is also clear that parents do not trust child services, and therefore do not seek assistance.

Booth (2000) goes as far as describing this as 'system abuse', in which the helping agent itself becomes a source of damage. The SSI became so concerned about poor joint working between children and adult services that it commissioned a special study to make recommendations for future improvement (Goodinge, 2000); in addition to the above points, it highlighted a lack of shared protocols for assessment, training and charging, so that parents were not penalised financially.

■ *Equal before the law?* Court procedures are not designed for the layperson let alone someone with learning difficulties; lawyers are not skilled in communicating with people with difficulties; and court procedures can be confusing and intimidating. Someone who does not speak English would be provided with an interpreter, and the pace of proceedings would reflect that need – not so for a parent with a learning difficulty. One Australian study discusses how, despite hard evidence being available in only 50 per cent of cases, 'compliance' in the sense of not opposing the case presented by the authorities is convenient for everyone but the parent: court business would grind to a halt if more cases were contested. Contesting a case results in children being removed pending a full hearing date, and parents rarely make good witnesses, but not contesting is seen by social workers as a lack of commitment to the children (McGaw and Newman, 2005).

Support and learning to be 'good enough' parents

It is now clear that the following interventions can assist in lessening the barriers for parents with learning difficulties and in enhancing their skills:

■ Social networks and support are key factors in assisting parents with learning difficulties to become and continue to be 'good enough' parents, as such interventions should pay attention to both strengthening networks and ensuring they are not disrupted.

■ Specialist assessment tools, such as those developed by McGaw et al (2007), should be used to assist in assessing support needs and identifying strengths as well as gaps.

■ Group work is effective if adjusted to the learning styles of the parent with learning difficulties to include concrete examples, modelling and role-play. If delivered in the home rather than the agency, problems of generalisation of learning can be avoided.

■ Long-term, multi-agency services and interventions work are required to avoid a revolving door cycle (Tarleton et al, 2006), together with information and resources adapted to their needs.

■ In light of parents' anxieties about statutory authorities and problems in understanding uncoordinated referral and eligibility processes, independent advocacy (MacIntyre and Stewart, 2008) should be provided.

Alice and Jimmy

Consider the situation of Alice and her long-standing boyfriend, James (Jimmy), who both have learning difficulties. How might some of the themes and issues discussed above apply to this family?

Alice and Jimmy attended special school and got to know each other at a day centre, but Jimmy was quickly bored and delighted to secure himself a place on a supported employment scheme collecting shopping trolleys at Asda. Alice began a part-time special programme in a local further education college three days a week. After a while she stopped attending the centre to look after her grandmother who had dementia, and with whom she, and later Jimmy, had lived. Her grandmother was then admitted to hospital where she died from a major stroke. The family was well liked in the neighbourhood. Alice and Jimmy were told they would have to give up the grandmother's house. They were pleased when the college helped Alice secure a housing association flat in another area, especially as she was expecting a baby. Although Alice and Jimmy had decorated the flat, Alice was worried about rubbish and needles in the stairwell, and she was lonely. The house was burgled and windows smashed; they weren't sure if this was because they had learning difficulties, or if it was just par for the course in this neighbourhood.

Alice was no longer in the catchment area for the college or the centre. The hospital contacted the social worker after the baby was born because Alice seemed unable to understand about routines and feeding, as well as being very disengaged from the baby. Alice told the social worker who asked to see them to go away and not come back because they were "all fine", but the midwife requested a children's hearing (Scottish legal tribunal for children and families). The baby was removed into foster care without a formal parenting assessment having taken place. Alice and Jimmy were devastated, especially when the social worker suggested Alice have an abortion if she ever became pregnant again.

This story is not unusual. Parents with learning difficulties can be viewed as incompetent, even when they are not, and as a result, both they and their children may be targeted rather than supported by 'caring' organisations. The assumption that people with learning difficulties will either be unable to successfully carry out such childrearing duties or to develop skills, even when there is evidence of adequate parenting, is not uncommon. There are instances recounted in the literature of parents having their children removed at or soon after birth without any assessment of their parenting needs (SCLD, 2009).

Many parents with learning difficulties, just like in the quote towards the start of this chapter, report that they feel themselves under scrutiny from the very start, and that they live in fear that they will lose their children. Booth and Booth (1993) tell of one mother's anxiety:

> Apart from undermining her self-esteem and sense of worth as a mother, she feels under constant pressure to prove herself to others and that any mistake she makes may result in her losing the children. She dare not admit to her difficulties but strenuously denies them for fear of the consequences. (p 389)

These issues are complex and multi-layered, and like most social work responsibilities, involve conflicting rights, safeguarding vulnerable individuals and challenging discrimination. Many of these issues are in permanent tension with one another, and there are no easy answers. However, the weight of negative attitudes and practices, and their accumulated impact on parents with learning difficulties, has resulted in ill informed, misguided and arguably oppressive practices. It will require a paradigmatic shift to change such practices. Again, in the words of McGaw and Newman (2005, p 1):

> ... the inability of those who cared for them to recognise their need for love and companionship, let alone parenthood, remains one of the least savoury aspects of welfare provision in the twentieth century.

Alice and Jimmy, a year on

Alice is pregnant again, doesn't want an abortion, and is sufficiently frightened of social work to suggest to Jimmy that they 'disappear'; by this she means just leave the area and tell no one where they are going. This worries Jimmy, not least because it will affect their (infrequent) contact visits with their first baby whom social workers wish to free for adoption. Jimmy confides in his job coach (not a social worker) from the supported employment agency, who happens to know of an advocacy project that agrees to help.

If you were a social worker and learned of this second pregnancy, how would you pick up from the last intervention when the first baby was born? In what ways might you intervene differently?

What did the advocate from the advocacy project do?

■ First, the advocate contacted a lawyer who instructed a parenting needs report with financial support from a large national charity. Social work was asked to address the recommendations of the report, but nothing happened as the argument raged as to whether this was a child care or adult care referral. So the charity in question provided support on an interim basis.

■ The advocate set about exploring options enabling the couple to move back to the grandmother's neighbourhood where they were well known. This was not easy, as they did not qualify for many housing points. They got lucky, as the advocate knew people in the community association who searched among their network for ideas. Many offers of support were forthcoming, but no accommodation, until one of the grandmother's friends, whose family had helped her buy the house, offered to rent it to them for one year initially, as the old lady was moving.

■ With a tailored parenting programme in place, a new home, a support circle drawn from the local community, an option of back-up from a lawyer, the advocate supported Alice and Jimmy to indicate they intended to keep this baby and to submit a request for improved access to their first child with a view to a planned return home.

Of course there is a long way to go here, and no guarantee that the outcome will be the desired one, from Alice or Jimmy's point of view. However, they are better positioned to do the best they can in a less hazardous environment with support from people who know them and live locally, as well as from a couple of key formal agencies. As a result, a new social worker, who happily has experience of working in both child and adult care, has visited them, and expressed a wish to help them succeed. She is exploring whether a direct payment might be possible to support Alice, alongside the parenting programme from the voluntary organisation, but unsurprisingly, given her statutory responsibilities, she is not making any promises. But she is trying to help.

This is fundamentally a rights perspective, but it also recognises that people learn best in situ, whether the focus is on becoming an effective householder, employee or parent. Resonating with ideas about a continuum of decision making, it is possible to envisage a range of approaches professionals might adopt, such as substitute, shared or supported parenting. This helps us get beyond the idea that individuals are good parents or bad parents, and immovably so. We need to take child welfare seriously, and we need to understand that IQ alone does not guarantee parental competence.

The support envisaged is multi-faceted along a continuum of informal and formal support, in individual and group contexts, drawing on practical resources from services and community networks. In the course of this journey, Alice and Jimmy have acquired a circle of supportive friends in a community they know well and which knows them. They also have some positive contact with services that will hopefully make for a slightly more level playing field when their second baby is born than was there for the birth of their first child.

In relation to people with learning difficulties, the idea of supported parenting or parenting with support can be seen as a response to the attitudinal barriers, presumptions of incompetence and inability to learn in the face of evidence to the contrary (McGaw and Newman, 2005), and setting higher tariffs of performance and expectations of parenting than would be expected of other groups of parents (Gath, 1988; SSI Unit, 1998). As such, it is directly comparable to the concepts of supported living and supported employment, where notions of 'readiness' as a passport for eligibility to live in the community or to have a job have been superseded by the development of 'support' as required and tailored to the individual.

Conclusion

For many adults with learning difficulties, in line with much of society, becoming a parent seems the next step from having a home, a job and a 'significant other' in one's life. For reasons associated with varying definitions of disability and information gathering between services, negative professional and public attitudes and lack of trust in services by service users, we don't know exactly how many adults with learning difficulties are parents. What we do know is that those who are parents are at a significant disadvantage; while they constitute 1 per cent of the population, one in six formal legal proceedings involve children from these families.

Presumption of incompetence, deficit working rather than focusing on strengths, lack of disability expertise in child protection services, and inaccessibility of legal procedures all constitute barriers for adults with learning difficulties who wish to become parents. While social workers cannot change attitudes overnight, they can harness their skills in facilitating social networks, accessing specialist parenting assessment tools, providing long-term support, ensuring multi-agency working, and engaging independent advocacy, which have all been shown to support adults with learning difficulties in the complex task that is parenting.

Just like the mainstream population, increasing numbers of adults with learning difficulties are surviving into old age. This is a new phenomenon in disability services, and the next chapter focuses on the challenges to be faced.

8 Growing older

This chapter begins by comparing the living arrangements and histories of five older people with an invitation to consider how they compare with those of older people without learning difficulties. It poses questions as to how services should respond to changes in the ageing demographics, especially longevity; as to the service implications of older people with learning difficulties with greater health needs, but also greater obstacles to accessing services than the general population; and as to the relative merits of generic elder services or specialist learning disability services for this age group. The possibility of individual budgets has brought particular opportunities to these individuals for greater control over their lives and more community participation. However, it also points to the need for clearer strategic planning to meet this expanding and diverse need, and the importance of listening to older people with learning difficulties themselves, as they are one of the groups that historically have been least heard.

Consider the stories of the following five people with learning difficulties. They are all the same age, but have had different experiences.

Billy Ruthven

Billy Ruthven was 58 years old when he left the learning disability hospital he had lived in for 45 years. For the five years since then, he has lived in a Housing Association flat in a highly desirable area in the city centre. He shares the flat with Frank, a man in his sixties, who, for over two decades, lived in the same ward as Billy. Both of them have minor mobility difficulties. In addition, Billy has a significant hearing impairment and wears a hearing aid, when his support staff remind him to do so. While he lived in the hospital he attended art therapy for many years. When he moved into the flat five years ago, he bought an easel, paints and other art materials, and not long after, he began renting studio space at a local artists studio collective. As well as continuing to paint, he has become a regular user of the printmaking facilities and now produces greetings cards, which he sells in aid of Cancer Research.

Margaret Taylor

Margaret Taylor was also 58 when she left hospital. She, too, had lived there for 40 years. Like Billy, she has some difficulty getting around, and for the last five years has used a walking frame. She is also losing her sight, and is no longer confident about walking, unless accompanied by a supporter. Margaret had become unhappy in her latter years in the hospital as several of the women in the ward moved out to new housing and established new lives in the community. She has now lived for five years in The Elms, a residential care home for older people. Although she has some family, she does not see them regularly – her nearest relative, a married niece, lives 80 miles away. She keeps herself informed of Margaret's wellbeing by phoning the home manager once a fortnight. She has her own family commitments and is not able to visit, other than at Christmas. Margaret spends most of her time in her room, listening to the Elvis Presley cassettes she bought with her pocket money when she lived in the hospital.

Ella Ramage

Ella Ramage was 58 when her dad, Albert, died five years ago. She and her mum, Cath, who is now 84, live together in the council house that has been the family home for 50 years. Ella has no brothers and sisters, and has lost touch with her friends from the day centre since she was informed at the age of 60 that she had reached retirement age, and could no longer attend there. She does go to church on Sunday, and until recently also attended the Women's Guild coffee morning on a Thursday. However, even that has now stopped – Cath is getting physically frail and extremely forgetful. The GP suspects vascular dementia, and is concerned about what will happen if there is a crisis. For now, it is more the case that Ella looks after Cath than vice versa.

Alice Woodford

Alice Woodford was 58 when she took up the tenancy of her ground floor, one-bedroom flat, five years ago. She is one of 10 people with learning difficulties in the immediate locality receiving support from a Locality Network manager who also lives on the estate. She is not the oldest person who is supported in the Network. The people in the Network meet together and support each other, and through them, Alice has become a member of a wildlife group, a flower arranging club, and is on the management committee of the Golden

Oldies, a social club that meets in the local community centre. She leads an active and satisfying life, but is being bothered by some local teenagers who are hanging about at night outside her flat. She is becoming anxious about going out after dark, and is beginning to miss out on committee meetings.

Gregor Cameron

Gregor Cameron has Down's syndrome and was diagnosed with Alzheimer's disease 10 years ago, when he was 53. He lived with his parents, Grzegorz and Dorothy, until he was 58. The family had begun to find his aggressive behaviour difficult and distressing, and so, with the assistance of their social worker, found a place in a semi-rural 15-person core and cluster residential service run by a voluntary sector dementia care provider. All of the people who live in the house have learning difficulties and dementia. The family does not have a car, and finds it difficult to spend time with Gregor. The care home staff think this is no bad thing, and will help him to settle.

It seems that Billy has a person–centred plan and is being assisted to take advantage of unpaid support and to be part of a valued community and business facility. He sees himself, and is seen by others, as a talented artist and is a member of the studio artists collective. He is no more or less disabled than Margaret, but she has a much less inclusive life. She may have been a victim of circumstance, and in a time of crisis 'placed' inappropriately as a person still in her fifties in a residential care facility that had a 'void'.

Neither Ella nor Alice have experienced institutional life. They have both lived their whole lives in the community. Ella, however, has had a very restricted social life, and she and her mother are now in a situation of double jeopardy, with Ella now effectively the primary carer. It is likely that no plans have been made for either of their futures, and they would both benefit from the creation of a circle of support, with some of the energy of the circle being put into the facilitation of a clear future plan for Ella. There may be complicated questions of capacity to be addressed, and it is the sort of situation that should really be tackled much earlier so that a will, discretionary trusts and powers of attorney can be effectively arranged. Alternatively, or even additionally, Ella could benefit from a neighbourhood network of the type that is clearly improving Alice's quality of life. Similarly to Billy, Alice is seen as a net contributor to her community rather than simply as a passive recipient of care and support. But life in the community still demands that attention is paid to risk management, and it will, of course, be important that the members of her network support her in continuing to attend her committee meetings, and perhaps work with the local youth to help them to understand the impact that their hanging around has had on Alice.

The service that Gregor lives in has split opinion – on the one hand, it can be seen as a congregate service, with all the likely tendencies to the development of institutional practices, but on the other, it can be viewed as supported living, albeit in five three-person flats in a block. Critics argue that it will never be part of the community; supporters, however, say that it has all the benefits of supported living, but with the added benefit of being provided by a specialist dementia care provider that is better at managing challenging behaviour.

Think spot

How do the lifestyles of these men and women compare with their peers who do not have learning difficulties? To what extent do you think that their experience of services is a contributing factor in their becoming 'old before their time'? Should older people with learning difficulties be in specialist services, or the same mainstream elder care services used by the rest of the population? How active a life could be supported for each of these individuals by well-planned and resourced services and community connections?

Increased longevity and its consequences for services

People with learning difficulties are living longer, and it is clear, therefore, that one of the most important challenges that services can anticipate is how to respond to this significant growth in the older age group.

The life expectancy of people with learning difficulties has increased over the course of the last 70 years. Indeed, in Emerson and Hatton's (2008b) report, *Estimating the future need for adult social services for people with learning disabilities in England*, it was estimated that the number of people with learning difficulties over the age of 60 would increase by over a third between 2001 and 2021. More recently, in 2011, the same authors reported that older people are one of the fastest growing groups of the learning disabled population (Emerson and Hatton, 2011b). The most recent predictions from the Learning Difficulties Public Health Observatory (Emerson et al, 2012) suggest that by 2030, the number of adults aged 70+ using social care services for people with learning difficulties will have more than doubled.

People with learning difficulties face many disadvantages in relation to health (DH, 2001a; Emerson and Baines, 2010; Scottish Government, 2013). Like the rest of the population, they have, however, benefited from improvements in public health and standards of living. The resultant increases in longevity mean that the average life expectancy for people with a learning disability has increased, and in particular, the life expectancy of people with Down's syndrome has risen, from 9 years in 1928 to over 40 years in the 1980s, and by 2001 it had been noted that some with Down's syndrome would live into their sixties (Wilkinson et al, 2006). Other people with learning difficulties are now living into their seventies and eighties (WHO, 2000).

This level of growth in the number of older people with learning difficulties has significant service and resource implications. Within the cost constraints being experienced by health and social care services, the statutory and voluntary sector must plan to ensure that this new population of older men and women with learning difficulties have access to, and are supported to use, age-appropriate supported living arrangements, appropriate domiciliary care and a range of universal services such as mainstream leisure facilities. Similarly, the very elderly parents of older men and women with learning difficulties are likely to need respite and other support services in order to continue to provide care for their sons or daughters.

People with learning difficulties are two-and-a-half times more likely to have health problems than other people, but the response of health services to these has been very poor. Older people with learning difficulties have usually already experienced difficulties with their health, and 'embark on the ageing process from a position of vulnerability' (Bigby, 2004, p 75). Ward (2012a) reports that they experience the same age-related physical and psychological changes as other older people (DH, 2001a; Emerson and Baines, 2010; Mencap, 2012), but as a result of poor levels of fitness, poor diet and lower levels of mobility, are likely to be at higher risk of obesity as well as such age-related diseases as diabetes, hypertension, heart disease, stroke, arthritis and respiratory disease (Emerson and Baines, 2010; RCN, 2013).

A small number of people with learning difficulties have genetic conditions that mean they will face specific health risks as they get older, such as people with Fragile X syndrome, who have an increased risk of musculoskeletal disorder, and people with Prader-Willi syndrome, who have an increased risk of diabetes, cardiovascular disease and obesity (Bigby, 1997). The prevalence of dementia in people with learning difficulties is two to three times more likely than in the general population (Strydom et al, 2009). Rates of dementia in adults with Down's syndrome are even higher, and may develop when people are in their late thirties and forties, and consequently they may need additional care and support in their later years (WHO, 2000). As well as experiencing an earlier onset of dementia, the rate of deterioration is more rapid and the presentation is different (featuring more behavioural changes than memory loss).

Although older people with learning difficulties are at a higher risk of other psychiatric disorders than their peers (two to four times more common than for other older people), there is evidence that these mental health conditions are less likely to be treated (Emerson and Baines, 2010).

Despite this general picture of the presence of additional health complications, with attendant extra support needs, a number of studies have identified that the uptake of health services by older people with learning difficulties is lower than that of their peers. This low uptake encompasses health screening, health promotion and health education opportunities (McConkey et al, 2004). Emerson and Baines (2010) give a shocking summary of this whole scenario, reporting that people with learning difficulties are 58 times more likely to die before the age of 50 than the rest of the population.

One of the consequences of the increased lifespan of people with learning difficulties is that today's generation of older people are the first for whom transition services are required to support movement from services provided to adults towards provision that is more suited to their changing needs as elders.

Who are these people and where do they live?

Older people with learning difficulties live in a wide range of settings, including:

- living with parents
- living with siblings
- living in residential services for older people
- living in specialist learning disability supported living or residential care.

Living with parents

Across the UK, two thirds of people with learning difficulties live with an ageing parent or parents (Foundation for People with Learning Difficulties, 2006). In England, 40 per cent live with a parent over 60, and 33 per cent live with a parent over 70 (Emerson and Hatton, 2008a). Many of these ageing family caregivers are doing so alone, and some are primary caregivers, caring for more than one person.

Most people with learning difficulties want to continue to live in their family home when they reach old age, and most ageing family carers want to continue caring for their son or daughter (Ryan et al, 2014).

However, many of them become frail and less able to cope with the physical aspects of caring, and as a result, the person with learning difficulties may come to adopt a caring role. Mutual caring and interdependence is therefore likely to be an increasing challenge to services.

Many families will need support to adjust to the changing roles being experienced by both the ageing parents and their sons or daughters with learning difficulties. Services for people with learning difficulties will have to embrace a more family-focused approach.

Not surprisingly, many parents are worried about that time in the future when they, as family carers, are no longer alive, or are unable to provide care (Walker and Walker, 1998). Sustained support is needed to help families do this (Walker and Magrill, 2002), but in reality, few initiatives have yet responded to this future planning challenge.

In part, this is because as many as 25 per cent of older people with learning difficulties living at home with older family carers are not known to services until there is a crisis. Consequently, there has been no formal planning for their future care (Ward, 2012b). There is a very real need to find ways of connecting with these families before they experience a crisis that results in the person living somewhere unsuitable.

There is some concern that people living at home with their ageing parents end up becoming old before their time because they have no choice but to share their parents' social life and social connections, and have few, if any, friends of their own. As family carers grow older and start to become more frail, and their social and support networks diminish, both generations risk becoming isolated and lonely (Magrill, 2007). One way of addressing this is by creating personal future plans and enduring circles of support of the type developed by Equal Futures in Scotland (www.equalfutures.org.uk). This approach is clearly beneficial, but has so far reached only a limited target group. An attempt to take the model to scale is being developed by Equal Futures in conjunction with the University of Ulster (Thompson and Taggart, 2014).

Living with siblings

At present, a significant number of adults with a learning disability live not with their parents, but with a sibling or other relative (Emerson and Hatton, 2008a). The role of siblings and other family members has become more important as greater numbers of people with learning difficulties outlive their parents. However, almost inevitably, the majority of siblings have not absorbed the detailed knowledge and experience of their relative, nor the familiarity with the services that their parents have acquired, and will therefore need to be supported to gain access to this information.

Living in residential services for older people

Best practice in learning disability has emphasised the importance of accessing the same services used by the rest of the population. Thus it is often the case that when people with learning difficulties reach old age, they are expected to be integrated into mainstream older people's services. The challenges that then arise include the tendency to limit opportunities to relatively active people with learning difficulties, and the question of whether staff in these settings have the training and expertise to work with people with learning difficulties.

However, people with learning difficulties placed in elder care settings are likely to be much younger than other residents, and the decision to place someone in such a service can be seen to result in unwelcome restrictions on the lifestyle of a person, who may, until then, have led a more inclusive life.

In 2005, an Australian study by Bigby and Balandin (cited in Slevin et al, 2011) examined the extent to which mainstream elder care services in the community were accessible to older people with learning disabilities. More than half of the services identified were accessed by a small number of people with learning difficulties, and overall, they found that there was a receptiveness to including these men and women in the generic services. They found that the issues for older people with learning difficulties differed little from those of other minority groups, and as a result, they proposed that staff in services for people with learning disabilities should have a role in brokering access to these mainstream services. In a review of the literature, Slevin et al (2011) report that there was limited consensus about whether services for older people with learning difficulties should be integrated within mainstream older people services, or whether their needs were best met by specialist learning disability services.

Like others, they believe that continued planning and collaboration between staff from learning disability services and those from older people services would benefit everyone.

In the absence of such collaboration, older men and women with learning difficulties may have to move on to another service setting when their needs change (Emerson and Baines, 2010). This can result in people with learning difficulties who do not meet the traditional age criteria for admission to residential care being inappropriately placed in care homes (often as an emergency measure) at a much younger age than would be considered for others in the community (LDAS, 2010).

LDAS Charter for Change

In part, arising from what is believed to be an inappropriate service response, and also, in part, arising from worries about the lack of governmental action on the commitment made in *The same as you?* to assist everyone with a learning disability to have a plan for the time when their family are no longer alive or no longer able to provide care, Learning Disability Alliance Scotland went on to work with partners to produce a charter for change concerned with improving the lives of older families, including people with learning difficulties:

1. Local government should collect accurate information on the numbers, needs and location of older carers and adults with learning difficulties living in the family home to facilitate good strategic planning.
2. Every adult with a learning disability living with an older carer should be able to have a person-centred plan that supports them in leading full lives, making and keeping friends, and keeping in touch with their families if they leave home.
3. In each local authority area there should be a dedicated officer for older families to provide local information, support access to services, to identify their needs and to plan for how they will change over time.
4. Every adult with a learning disability living with an older carer should be able to have an Individual Emergency Plan, which identifies what could be done in specific crisis situations.
5. Every family with older carers across Scotland should have the opportunity to access independent advocacy services.

Source: Adapted from LDAS (2010)

Think spot

In 2010, Learning Disability Alliance Scotland reported that there were nearly 1,000 people with learning difficulties who were stuck in large residential homes for the elderly, some the size of small hospitals, not because they needed to be, but because it was both convenient and cheaper. Studies suggest that life in care homes is essentially passive, with almost 50 per cent of residents' time spent asleep, socially withdrawn or inactive, and only 14 per cent spent in some form of communication with others. Only 3 per cent of time is spent in any constructive activity.

Many of the people stuck in these homes were under the age of 55, with many years of healthy life ahead. Research by Higgins and Mansell in

2009 found that people with learning difficulties living in care homes for older people:

> did fewer activities in the home than people who lived in learning disability homes;
> went out of the home less than people who lived in learning disability homes.

Do you think that this is the right sort of placement for older people with learning difficulties?

Are there any circumstances in which you think this could be an appropriate placement for a person with learning difficulties who has not yet reached retirement age?

Living in specialist learning disability supported living or residential care

Many older people with learning difficulties who are placed in supported living services have little control over where they live, with whom they live, or how they are supported. Of the 30 per cent of adults with learning difficulties who live in specialist residential care, a high proportion are over the age of 45. Although these services are designed for people with learning difficulties, there is, as yet, little training in the specific skills required to meet the needs of older residents with learning difficulties. As we discuss later, it is as yet unclear whether upskilling and adapting mainstream supported living services is the best way forward in meeting the needs of this new older population.

Collaboration between specialist learning disability services and generic elder care services

In a comprehensive literature review, Llewellyn et al (cited in Slevin et al, 2011) concluded that there was general consensus that learning disability services should be the main providers of care for older people with a learning disability. In the more particular situation of older people with learning difficulties who additionally have dementia, the majority view was that these individuals should have the same access to dementia services as those without learning difficulties. Much of the research points to the need for greater coordination between learning disability services and mainstream dementia services (Hatzidimitriadou and Milne, 2005; Kalsy et al, 2005; McCallion et al, 2005; Forbat, 2006).

In an earlier Northern Ireland-based study of adults with learning difficulties and dementia, Davies et al (2002) reached similar conclusions, and also recommended multi-agency and multi-disciplinary collaboration. Similarly, Janicki et al (1998) found that the pooling of resources among learning disability specific services and elder care services produced viable and effective programmes for both populations.

Specialist training for staff in both types of setting

If staff in mainstream services for adults with learning difficulties are going to be effective at meeting and supporting older people through the different stages of dementia, and even becoming involved in end-of-life care, they will need additional training. On a similar basis, dementia staff and palliative care staff will also need training and support if required to provide dementia support or end-of-life care for older people with learning difficulties.

Bigby (2010, p 11) conclude that the specialist service system for people with learning difficulties must:

> ... reorient to incorporate knowledge and expertise around age-related support needs ... and take responsibility for the development of specialist age-related services. It may also give the disability sector a much clearer mandate to lead and adequately resource partnerships with existing services [older persons' care programme] or organizations.

Direct payments and self-directed support: the way forward?

The direct payment scheme was introduced to allow individuals and their families to choose and direct their own supports, and Slevin et al (2011) have found growing evidence to illustrate the success of the schemes for older family carers in both the UK and the US (Stainton and Boyce, 2004; Heller and Caldwell, 2005; Caldwell, 2007; Caldwell and Heller, 2007). Older family carers who have been involved report that they experienced a sense of empowerment through increased choice; improved flexibility in the way support was provided; and a greater sense of trust when they were able to employ PAs. They also experienced greater confidence and optimism and reduced anxiety about going out to work or going out socially. Their relative with learning difficulties also reported satisfaction as a result of improved social integration.

Clearer strategic direction and priorities

Ward (2012b) identifies some key areas for development and investment in services and supports for older people with learning difficulties:

- Identify older people with learning difficulties and their family carers through a Joint Strategic Needs Assessment.
- Invest in person-centred planning for future needs for families growing older together and in supported living or residential care.
- Join up practice across learning disability and older people's services.
- Equip the workforce to be aware of the age-related needs of people with a learning disability so they can make adjustments to practice.
- Continue to listen and to learn from what older people with learning difficulties and their families have to say.

In a similar vein, the Northern Ireland *Learning disability service framework* (Northern Ireland Executive, 2011) proposes that:

- All people with a learning difficulty over the age of 50 should have the impact of ageing taken into account in having their future needs assessed and proactively managed.
- People with a learning difficulty should be enabled to remain in their own home with their family carer for as long as possible, with appropriate care and support to do so.
- People with a learning disability have the same needs for autonomy, continuity of support, relationships and leisure as other older people.
- All people with a learning difficulty should have access to dementia services at whatever age it becomes appropriate for them.

Listening to the views of older people with learning difficulties themselves

At the root of all of this it is essential that any changes proposed clearly reflect the views of older adults with learning difficulties themselves. What we know is that the priority concerns of older adults with learning difficulties are similar to those of other older adults. The situation is more complicated for some older adults with learning difficulties because they are, for the most part, more dependent on family care as well as paid staff support through a variety of agencies. However, older people with learning difficulties tell us that they value the opportunity to speak for themselves, and it is important that services continue to invest in self-advocacy as people age. It is also important to invest in support and advocacy services for older families, as they are often isolated and vulnerable, and need support to plan for the future (Ward, 2012b).

Conclusion

As in society as a whole, the population profile of people with learning difficulties is changing, and it is an ageing one. In general, adults with learning difficulties experience comparable age-related changes to everyone else, but they tend to occur earlier, and they are more likely to have additional complications. There are more older people with learning difficulties from BME communities, many with complex health needs, and as they age, these men and women will present new challenges for services (Emerson and Hatton, 2011b).

Those surviving into their seventies and eighties today are the first-generation adults with learning difficulties to face the transition from adult services into those required for elders. There is an ongoing debate about the relative merits of services integrated into the mainstream ageing or specialist disability services, with the most recent consensus being that the latter should be the main provider, with greater cross-sector cooperation, especially in relation to dementia. Some urgency attaches to this, as most older people live with their families, and as many as 25 per cent are not known to services until there is a crisis. Social workers are well placed to respond to the identified key areas for development – Joint Strategic Needs Assessments for adults with learning difficulties and their families; investment in person-centred planning, with particular reference to long-term future planning; joined-up professional practice; listening to and learning from service users; and workforce training beyond the traditional silos of practice. The profile of older people with learning difficulties in the future will be even more diverse and challenging than it is today.

Implicit in all the preceding chapters has been the question of how capacity or incapacity relates to the issues under discussion, and how the related issues of risk and protection are addressed. This is the subject of the next chapter.

9 Capacity, risk and protection

> This chapter is concerned with the ability of people with learning difficulties to make 'informed' decisions, often referred to as 'capacity', and how this interacts with service delivery, particularly in relation to user choice, risk taking and safeguarding. These issues have been gaining prominence in recent years, as long-stay 'mental handicap' hospitals were closed in favour of community living arrangements; as policies of personalisation of support, individualised funding and co-production have evolved; as user expectations of 'having a say' and control over their lives have increased; and as the rights agenda has moved centre stage, permeating all aspects of contemporary living. The debate as to how autonomy and keeping people safe can be best promoted spans all areas of welfare, but these concerns have a particular resonance for people with learning disabilities who, as a group of service users, are often viewed as 'not-quite-adult' and who may, as a result, be at risk of being denied choices and opportunities.

The chapter is divided into four sections in line with these four themes:

- capacity
- risk
- recognising abuse
- protection from abuse: safeguarding.

> ... giving people choice without sufficient support merely sets them up to fail (and massively increases risk). Thus, the assumption throughout is that people need meaningful support to think through and exercise choice, and that this support needs to be just as tailored to their needs and individual circumstances as their subsequent 'services'.... Personalisation can be a way to improve safeguarding and can enable positive risk-taking – but only with adequate and tailored support. (Glasby, 2011, p 14)

Capacity

If individuals are deemed not to have capacity, choices are likely to be limited, and not only in law. Research suggests that those areas of choice practised by people with a learning difficulty tend to be domestic and associated with daily living (Stalker and Harris, 1998), such as what to wear or the selection of television programmes, rather than impinging on the big decisions in life, such as where to live, how to spend money, or whether sterilisation can proceed or not. However, recent developments in both legislation and policy have enabled a wider repertoire of responses from professionals.

What is meant by 'capacity', and why, in general, is capacity such a central concept in professional practice?

Think spot

Decisions, decisions!

Can you think of a time in your life when you wanted to make an important choice or decision that was contested?

Why was it contested? By who? What were the deciding factors? What did you need to make it possible to take this decision? How might this differ if you relied on services?

Jot down your ideas for easy comparison later.

Historically, the capacity to make decisions was seen as a 'fixed' characteristic of the individual, and people were deemed either to possess this capacity or not, irrespective of circumstance. We now think of 'capacity' as the ability to take *particular* decisions, and to act on them at a *particular* time. This means that the capacity to take decisions might vary with someone's mental state, or improve as life skills are acquired, or deteriorate as dementia progresses, for example, or be an unchanging feature from birth. It can also mean that an individual might be able to make small daily decisions about what to eat, but require others to make life-changing decisions about where to live or how to use finances.

This shift in current thinking away from viewing capacity as a characteristic independent of its context has been assisted by the development of the 'functional' approach to decision making as opposed to the 'status' approach based on clinical, individual diagnosis (Suto et al, 2005). These authors (Suto et al) have undertaken research as the basis of developing a framework for assessing capacity to make financial decisions. Some of their findings are particularly noteworthy in the contemporary context of personalisation and individual budgets, and confirm, for example, that:

■ variability of capacity to make decisions about money occurs among all adults, disabled or not;

■ improvement in making decisions is increased with opportunities to do so; and

■ there is a misleading impact on judgement of 'appearances' and of situational factors, such as place, feelings and circumstances.

Suto et al conclude that 'decision-making abilities and capacity are not fixed and can be improved' (2005, p 7), and furthermore, that these skills can be taught, and the greater the number of opportunities to make choices, the greater the uptake. The process of making decisions has a number of pre-requisites, such as access to information, ability to communicate, to act on and retain decisions, and a familiarity with and understanding of alternative options. If capacity is not inherent, any of these processes can be compromised by a variety of external factors unrelated to individual cognition and diagnosis.

Think spot

Decisions in context

Were any of these considerations present in the decision you identified in the 'Think spot' earlier in this chapter? Was age and/or experience a factor? Did you consult others, and if so, why? Had you taken such a decision before and felt confident about your abilities? Were you seen as less able to make a 'good' decision because you were a child, inexperienced, or under stress?

Women in France only achieved full voting rights in 1947, and right-to-vote campaigns by people with learning difficulties were still being mounted in the UK in the 1980s. The modern concepts of capacity are evident in the previous sentence, and are reflected in recent legislation.

Legal and policy context of capacity

The policy 'vision' (HM Government, 2007; DH, 2010a, 2011b) is one that places the idea of co-production at the centre of contact between those requiring support and those offering it. This has culminated in the personalisation agenda, which embodies a shift in the balance of power and decision making between professionals and users of services, from paternalism to empowerment, and from professional expert opinion towards people as 'expert in their own problems'.

However, the contemporary personalisation 'orthodoxy' (Needham, 2011) has not been without its critics (Jordan, 2004; Ferguson, 2007, 2012). One dimension of the critique that resonates with the discussion in this chapter is how the model of individual service control can be applied in circumstances where someone who uses services has difficulty in making decisions or may be at risk of harm. Clearly, in order to realise the ambitions of the inclusion and personalisation agendas for increasing user control and choice on the one hand, and achieving co-production and self-management on the other, individuals require:

- the capacity or ability to make decisions and choices; or
- provision of the necessary support through legislation and services to make such decisions and choices; and
- the necessary safeguards in place in situations of risk.

Presumption of competence

The Adults with Incapacity (Scotland) Act 2000 and the Mental Capacity Act 2005 reflect an evolution in thinking, from an 'all or nothing' concept of capacity to a more finely grained and situation-specific one. While there are some differences between these two Acts, the broad intentions are shared. Both Acts set out to *empower*. As the Foreword to the Code of Practice for the 2005 Act states, the legislation should empower people to:

> ... make decisions for themselves wherever possible ... and protect people who lack capacity by providing a flexible framework that places individuals at the heart of the decision-making process. (DCA, 2007, p 1)

Legislation now requires all professionals, and indeed, family members, to assume that an individual is competent to make a decision unless otherwise established, and to explore all avenues to support an individual to make their own decisions, possibly by the provision of advocacy or use of communication technology. This is referred to in the literature as the 'presumption of competence'. This position stands in clear distinction from the historical assumption of incompetence based solely on the diagnostic label of learning difficulties, as can be seen below. For an intervention to be justified, it must take into account the preferences of this individual, be in their 'best interests', represent the 'least restrictive' option, and be free from 'undue pressure'.

Mental Capacity Act 2005: five statutory principles

1. A person must be assumed to have capacity, unless it is established that they lack capacity.
2. A person is not to be treated as unable to make a decision, unless all practicable steps to help them to do so have been taken without success.
3. A person is not to be treated as unable to make a decision merely because they make an unwise decision.
4. An act done, or decision made, under this Act for or on behalf of a person who lacks capacity must be done, or made, in their best interests.
5. Before the act is done, or the decision is made, regard must be had as to whether the purpose for which it is needed can be as effectively achieved in a way that is less restrictive of the person's rights and freedom of action.

The principles underlying the Scottish legislation (Adults with Incapacity (Scotland) Act 2000) also require that any intervention should benefit the adult; take account of the adult's past and present wishes; encourage the adult to use existing skills or develop new skills; and take account of the views of others with an interest in the adult's welfare.

Further, an individual cannot be assumed to lack capacity because they make an unwise decision. This is often a difficult area for family members who may have had a life-long responsibility for their relative, and for professional carers who have a duty of care.

The traditional response to people who are deemed in law to be lacking in competence, or 'incapax', has been 'substitute decision making' or deciding in their 'best interests'. The provisions for this approach are set out below, together with some other mechanisms, in particular, independent advocacy, which is well established in good practice with people with learning difficulties, but has also begun to feature in legislation. Over time there has been a shift from a benevolent but paternalistic approach in which families, professionals and those in legal authority were deemed to 'know best' (that is, reliance on substitute decision makers acting in the 'best interests' of the individual), to one that recognises that those close to the individual, whether family or professionals, have conflicts of interests, and therefore assumes that independent representation or advocacy may be required, along with clear mechanisms for monitoring professional behaviour and support for the individual to make their own decisions.

Of course, much of the time professionals did and do act in well-intentioned ways on behalf of the people they support, and indeed, they may advocate on their behalf for resources and services. However, professionals and services are subject to other imperatives, such as finance, staffing, risk-averse policies, large workloads and the competing demands of service users, and all of these factors can conspire to have an impact on decisions taken. In light of the history of services for and attitudes towards people with learning difficulties, it is not surprising that paternalistic practices persisted. The Mental Health Acts 1959 and 1960 replaced the detention measures under the Mental Deficiency Act 1913, but created powers for 'guardianship' that were essentially those of a parent or 'tutor'. The philosophies of normalisation began to challenge the need for such absolute powers of intervention, and in the 1983/84 Mental Health Acts, they were replaced by powers giving the guardian rights of access, power to specify residence and powers to require attendance at treatment and services. Financial guardianship was not covered by this legislation, but fell to court-appointed curators charged primarily with preserving any inheritance. Social workers, particularly in the absence of family members, often held the guardianship role. At a practical level this fragmentation of arrangements was unhelpful, implying that financial and welfare matters could be treated separately.

These provisions came under increasing criticism for failing to recognise degrees of capacity and the influence of situational factors. In other words, if an individual was deemed 'incapax', this applied as much to deciding to have a haircut as to deciding to stop attending a day centre; 'gradations' of intervention were not an option. Understandably professionals became increasingly reluctant to use such draconian powers. Critics took the view that they failed to recognise that people with learning difficulties could become more able to make informed decisions given experience, opportunity and support.

Strengthening the voice of people with learning difficulties

It was only with the Adults with Incapacity (Scotland) Act 2000 and the Mental Capacity Act 2005 in England that an updated legal framework came into being that set out to address these problems by:

■ reinforcing the presumption of competence applied to the general population; in other words, incapacity should not be assumed to exist by virtue of a diagnosis or label;

■ making provisions that cover both welfare and finance arrangements; and

■ introducing a 'menu of powers', including single intervention orders, reflecting contemporary thinking about degrees of capacity.

The intention of these Acts is that judgements about the 'best interests' of the individual should take into account their known preferences, as well as making clear efforts to involve them in any decision taken about them. There are some differences between legislation north and south of the border, but the broad intentions are shared across the UK. The English legislation specifically underlines the importance of using a 'functional' approach to the assessment of capacity.

Furthermore, it is expected that individuals will be given support to make decisions; that a 'best interest' and 'least restrictive' standard is used if someone else makes decisions; and that professionals will have a duty to follow the Code of Practice. There is provision in England and Wales for a new independent mental capacity advocate who supports and represents the individual in the decision-making process.

Supported decision-making

Values Into Action in England proposed the adoption of a set of arrangements based on the British Columbia model in Canada (see below) (Beamer with Brookes, 2001). These challenge not only traditional approaches to incapacity and decision making, but draw attention to the significance of turning such processes on their heads:

> ... the key factor is not capacity but support. Rather than basing the legal system on deciding who has and who has not got capacity, why not turn it around and base it on a right to support? From this perspective, where someone lands on a continuum of capacity is not half as important as the amount and type of support they get to build to build preferences into decisions. (Beamer with Brookes, 2001, p 21)

In the UK the most established provision for supporting individuals to have a say and some control over decision making about their lives has been advocacy in its various guises. More recently, the increasing prominence of advocacy and the development of circles of support and person-centred planning have added further ballast to the endeavour, but there is no legal basis for their use, except in certain aspects of the mental health legislation. In this context, developments in the Canadian legislation are noteworthy.

Canadian Representation Agreement Act 2000

This legislation in British Columbia, Canada, gives people with a learning difficulty the legal right to nominate a representative with legal status to act as a 'conduit' for the expression of their wishes.

What is particularly interesting and impressive is that this is a generic piece of legislation – in other words, it applies to all Canadian citizens, and not just those with disabilities. This sits well within the social rather than medical model of disability in its attempt to address structural exclusion rather than individual deficit.

While we are beginning to move towards this in the UK, with provision for independent advocates, our legislation is not equalities-based after the Canadian example. We have not crossed that conceptual Rubicon which recognises that in providing for all citizens, crude distinctions between those who 'can' and those who 'can't' become less relevant.

On the basis of information about the legislation in British Columbia, Values Into Action made proposals that placed individuals at the centre of decision making supported by a group of people, such as a circle of support, which could also act as trustees and be monitored by a regulatory body operating as a streamlined alternative to the Court of Protection in England (Etmanski et al, 2015: forthcoming).

While circles of support have no legal basis, they may take on the role of Independent Living Trusts, a formal and legally recognised arrangement for assisting the management of an individual's finances and assets. Social workers who are serious about enabling an individual to gain control over their life and decision making associated with it would do well to explore how circles of support can be encouraged. However, they should expect challenge from colleagues, both in social work and other disciplines. This is not about being a good or a bad professional; the perspectives are different, and inherently contain the potential for conflict. As professionals, social workers need to learn to welcome this as both enriching and safeguarding for the lives of individuals whose lives have often contained little of either.

We return now, however, to the most widespread resource for promoting participation in and control over decision making that is available to professionals currently in the UK, namely, independent advocacy.

Independent advocacy

In recent years, the development of advocacy in relation to 'vulnerable' adults, particularly those with learning difficulties, has been one example of a response to realise the ambition of involving people in making decisions about their lives. Wolfensberger (1997) has described this as one individual with a 'minimal conflict of interest' acting on behalf of other(s), as if they were acting to defend their own interests.

It was developed as a protective device as much as anything else in the face of dehumanising regimes in many institutions of the day. This is reflected in the early use of the term 'protégé' (partner) to describe the service user in the advocacy partnership. To do this effectively requires a number of prerequisites, but independence from the service provider – intellectually, organisationally and above all, financially – is a fundamental, quintessential feature.

Some would say that *citizen advocacy*, as it came to be known, was the archetypal form of advocacy. Here, one ordinary, unpaid citizen ensures that one service user or 'partner', who is at risk of being ignored, is heard 'with a self-sacrificing vigour and vehemence' (Williams and Schoultz, 1979, p 92). Other characteristics include a long-term, altruistic relationship that carries with it the invitation to join the advocate's family and social network, thereby promoting social inclusion. Its proponents have been highly influential in the field, and even described as 'passionate' (Forbat and Atkinson, 2005), but commissioners find it difficult to do business with because citizen advocacy projects typically cater for small numbers, and work in ways that don't sit easily with the contract culture. Some commentators think citizen advocacy is best viewed as a form of community capacity building or 'community vision' (McKnight, 1995), which may be of particular interest in the contemporary climate of co-production and personalisation. A critical perspective is provided by Walmsley (2002) of citizen advocacy's philosophical roots in normalisation, and its privileging of the contribution of a non-disabled person.

Self-advocacy, either on an individual, or more often on a collective, basis, clearly involves individuals speaking up directly for themselves, but also carries with it the possibility of enhanced self-esteem, positive identity and even political solidarity and success. Although modelled on self-help, most advocacy groups within learning difficulty, unlike the activist groups typical of the physical disability movement, have a non-disabled supporter available to the ongoing membership of the group.

The role of non-disabled people within learning difficulty advocacy, and the extent to which they act only as a mouthpiece, has been the source of much contention, and is an issue in both forms of advocacy (Kendrick, 1994; Walmsley, 2002). It is particularly sharply defined in citizen advocacy when individuals are unable to express themselves or communicate their views in readily understood ways. Advocates may be ordinary people without professional qualifications, but to meet citizen advocacy standards, they need integrity and skills a-plenty. This dimension of advocacy may increase in significance as self-directed support becomes more widely used with people requiring support to make their views heard.

A further form of advocacy is often referred to as *professional advocacy*. This has proved popular with commissioners of services, providing a basis on which to build mandated advocacy introduced by the mental health legislation. While financially and organisationally independent, professional advocacy projects are operationally and contractually much closer to conventional services, with caseloads, clearly stated and time-limited objectives, records, supervision, and commonly, although not exclusively, offering paid employment to advocates. Unlike professional advocacy projects, most citizen advocacy projects would resist being called an advocacy 'service', preferring the term advocacy 'resource'.

Risk

The promotion of opportunity and choice by professionals in response to good practice considerations and developments in contemporary law and policy brings with it questions of risk, risk taking and risk management.

Rather like the question of capacity, the concept of risk has been an evolving and increasingly prominent one in social work practice. 'Who assesses risk and how that is managed' is now a major agenda in adult social care.

In relation to people with learning difficulties, who decides what is reasonable, or 'informed' risk taking, is intimately tied in with the previous discussion about capacity and the rights of individuals to make their own decisions. In this section, we therefore explore:

- concepts of risk;
- implications for social work, and in particular, working with people with learning difficulties; and
- some practice considerations – risk assessment, risk management, defensible practice as opposed to defensive practice, and risk-averse service cultures.

With the opportunities offered by policy trends that promote choice, personalisation and aspirations for citizenship and social inclusion come concerns about protection, abuse and exploitation. However, the extent to which external forces such as the law, services and professionals, relatives and advocates should mediate these decisions or even intervene is an important question for social workers. Striving to achieve a 'proper' balance between autonomy and protection, care and control, in a changing context of expectations and services requires skilful judgement, especially in the risk-averse culture in which most social work occurs. It is important to remember that natural supports, such as concerned neighbours and friends, as well as most families, are major sources of safeguards for vulnerable people. In this context, advocacy and circles of support are more than devices for making decisions; they are devices for keeping people safe, or safer.

Think spot

Thinking about risk

... risk is a barometer of ordinary living, and is as much to do with opportunities as threats. (Manthorpe et al, 1997, p 80)

Identify a 'risk' you wanted to take as a young person, or a 'risky' situation you experienced. Consider the above comment in relation to the risk identified.

> Why was it a risk? Did others agree?
> What were the opportunities and threats? Did everyone agree? Was there a 'trade-off'?
> How far could these risks be seen as part of 'ordinary life'/growing up?
> Was there a compromise or a 'safety net'?
> What did you learn as a result of this experience?

The idea that risk and risk taking is inherent in daily living is a commonplace one. The idea that life circumstances encompass both threats and opportunities can also be found in discussions about danger and crisis, as well as risk; indeed, these terms are sometimes conflated in our thinking or used interchangeably. There are often companion discussions about striking a balance between opportunities and threats, providing support to reasonable risk taking. Clichés such as 'no gain without pain' and 'going under a bus' abound, conveying the idea that tragedies have to be expected to occur.

It is likely that the risk situation you identified contained many of these threads – different perspectives on what constitutes a risk; how 'normative or desirable' they are; how dangerous and whether they are 'worth the risk'; and what degree of support, if any, is required. In other words, 'risk' is rarely uncontested, usually requires negotiation and navigation, often has a potential pay-off, and is sufficiently the 'stuff of life' for you not to have any difficulty identifying such an experience.

Risk: an evolving concept

Unpacking the concept of risk reveals an evolving and multi-layered concept rather than an absolute and objective one. In view of current formulations of risk that involve predictions of dangerousness or adverse outcomes, it is useful to remind ourselves of this. Under the impact of the science of statistics and the influence of 'rationality' as an explanation for events in the natural world, Lupton (1999) suggests that risk, being a matter of calculation and probability, is a neutral concept. It did not acquire any positive or negative connotations until the last century. In recent times, risk 'as danger' has become a central theme in our 'globalised' society, where diseases such as swine flu or Ebola have the potential to become pandemics in days through air travel – it has been argued that we are evolving into a risk-sensitive society (Beck, 1992) with 'risk-averse practices', that is, risk avoidance, notably in the public sector.

In an interesting discussion of the 'multi-faceted' nature of risk, Stalker (2003) suggests that in addition to 'danger', the idea is associated with 'vulnerability' and 'uncertainty'. Accepting the argument that risk is multi-faceted rather than inherently neutral, it follows that risk can be seen as a socially constructed idea, open to different 'cultural and political' interpretations (Douglas, 1992). Furthermore, it can also be seen to be open to individual opinions about risk, whether professional or personal. More recently attention has been drawn to the neglect of user perspectives and difference in judgements between users and professionals as to what constitutes 'risk' (Douglas, 1992). This fluidity may be at odds with an environment preoccupied with safety and certainty, and intent on seeking to avoid or avert danger.

We would take the argument further, and stretch the continuum to embrace what Perske called many years ago the 'dignity of risk' (1972). This is the notion of positive rather than negative risk, and is related to the philosophical argument that risk is part of living; to attempt to eliminate it is neither possible nor desirable. In practice terms, the concept of 'planned (or positive) risk taking' is beginning to emerge as a counterpoint within defensive risk management cultures (Titterton, 2005), and has particular relevance to the implementation of self-directed support.

As the concept of risk has evolved, it has also become more contested – between experts and non-experts, in what George Bernard Shaw termed a 'conspiracy against the laity', as well as between experts with differing knowledge and value bases, as reflected in the 'social' and 'medical' models of disability, for example. Positive risk taking or risk enablement is particularly contentious in situations where the capacity of the individual is in question.

What does this mean for the practice of social work and, in particular, in the field of learning difficulties, in an era of personalisation, co-production and community participation?

Risk, learning difficulties and social work

Within social work practice, the concept of risk has never been viewed as neutral; negative connotations pervade all discussions of risk, from Brearley's (1982) early seminal text onwards. Twenty-five years ago there were few references to risk in social work practice and training, but the discourse of risk has become a predominant one in all aspects of contemporary social work. With hindsight, one notable feature of the NHS and Community Care Act 1990 is the absence of reference to risk within it, and in the subsequent care management guidance (Waterson, 1999). Notwithstanding the pre-eminent concern with the protection of children (Scottish Executive, 2002; Laming, 2003; Haringey Local Children's Safeguarding Committee, 2009; Haringey Local Child Safeguarding Board, 2010), the consideration of risk is increasingly dominant in adult care. The impact on adult care can be seen in the instigation of the inquiry into the circumstances of Ms H in the Scottish Borders (Scottish Government, 2004) that revealed abuse, exploitation and professional neglect stretching over years; in serious case reviews such as the one following the murder of Steven Hoskin, a man with learning difficulties; and in the healthcare 'scandals' described earlier (Flynn, 2007).

Commentators have suggested that together with a proliferation of professional literature on risk, the concept now even colours our perception of 'community' and what this means. In relation to social work practice itself, some writers have gone so far as to suggest that risk, in the sense of dangerousness rather than need, is now a prime criterion for eligibility for services. As Stalker crisply puts it,

> ... risk has replaced welfare as social work's raison d'être. (2003, p 227)

This statement has major implications for the future of the profession of social work, and injects a tension into the heart of the argument in favour of an increasingly personalised and capacity-building interpretation of the role of social workers in adult care.

Malcolm's story

Malcolm is in his forties, has a learning difficulty and autism, and lived for many years in a residential community in a rural setting. His parents are closely involved with his life, and supported his request first, to move back to the city to a group home with 24-hour day support, and then, to his own flat rented from a friend of his parents. He now has 35 hours a week support, including 18 hours with a one-on-one supported employment worker. In recent months, he has become increasingly agitated. He has punched holes in the wall of the flat and pulled out electrical connections; he has thrown a cup of coffee over someone in a café who he said was looking at him; and he has reported being the target of sexual advances from a friend for money. These incidents always occur when he is on his own and when he goes out, after the support worker leaves.

Think spot

Drawing on the concepts outlined above, consider independently how you would rate the risks. How might you manage them, and what would constitute defensible practice? As a care manager, what considerations would you take into account in the impending review of Malcolm's care package as a result of the introduction of self-directed support?

Context

Malcolm has never been subject to any statutory measures, and has always been thought unlikely to be so without significant deterioration in his mental health, or increasing levels of risk of harm to himself or others. Staff have organised a multi-agency review (including Malcolm and his parents) in line with agency policy, which coincides with the introduction of self-directed support.

Risk assessment and management

- Malcolm's social worker is worried about self-injury as a consequence of his recent destructive outbursts in his flat, and is now unsure about his ability to protect himself in the open environment of the town; a clinical psychologist is spending time with him when he goes into town to assess what happens, and to develop strategies when he is on his own.
- Support staff have never been attacked and feel safe; they are talking to him about alternative living arrangements, such as sharing a flat with someone he knows and likes and who is very quiet, unlike most of the residents he knew when in the group home.

■   Neighbours might start to be worried about noise levels and possible fires; fire precautions have been reviewed; neighbours have not complained as yet about the noise when he is upset. Should he stay in the flat, additional noise reduction measures could be considered.

■   The police were called when he threw coffee at a member of the public. He was charged, but an assessment requested by the procurator fiscal (who makes the decisions to proceed with prosecutions in Scotland) suggested he was not capable of understanding the legal process; a further psychological assessment has been undertaken, revealing that out of the context of group living he was less capable than had been previously judged. This could open the way for guardianship in the future.

Options

■   *Twenty-four-hour support:* Malcolm's social worker says there is no finance to provide 24-hour support if he lives on his own.

■   *Group home:* Malcolm's parents have raised this idea, but Malcolm does not wish to live in a group home. His social worker sees guardianship as a last resort, although the discussions of this have resulted in Malcolm's two brothers becoming more active.

■   *Least restrictive option:* the social worker has a duty to consider this – including smart technology such as a pressure sensitive doormat switch to alert staff when he leaves the flat at known risk times.

■   *Exploring vacancies* within a core and cluster development.

■   *Sharing a flat* with one other person.

■   In an emergency there is a *temporary 24-hour care* placement.

■   Malcolm's parents have just downsized, but Malcolm's brother, who may act as guardian, may also offer a temporary room; this brother is working with Malcolm and the psychologist to learn how to use a special mobile phone when Malcolm gets agitated on his own.

Defensible practice

This situation is a complex balance of shared decision making that explores simultaneously why this change in behaviour has occurred and what immediate supportive measure can be taken both to enhance understanding and to respond to emerging problems/risks; that explores and anticipates a range of longer-term options depending on the impact of interim measures; that engages with the increasing reservations of the parents but builds alliances with newly available family resources in the form of the brothers; and that takes into account the policy and legal context, and in particular, pays attention to Malcolm's interests and rights. The following section explores what tools and concepts have been developed in professional practice as an aid to decision making in situations such as Malcolm's.

Risk as a concept in professional practice

At the centre of the discussion here is the extent to which people with learning difficulties can expect to exercise rights enjoyed by others in society, and on what basis. Tied up with the question of autonomy and the exercise of choice is the question of risk – to self and to others. If risk is part of everyday life, to what extent do people with learning difficulties have the right to take risks with their lives similar to those of the general population? And to what extent and in what circumstances can professionals be held accountable?

Risk is a double-edged concept that presents opportunities and dangers for professionals as much as individuals in their personal lives. The waters are no longer uncharted but remain hazardous, and the intent behind the developing models of risk assessment and management is to provide the necessary steerage. As suggested by Titterton (2005, p 26), the

> ... professional art of risk-taking lies in the weighing up of likely outcomes and the use of professional judgment guided by systematic methods of risk assessment and risk management.

The realisation of the aspirations in the lives of service users quoted at the beginning of this chapter relies on the development of a conceptual and practical framework that elucidates what might be called 'defensible' practice. One approach is considered in the following section.

Risk assessment, risk management and defensible risk taking

It is a measure of how the social work world has changed in the last 10 years that the discourse of risk is now pivotal in most practice discussions, and that policy and legislation has been introduced, such as the Adult Protection and Support (Scotland) Act 2007, the Mental Capacity Act 2005 Deprivation of Liberty Safeguards (Ministry of Justice, 2008), *No Secrets* review (Home Office/DH, 2000), and *Caring for our future: Reforming care and support* (DH, 2012c).

Some commentators (Kemshall, 2002; Carson, 2008; Titterton, 2011) have concluded that this has led to the adoption of an excessively conservative approach to risk – born from a fear of being in breach of the 'duty of care' and of being sued accordingly. They argue that such 'covering the organisation's back' results in excessively bureaucratic and routinised assessment patterns as a defence against anxiety. There is a temptation, partly resulting from the way accounts now appear in the literature, to treat risk assessment and management as separate and different from other aspects of assessment and intervention, reifying it as something special done by experts. If risk is part of everyday life, it will be part of every assessment, whether or not it is classified in these terms. The development of risk management frameworks has been slower than that of risk assessment, constrained by the public safety and 'blame culture' agendas, but also reflecting the pre-eminence of risk assessment within the profession as a key task that distinguishes its operatives from unqualified care workers. As Davis (1996) and Ryan (1996) point out, the 'defensive' surveillance strand is slowing, being matched by a developmental agenda to promote autonomy, choice and taking control. Central to positive risk taking, however, is the explicit management of that process, particularly in the field of learning difficulties, where traditional expectations for autonomy are low and service barriers high.

Accepting the argument that risk elimination is not the objective but rather the minimisation of harm, a cluster of helpful questions and key concepts systematically applied can assist in informed consideration of the balance of risks, of the options available at the time, and of the dilemmas faced. Consider the issues (below) identified by commentators in the field in relation to Malcolm's review discussion.

Considerations for defensible risk taking in practice

What is the risk? Ask what is the nature of the risk – how significant and how likely. Identify and record the likelihood of positive and harmful outcomes. Do you have the full information? Check its accuracy. What is known about trigger factors?

Who is it a risk for? Is it for the individual, relatives, neighbours or the professionals? Consider your agency risk policy, and if there isn't one, what the implications of that might be. Consider the wider policy and potential legal provisions. What past experience or personal attitudes may be at play?

Partnership, communication and comprehensive consultation should be prioritised between all 'stakeholders' – individual, family, colleagues and other agencies. Exploit the coordinating role of the adult protection/safeguarding committee.

Is capacity an issue? Explore why. How recently has this judgement been reviewed? Is/should there be an advocate? How strongly does the individual feel about taking this risk? What benefits might accrue by taking the risk?

Decisions, when taken, should be recorded. If there is no consensus, this should also be recorded, along with the reasons why.

Draw up a risk management plan. The key elements should be noted – who is involved; who is responsible for what; what steps are required for minimising harm and maximising benefit; establish timescales; what safety net is in place in the event of adverse outcomes; who is responsible – individuals/agencies? Who is recording and monitoring?

Review: establish dates in advance when the plan will be reviewed; formally note learning from the outcomes, positive or negative.

The answers to the above questions form the building blocks for a 'defensible' rather than defensive practice in risk taking. The concept of 'defensibility' has been developed as a 'bridging' concept, linking the inevitability of a serious incident happening with best practice/best professional judgement (Fife Council, 2009; Webb, 2006; SCIE, 2010; Glasby, 2011). In other words, being able to set out the rationale for the decision, underpinned by 'best practice' knowledge, the 'foreseeability' of the incident and the quality of professional resources and response. These 'building blocks' can be set out as a grid or spreadsheet for ease of tracking decision making and differing accountabilities.

Furthermore, decisions should be 'defensible' in terms of the 'least restrictive option'; in other words, why is this person not able to take the risks deemed suitable for other members of society? These are central concepts for ensuring that undue constraint and restraint do not overwhelm individual lives to the point where the assessment and management of risk becomes the new form of 'institutionalisation' (Titterton, 2005, p 29).

When it comes to considerations of risk, people with learning difficulties have tended to be caught at the extremes, either perceived as individuals unable to make judgements about risk, or as posing risks to others. Both of these perceptions result in surveillance, benign or otherwise, as a feature of their lives. One of the stated key principles underlying the change agenda created by *Valuing People* and *The same as you?* was 'choice', which has been expressed in the gathering momentum for services that reflect community membership, participation and citizenship, and in debates about risks, rights and responsibilities, where boundaries have to be re-negotiated. Being responsible for personal money and taking decisions about how to spend it, and being able to develop friendships and engage in intimate relationships, brings its own hazards, and raises the potential for exploitation. Risk assessment and risk management functions are perhaps prime danger zones in which restrictive practices may become reinstated in learning disability practice. It would be ironic if having dissolved some of the 'bricks and mortar' barriers to participation in the shape of institutions, new and less visible ones were erected as a consequence of defensive practices in services.

Recognising abuse

However empowering and compelling the aspirations might be for living independent and fulfilling lives, people with learning difficulties may have personal histories or be in circumstances that place them at particular risk of harm, and indeed, potentially, of abuse.

In this section aspects of particular relevance to the themes in this book are identified:

- What is abuse? Of particular relevance here is:
    - institutional/service abuse
    - financial abuse
    - sexual abuse.

Some of the risks may be amplified in the current policy and practice climate of personalisation and independent living. This particular tension between duty of care and respect for personal autonomy is a major topic of contention, especially where the consent of the adult is overridden.

What is meant by abuse?

The understanding of abuse has evolved from one comprising physical, psychological, sexual and financial abuse, to one that incorporates discriminatory and institutional abuse, and the idea of acts of omission and commission that includes neglect and inappropriate medicating (ADSS and NAPSAC, 1996; Home Office/DH, 2000). Underlying all of these ideas, however, is the concept of power and its improper exercise, which assumes a particular and complex form with regard to adults. This arises from the way in which matters of consent, informed consent and adult autonomy influence judgements about intervention, as discussed earlier.

Practitioners might consider the following.

Issues of consent

Did the user give their consent? If not, they are entitled to the protection of the law (in cases of, for example, sexual assault), just like anyone else. Has a criminal offence been committed?

Is the user capable of giving consent (or does the law regard them as 'incapax')? Do you have a professional assessment to inform you about their understanding or capacity?

Should apparent consent be disregarded because it was the result of exploitation, undue pressure, or fear of reprisal, and hence not meaningful?

Source: J. Aylett, presentation at the University of Edinburgh (2009)

Commentators argue that physical abuse often dominates as part of a cluster of other violations, for example, financial, sexual and neglect, citing among others one study that identifies perpetrators as other service users (12), staff (15) and relatives (11) (Brown and Stein, 1998; Cambridge, 1998). In other words, there can be no complacency – just because an individual lives in one place rather than another does not mean that they are safe from abuse. Indeed, recent prison sentences for 11 staff working at Winterbourne View hospital demonstrate that abuse of people with disabilities is an ongoing problem that changes in service cultures have not eradicated. Disability 'hate crimes', often perpetrated by members of the public, are now an offence under section 146 of the Criminal Justice Act 2003, but persist at a high level, despite the claim by government that 70 per cent of the British public feel that attitudes towards disabled people have improved since the London Paralympic Games in 2012 (Disability Rights UK, 2014).

Individualised forms of care, delivered in private rather than public spaces, have generated concerns both about risk and the potential abuse of service users, and about conditions of employment for PAs in an essentially privatised workforce (Ferguson, 2007; Duffy et al, 2010).

Whatever the context in which acts of 'aggression' occur, practitioners should bear in mind the following four dimensions in an investigation.

> ## Investigating an abuse allegation
>
> ■ *Establish matters of fact:* what actually happened, the nature and extent of any abuse, who or what is to blame, and whether any individual, group or agency should be called to account.
> ■ *Access what is needed* to make and keep the vulnerable adult safe, and to assist them to recover from any trauma they have experienced.
> ■ *Take appropriate action* against the person alleged responsible, and where possible, prevent them being in a position to harm other vulnerable adults in future.
> ■ *Evaluate* whether the service (assuming such involvement) has acted promptly and properly in seeking to prevent and respond to abuse or poor practice, and take appropriate remedial action to assure the safety of other service users.
>
> *Source:* J. Aylett, presentation at the University of Edinburgh (2009)

In addition, there now exists an extensive literature on the abuse of adults as well as children. What follows is a selective reflection on the issues that are particularly relevant in the current policy climate.

Institutional abuse and the limitations of regulation

A marker in the recognition of the importance of regulation as a bulwark against maltreatment and abuse, the hospital scandals described in John Martin's book (1984) were an important driver in the ultimate closure of what were then called 'mental handicap' hospitals. The first inquiry at Ely Hospital was typical of what followed in others. It revealed both specific and general allegations of cruelty and inhumane treatment, 'pilfering' of food and possessions, indifference to complaints and lack of care by the physician superintendent. This account in such everyday language actually refers to beating with a thick stick, hosing down in outside yards with cold water, using strong patients as 'enforcers' and assorted sets of false teeth for communal use. Martin's coruscating expression for this was 'corruption of care' (1984, p 87) by those charged with a duty of care.

Community care was intended to herald a new era of enlightened care for people with disabilities, but we know that abuse still occurs, some of it depressingly reminiscent of 50 years ago, such as at Winterbourne View (2011), Budock Hospital, Cornwall (2006), or Longcare, Buckinghamshire (1998). While the traditional institutions, such as those with which Martin was concerned, have declined, private sector care settings have increased

(Peace et al, 1997), prompting the description 'personal fiefdoms of clinicians' (Butler and Drakeford, 2003). The abuse perpetrated systematically at Winterbourne View is indicative of its endemic and enduring nature, and a devastating indictment of our care system. Further, there is evidence of the importation of institutional practices into community-based provision (Emerson and Hatton, 2005; Kinsella, 2005). With this must come a concern about management practices that are restrictive and potentially abusive.

Contemporary inquiries still unearth examples of cruelty by individual staff, but the emphasis seems to be much more on systemic failures, as in Budock Hospital, for example, where proper referrals for community care assessments and procedures for joint planning were not in place. Whether in response to the man at Budock who spent 16 hours a day tied to a chair, in part due to inadequate staff training, or to systems failures due to lack of communication between health and social services, social work as commissioners and funders of services such as Longcare, and social workers as reviewers of the care provided to individuals, cannot afford to underestimate their responsibility in this sphere.

The creation of an external inspection system (Hospital Advisory Service) for the first time in the wake of the Ely Inquiry has been strengthened by further regulatory bodies in the shape of councils and care commissions to act as a safeguard for vulnerable people, both against individual workers and service systems. The lack of response to Winterbourne complaints of the current regulatory body, the Care Commission, however, is deeply concerning, and suggests the increasing 'regulatory tide' (Schwartz, 1999) has not resolved the problem.

Registration of community-based professionals has proved no more fool-proof than inspection systems. The inquiry in the Scottish Borders into the circumstances of Ms H (Scottish Government, 2004) made clear the extent and long-established nature of multiple abuses, and the extensive contact with a variety of professionals during that time. Finally, after 19 years, it was a friend and not a professional whose action in making an emergency call for an ambulance brought concerted action. What this tells us is that any amount of surveillance by professionals cannot necessarily be relied on to deliver safety. This is not an anti-professional argument, but one underlining the importance of people being surrounded by friends and family to be truly protected. It is the job of social workers as professionals to see that professional support and an informal support network are in place and complement each other. As professionals, it is important that social workers' decisions don't undermine informal networks, and that if these are absent, they consider adopting a person-centred planning approach and develop strategies to create alternatives, such as circles of support, connections into LAC and links with advocacy.

Financial abuse

There have always been concerns about financial abuse, but this is an area of increasing focus as personalisation policies are implemented and individual budget holding takes root.

There are some fundamental problems that compound any discussion of financial abuse per se, which are that people with disabilities and support requirements are generally poorer than the general population, having 'low incomes and higher outgoings' (Williams et al, 2007, p 7); their individual income is often intertwined with the family income (Bewley, 1997); and many have both limited understanding of how money works and of how financial services, such as the Post Office, banks and benefits agencies, operate (Williams et al, 2007).

Williams et al (2007) point to the literature, suggesting that the income of people with disabilities is £200 per week less than required for a reasonable lifestyle. Only 10 per cent of people with learning disabilities have a paid job that might boost income significantly under certain circumstances. Many people reported being frightened of handling money, and 74 per cent relied on carers and family to handle their money for them and were given pocket money, further reducing their experience of handling money. While families reported positively on direct payments, even they found the management of them confusing, with little available help and advice.

This state of affairs makes people particularly vulnerable to loan sharks, 'cold calling' and getting into debt. Financial agencies such as the Citizens' Advice Bureau Advice Shops are unlikely to have any specific initiatives targeted at this section of the population (Williams et al, 2007). It is not difficult to conclude that whatever the advantages of personalisation, we have the flimsiest foundation and skills set for individuals (not just those with learning difficulties), for assuming increased responsibilities for managing money in lieu of care services. Some further education colleges offer courses on handling money, but there is a huge need for direct training and training/ advice for those supporting people, family and carers alike.

Taken in this light, the introduction of individual budgets only increases concern about financial exploitation and abuse. Recent studies undertaken in both England and Wales, and in Scotland on the implementation of self-directed support and personal budgets, have revealed a shortfall in consideration of the policy and practice interface between safeguarding/ adult protection and the allocation of money in lieu of services (Hunter et al, 2012b). The process was described as 'twin-tracking', with the two policies being implemented in parallel with underdeveloped crossover in protocols and joint training, for example.

This anxiety is beginning to be documented in the literature by practitioners (Manthorpe and Samsi, 2012) and by users and carers (Caldwell,

2007). Calls for greater controls to minimise risks emerged from the Ipsos MORI (2011) study of user experiences of personal budgets (mainly direct payments). And there are concerns that the arrangements may result in fraud and abuse by unscrupulous family members (Henwood and Hudson, 2007; Manthorpe and Samsi, 2012). That said, the Audit Commission has compared £855 million public procurement fraud against £2.2 million in personal budgets out of a social care budget of £16 billion (cited in Hunter et al, 2012). Duffy et al (2010) and Fox (2012) provide a counter-argument, that personal budgets may yet prove to be a safer way of managing public money and of reducing vulnerability to abuse compared with traditional services.

The implementation of personalisation will need to address the tension between choice and protection if the bureaucratisation of direct payments and subsequent under-use is to be avoided. The strengthening of family and support networks through the themes mentioned in this section, such as person-centred planning and community capacity development, have a contribution to make.

Sexual abuse

Since the formal introduction of community care, it has become clear that people with learning difficulties are no more 'safe' from abuse in the community and in their own families than in the old-style 'mental handicap' institutions. We also know that acts of aggression, intimidation and exploitation towards people with learning disabilities tend to be reinterpreted as abuse rather than rape, as financial exploitation rather than theft, and as 'disclosure' rather than reporting crime (Williams, 1995). However, concern about sexual abuse has been growing, along with recognition of its complexity where matters of intimate care are not restricted to same-sex workers; where informed consent is in dispute; when matters of choice and 'undue pressure' are ambiguous; and where poor education for embarking on 'safe sex' and intimacy is pervasive.

McCormack et al's longitudinal study (2005) concludes that the confirmed incidence of sexual abuse is high (47 per cent) among those with a learning disability. This study is of interest in its practice implications, by confirming the pre-eminence of men among the perpetrators (94 per cent), and notably that the majority of these men (56 per cent) were other service users, and that half of the reports were made by victims themselves (42 per cent). Evidence generally supports the view that sexual abuse is likely to be a pattern rather than an isolated incident, will involve single perpetrators, and permissive organisational cultures (Brown, 1999).

In practice terms, this means that services have to be alert to the possibility of abuse by other services users, especially men, as well as family and staff. Where an instance comes to light, it is important not to treat it as an isolated incident, as others may have been abused by the same person. It is important to recognise that in some organisations there may be a culture of permissiveness that can be based on a perception of consensual activity between service users as well as the staff perpetrators. The development of guidelines and a policy for dealing with peer abuse, especially in a shared setting, must be a priority. The high incidence of reporting by service users is encouraging, and points to the significance of training and support. However, levels of prosecution remain unacceptably low and victim support underdeveloped.

In summary, Figure 9.1 below, developed by Hilary Brown, summarises and illustrates the complexity and range of the task facing social workers and others working in the adult support and protection field.

Figure 9.1: Map showing constellations of abuse and sources of heightened risk to 'vulnerable' groups

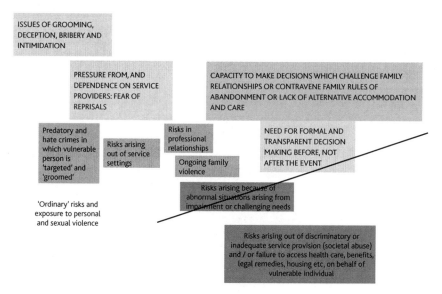

Source: H. Brown, presentation at the University of Edinburgh (2008)

Protection from abuse: safeguarding

At this point it is worth pausing to take account of the underpinning statutory framework that has developed apace to match changing expectations with respect to both protection and autonomy.

First, it is important to note that there is no law about risk taking per se, and that the legal concept is one of 'negligence' (Carson, 2008); services are usually preoccupied with 'risk avoidance' from fear that they might be sued for failing in their 'duty of care'. It is rare to see prominence given to Carson's (1996) argument that a narrow, defensive and unduly restrictive interpretation of risk might be equally negligent and liable if workers have failed to take into account the importance of self-determination and inclusive, least restrictive, options. He makes several helpful points that proving negligence involves a view about comparability of the action with accepted professional conventions; reasonableness in relation to the duty of care; and avoidance of the 'hindsight fallacy'. This underlines the importance of a broader definition of risk that sets potential benefits alongside potential harms.

Unlike children's legislation, there is no single over-arching Act in adult care, but a 'raft' of community-care related legislation, although a recent White Paper and draft Bill in England, *Caring for our future: Reforming care and support* (DH, 2012c), seeks to remedy this through reform and calibration across sectors over the period until 2016. For the moment, however, practitioners are potentially required not only to draw on a range of Acts in relation to deciding the most effective intervention in a single case, but must also have 'due regard' for the general principles and guidance underlying them. For example, the Millan report (Scottish Executive, 2001), whose 10 principles[1] are central to the more recent Mental Health (Care and Treatment) (Scotland) Act 2003, are perhaps the clearest example of this kind of ethical signposting. They also reflect the impact of the Human Rights Act 1998 that applies across all jurisdictions, with which all domestic law and interpretations of that law must comply or be 'compatible', and which is only slowly gaining the requisite profile and understanding in the minds of practitioners as they go about their daily business. From the point of view of adult safeguarding or protection, the Adult Support and Protection (Scotland) Act 2007 requires any intervention to 'provide benefit' and be likely to be 'the least restrictive' among the options available.

It is also clear that the Human Rights Act 1998 will become more prominent in due course, as welfare decisions are tested in court for their 'proportionality' in particular, as well as for being 'lawful' and 'justified'. While the general principles mentioned give prominence to the 'least restrictive' options in professional decision making, individuals themselves may have recourse to the Human Rights Act if they feel 'overprotected', however benignly, for example, in asserting the right to support for family life (Article 8).

Welfare law throughout the UK has many commonalities despite some notable differences in Scots law. In Scotland there are three key Acts: the Adult Support and Protection (Scotland) Act 2007, Adults with Incapacity (Scotland) Act 2000 and the Mental Health (Care and Treatment) (Scotland) Act 2003. In England and Wales, there are broadly similar principles underpinning the legislation (the Mental Capacity Act 2005 and Mental Health Act 2007), although there are some specific differences with English legislation, such as the widening of the approved social worker role to include an approved mental health professional in the assessment of detention; the introduction of an assessment and safeguarding role for social workers under the *Mental Capacity Act 2005 Deprivation of Liberty Safeguards* guidance (Ministry of Justice, 2009) (following the Bournewood judgment, *HL v UK* 2004); and the lack of 'named person' directly appointed by the 'patient' in Scotland. In terms of safeguarding adults, the most significant exception is the enactment in Scotland of the Adult Support and Protection (Scotland) Act 2007 that gives expression to, but goes beyond, the concerns, in terms of duties to investigate and intervene, as expressed in the *No Secrets* guidance in England (Home Office/DH, 2000). This has currently been reviewed to give mandatory powers to safeguarding committees, but does not include intervention in the affairs of a capable person who meets the criteria and is judged to be under duress (DH, 2009b).

Safeguarding and incapable, detained, vulnerable adults

Some adults who are at risk of harm or vulnerable will be deemed not capable of taking decisions on their own behalf, and come under the Adults with Incapacity (Scotland) Act 2000 or the Mental Capacity Act 2005. So the current legislation, while it sets out to protect people with impaired capacity, actually offers a menu of interventions that have to be 'of benefit' to the individual; be the 'least restrictive' option; take into account the past and present wishes of the individuals and significant others; and encourage maintenance of skills. Although this is the guardianship legislation, and as such provides for substitute decision-making powers, it is evident that the principles intend to maximise the self-determination and minimise the restriction of the individuals in question. Such considerations are generally relevant in assessing risk and defending decisions about risks. The intent of robust support for individual autonomy is further evident in the provisions for independent advocacy under the Mental Capacity Act 2005 and the Mental Health (Care and Treatment) (Scotland) Act 2003.

However, it is important to remember that not all adults who live in abusive or hazardous situations are 'incapable', although professionals may consider them to be 'vulnerable' or 'at risk' of harm, abuse or neglect. In such circumstances, the adult has the right to choose; professionals do not have automatic rights to intervene, although they may attempt to negotiate, persuade and support. If professionals cannot get access to individuals suspected of being in harmful situations, or have reason to believe they are under undue pressure not to cooperate, the Adult Support and Protection (Scotland) Act 2007 provides for assessment, intervention and removal if necessary, of the perpetrator, and as a last resort, forced entry. Again, the legislation requires interventions to be of benefit to the adult, be the least restrictive, and have regard to carer/guardian wishes. This Act introduces important safeguards, especially for vulnerable individuals who co-reside with the suspected perpetrator. However, as a counterbalance to allowing even limited intervention in the lives of adults without consent but on their behalf, it does not allow detention against their will, and once removed from the situation, individuals can only be interviewed with their agreement. The controversy generated in Scotland by this statute is one that reverberated through the *No Secrets* review in England (Cambridge, 1998; Flynn, 2007), although it has been argued in High Court that the common law 'declaratory relief' was relevant in these circumstances. Following the *No Secrets* review, the government plans to consult on this again, but points out the recent ruling of the High Court confirming the option to use declaratory relief (*DL v A Local Authority* 2012, EWCA Civ. 253).

Many practitioners will find the broad UK provisions enormously helpful in their everyday practice. However, in addition to plugging a gap in provisions underpinning intervention in the lives of vulnerable adults, they do open up the possibility of over-protective, defensive and unimaginative practice for fear of being sued. There is no recognition of 'over-protection' in the legislation, but there is a possibility of perverse effects from well-intentioned legislation aimed at increasing protection becoming a risk itself in the lives of people with learning disabilities, resulting in greater restriction.

In this context, practitioners should realise that their direct practice in the interpretation of the law must also be compliant. It is important that they understand how this legislation might take precedence. One well-publicised example of this was the Bournewood judgment (European Court of Human Rights, *HL v UK*, 5 October 2004, mentioned above), where a man with a learning disability (and unable to give consent) was detained in hospital under the English common law of 'necessity'. Under Article 5 of the Human Rights Act 1998, it was judged that he had been deprived of his liberty because he was not free to leave, as staff effectively controlled his environment. This led directly to a legislative amendment introducing the Deprivation of Liberty safeguards that builds in a series of formal requirements before acting in the individual's 'best interests' (SCIE, 2010).

If choice and supporting individuals to make decisions as independently as possible is a major policy and practice aspiration, how does this impinge on considerations of risk? How are people 'safeguarded', especially if capacity is uncertain or 'duress' is present, leading to the unavoidable tension between individual control and risk management? This issue is particularly pressing in risk–averse service cultures. How can risk, protecting individuals 'at risk' from harm while promoting positive risk taking and risk enablement, be tackled?

Adult protection is emerging as a distinct area of practice, rather like child protection. However, this separation could create other problems. There is a danger that a 'technology' of risk will be developed around forms of assessment, and intervention will occur at the expense of embedding practice in social and family contexts, building on the natural safeguards of family, friends, advocacy and community capacity to support people. The challenge for social work practice is to balance understandable user demands for autonomy and choice and the accompanying increased exposure to risk, with meeting increased public expectations for the protection of vulnerable individuals.

Conclusion

People with learning difficulties, children and adults are at greater risk of harm than the general population for a range of reasons that include some personal characteristics, service cultures and their organisation and social attitudes. In an era of personalisation, they are also at greater risk of exclusion from decision-making processes that emphasise user centrality. Complications in understanding and judgement associated with learning disabilities impinge on individual decision making. On the positive side, the concept of capacity in law and in practice has evolved from being an 'all or nothing' concept, that is, an individual has capacity or not, to one that allows for gradations of decision making and a menu of powers for intervention.

Together with the provision of the necessary support to make those decisions, it is important to offer safeguarding and protection to individuals who may be at risk. These potential hazards are further compounded by service cultures, which, in an attempt to protect, actually limit individual experience and professional practice from learning by their mistakes. In the literature there are now more readily available discussions of how to move from 'defensive' risk taking to 'defensible' risk taking in practice. These are of critical importance in managing the tension between choice and individual autonomy, especially in risk-averse service cultures. In the past, discussions of abuse have tended to focus on physical and institutional abuse. However, in an era of individual budgets and dispersed supported living, financial abuse has acquired greater prominence, together with an increased concern for sexual abuse in a group of people who are vulnerable to 'undue pressure' at the hands of unscrupulous others.

Finally, social attitudes towards learning disability tend to assume any complaints result from a lack of understanding and are not taken seriously. In order to break into this vicious circle, attitudes and practices need to be alert to the importance of providing opportunities for learning; afford opportunities to take risk in the context of supported decision making; to be believed through word or action that harmful experiences can and do happen, that the dissolution of the Victorian institutions was only the start and not the end of the journey to an ordinary and better quality of life. As indicated by all the policy documents and good practice described in earlier chapters, achieving this 'good life' and positive outcomes requires not only good services that are 'personalised', but also the active support and strengthening of valued connections with relatives, friends and local communities. How this can be achieved, particularly in the current climate of retrenchment, is increasingly pressing.

Questions of understanding and the ability to give informed consent are nowhere more vital than in the consideration of people who, in addition to a learning difficulty, have additional characteristics or features in their lives that intensify the potential risks they face. Consideration is given in the next chapter to some of these individuals.

Note
[1] Non-discrimination; equality; respect for diversity; reciprocity (under compulsion); informal care; participation; respect for carers; least restrictive alternative; benefit; and child welfare pre-eminence.

10 Supporting people with complex needs

In this chapter we consider the circumstances of people with complex needs as illustrated by people with learning difficulties who come into contact with the criminal justice system, who additionally have mental health concerns or behaviour that challenges services, and individuals with profound and multiple learning disabilities. Definitions of 'multiple and complex' needs are explored, and the consequences for the provision of support. We discuss why the needs of people with complex needs are at risk of being underestimated or ignored, and how person-centred and individualised approaches are critical in meeting the particular combination of needs presented. Case studies are used to illustrate how this can be achieved.

The term 'complex needs' is used to mean different things by different authors (see, for example, Gallimore et al, 2008). What the various definitions of 'multiple' and 'complex' needs tend to have in common are the concepts of:

- breadth or range of need (that is, that individuals have a multiplicity of inter-related needs), and
- depth or severity of need (often described as profound, severe, serious or intense needs).

Rankin and Regan (2004) suggest that people with complex needs are characterised by multiple interconnected needs that can only be effectively addressed if both health and social care services respond. They and their families are likely to have to deal with issues arising from a learning disability, mental health problems and other complications. It is also likely that they will be living in areas of deprivation, and may not have suitable housing or meaningful daily activity. A unique, individualised and personal service response has to be developed in order to tackle the particular combination of health and social care needs each individual presents with.

Regardless of their particular combination of need, the Pathways to Health Access project in Lothian found that families shared a desire for their services to have the following features:

- simple, quick access to services at the time they are needed;
- a single point of access to services or one service that will respond to all needs – thus avoiding repeated assessments;
- respect from staff;
- staff behaviour that is culturally sensitive, equal, fair and non-judgemental;
- consistent and positive relationships with staff offering long-term support, with handovers of casework when staffing does change;
- effective joint working and communication between services;
- information about the services available, their remit, and how to access them;
- a flexible approach to each client, as what works for one client may not work for another;
- support with the practicalities of everyday life;
- peer support; and
- involvement in decision making (Gallimore et al, 2008, p 15).

We propose to look at three different groups of men and women with learning disabilities who are characterised by the breadth and depth of their multiple support needs:

- people with a learning disability who are at risk of encountering the criminal justice system
- people with a learning disability who have a mental illness and/or behaviour that challenges services, and
- people with profound and multiple learning disabilities.

People with a learning disability who are at risk of encountering the criminal justice system

Over the last 30 years, significant numbers of people with learning difficulties who, in former times, would have lived in long-stay hospitals, now live in the community. The demise of the old institutional services means that it is no longer possible to use hospital 'beds' as a convenient, although often not appropriate, way of conducting a short-term assessment, or gaining easy-to-access 'respite'. It also means that new options need to be found to respond to inappropriate sexual behaviour, challenging behaviours, chaotic lifestyles and/or decreased capacity for decision making. While in a previous era the courts or other public bodies would often play for time and place people in such settings for observation or assessment, the reality, for many of these people, was that these short-term measures turned into an entire lifetime of isolation and segregation.

While person-centredness has created a clear focus and philosophy for how support is provided in the community, one group of people with complex support needs that has been largely passed by in that process comprises of those with leaning disabilities who have offended or are thought likely to offend. For many of these people, life is still typified by living in locked wards on the remnants of old long-stay hospital sites, or in medium secure units around the country, often referred to as forensic units. In most cases they are run by the NHS, and in many cases, people live very isolated lives that fail to reach any of the quality measures of *Valuing People*, *The same as you?* or *The keys to life*.

Offenders who have a learning disability are typically young males with borderline/mild learning disability. They do not often come to the attention of health and social services until they offend, and referral is then often from the criminal justice system. These offenders generally share a number of other significant risk factors, which include:

- having a history of anti-social behaviour
- using substances hazardously
- having a mental health problem
- being loners   they have few friends
- having experience of physical and/or sexual abuse
- being unemployed
- living within family units that are dysfunctional with multiple losses, and
- being raised in a socially deprived area (Winter et al, 1997; Murphy and Mason, 1999; Simpson and Hogg, 2001).

In sum, they present with multiple problems, and do not fit the profile of those usually served by the learning disability programme of care. Neither has the bulk of staff in these learning disability services the right training or experience to best support them.

One of the challenges faced when planning and developing services for people with learning disabilities who come into contact with the criminal justice system, or who are at risk of doing so, is the limited data available on the exact numbers falling within this group. In Scotland, for example, it is estimated that there are some 2,500 individuals with learning disabilities with a pattern of involvement with the criminal justice system, a proportion of whom might require access to specialist services ranging from outpatient and day services through to prison and secure facilities. More men with learning disabilities demonstrate offending behaviour, and there has been a limited focus on women with learning disabilities (Rowley, 2008).

The assessment of the risk of potential re-offending is important, particularly where there is a history of violent and sexual offences. It is important that these risk assessments have been validated, and that they are viewed as only part of a more comprehensive assessment. Multi-agency protocols and procedures must be in place. There is also a need for research on the effectiveness of risk assessments. We must be confident that there is robust evidence to support decisions that restrict an individual's liberty or lifestyle.

In Fife, the Significant Risk Advisory Group (SRAG) has, for some years, been an integral part of the spectrum of specialist learning disability services. It plays a central role in directing the management of the care of offenders with learning disabilities. It is a multi-disciplinary group comprising representatives from the health service, the local authority and criminal justice service, and has representation from service providers involved in the care of individuals.

Broadly, the function of the group is to review and advise on the development and implementation of care plans for offenders with learning disabilities living in community settings. The identification of potential risks associated with individual service users is undertaken, and strategies are integrated within their care plan, as implemented by service providers. Changes to care plans can only be made following a review by SRAG, and it is an integral part of service-level agreements that participation and compliance with treatment and care plans will occur.

Source: Adapted from Rowley (2008)

The SRAG arrangements foreshadowed the multi-agency public protection arrangements (MAPPA) that were introduced to manage high-tariff offenders such as sex offenders (Ministry of Justice et al, 2014; Scottish Government, no date). There has been some discussion about extending MAPPA to embrace both child and adult protection committees. While they remain separate for the moment, there is overlap and cooperation between them. In the meantime, SRAG continues to operate in some parts of Scotland in parallel to the more widely adopted MAPPA, so that 'lower-tariff' offenders, who might also be deemed vulnerable adults, are systematically reviewed and supported.

There are examples of service providers across the whole of the UK working effectively with people with challenging behaviour, and making a difference to their quality of life. If their success and innovation is to be replicated, we agree with Kinsella (2000) that the following service components are required:

■ Consensus that present arrangements are not working well and are not sufficiently person-centred.

■ Senior managers across all sectors must come together to provide coherent and visible leadership in this area.

■ A systematic and congruent approach must be developed that:
> ensures that people do not get stuck in medium secure units – the system must not only enable them to move out, but also support them to move back if necessary;
> uses an agreed person-centred and outcomes-focused risk-taking approach;
> is committed to working across disciplinary and agency boundaries to tackle difficulties;
> has resources and is flexible enough to be able to provide short breaks for people when required;
> provides more person-centred clinical support;
> is based on relationships and shared practical tools and working protocols between the police, court diversion schemes, probation and social services.

■ Service providers must be engaged on the basis of detailed individual specifications.

■ Commissioners and providers must be committed to regular and rigorous evaluation.

■ The development of competent providers that can deliver person-centred supports, that constantly focus on improving person-centred approaches by staff at all levels, and that are open to organisational change if necessary.

■ Commissioners and providers should have a shared understanding of the financing of the services to be provided.

Helping people know about No One Knows

This programme, run by the Prison Reform Trust, aimed at highlighting the needs of offenders with learning disabilities. In 2008, KeyRing helped establish the Working for Justice group. Many of the members of this group were also members of KeyRing housing networks from across the country. They collected the views and experiences of people with learning disabilities to help with the project planning and the approach the No One Knows programme should take.

The group became particularly expert in working with organisations and agencies involved in the criminal justice system to make it more accessible for people with learning disabilities. A striking example of the impact of their involvement can be seen in their work with the Criminal Complaints Review Commission (CCRC) to produce a new easy-read application form. Since the

Commission started to use this version of the form in early 2012, the volume of applications received has doubled, and it seems that the reason for this increased uptake is through the use of the easy-read form by other previously under-represented groups of people who could be viewed as being vulnerable. As a consequence of this more accessible format, the system has not only received more applications by people with learning disabilities, but also more applications from other vulnerable minority groups, including people already in prison. The impact has been such that the easy-read version is now the only form that is available to download, and is the only format sent out, and the agency now only uses easy-read leaflets and posters.

People with a learning disability who have a mental illness and/or behaviour that challenges services

It is estimated that one in four of the general population experience a problem with mental health in any one year, and most people can expect to have some challenges in their emotional wellbeing at some point in their life. People with learning disabilities are no different. For children and young people, the prevalence rate of a diagnosable psychiatric disorder is 36 per cent in children and adolescents with learning disabilities, compared with 8 per cent in those who do not have a learning disability. These young people are also 33 times more likely to be on the autistic spectrum, and are much more likely than others to have emotional and conduct disorders. The complex nature of their interlocking and multiple needs is demonstrated further by the fact that these young people are much more likely than others to live in poverty, to have few friends, and to have additional long-term health problems such as epilepsy and sensory impairment (Emerson and Baines, 2010).

The overall prevalence of mental health problems in people with a learning disability is significantly higher than that of the general population, with most studies pointing to a prevalence rate of somewhere between 30 and 50 per cent. For reasons that we do not yet fully understand, particular conditions have a higher prevalence among people with learning disabilities. For example, while only 1 per cent of the general population develop schizophrenia, we know that approximately 3 per cent of people with a mild learning disability do. Rates of depression and anxiety are also higher. There is an increasing awareness, too, of how attention deficit and hyperactivity disorder (ADHD) can affect people long into adulthood (see http://www.nimh.nih.gov/health/topics/attention-deficit-hyperactivity-disorder-adhd/index.shtml).

Eric Emerson's definition of behaviour that challenges services is widely used. He defines it as:

Culturally abnormal behaviour of such intensity, frequency or duration that the physical safety of the person or others is placed in serious jeopardy, or behaviour which is likely to seriously limit the use of, or deny access to ordinary community facilities. (Emerson, 1995, pp 4-5)

Recent studies suggest that between 12-17 per cent of people with a learning disability will display behaviour that is challenging to services. Approximately 40-60 per cent of these will show more severe problems including physical aggression, self-injury and destructiveness towards the environment. Challenging behaviour is more likely to be presented by men, especially in the age range 15-35, in those having a more severe intellectual disability, and in those who have additional sensory impairment (see Health Evidence Bulletin Wales, http://hebw.cf.ac.uk/learningdisabilities/chapter4.htm).

In the Valuing People (2002) review of the research evidence on the health needs of people with learning difficulties, it was noted that people with mental health problems and borderline intellectual functioning are particularly difficult to treat. It was also noted that because of the poor track record of communication between specialist psychiatrists in mental health and learning disability, some people with learning difficulties were unlikely to be in receipt of any formal service for their mental health (Hassiotis et al, 2008).

There is no reason why people who present these challenges to services should not be treated as individuals. Services should adopt a person-centred planning approach to designing support, and avoid a blame culture where the person with the learning disability is considered responsible for the problem. In order to ensure that services are specific to the individual and designed to meet their particular needs, person-centred planning should be adopted among all services providing for people with complex needs. To ensure quality and equity of specialist support services, there needs to be a consistency of approach.

… personal budgets have been hugely important in making life-changing differences to people using care services, and driving a shift from a service-centred, paternalistic care system to one where the individual is in control. But even the greatest proponents of personal budgets recognise that they are necessary but not sufficient for personalisation. Several other factors have to be in place. (Wood, 2011, p 12)

People with profound and multiple learning disabilities

Finally, we consider the group of people with perhaps the most complex needs, people with profound and multiple learning disabilities. These men and women experience a range of significant health needs that bring them into frequent contact with healthcare services; the range and complexity of their health needs increases with the severity of learning disability.

Sight and hearing problems are common in people with learning disabilities (RCN, 2013), and it is believed that the majority of people with profound and multiple learning disabilities also have severe sensory and communication difficulties (Mansell, 2010).

Mencap (2001, 2006) stresses that families caring for a son or daughter with profound intellectual and multiple disabilities face an exceptionally heavy responsibility:

- sixty per cent of parents of children and adults with profound intellectual and multiple disabilities spend more than 10 hours per day receiving essential physical care;
- a third of these parents said that their caring role was a continuous task – 24 hours a day, seven days a week;
- fifty per cent of parents spend more than eight hours per day on therapeutic and educational activities;
- parents are woken up, on average, three times a night by the need to care for their son or daughter.

Given our knowledge of the above, it is shocking to discover that a further survey from Mencap (2006) found that 70 per cent of families reported that they were at, or nearly at, breaking point because of the lack of short-break services. Almost half of them were still entirely reliant on their own family for help with practical care tasks because they did not get any formal service support. Only about a quarter got any more than two hours a week home-based care support.

Emerson and Hatton (2008b) estimated that in England in 2008 there were just over 16,000 adults with profound intellectual and multiple disabilities. They go on to estimate that the number of adults with profound intellectual and multiple disabilities will increase, on average, by 1.8 per cent each year to 2026, when the total number will be just over 22,000. In an 'average' area in England, with a population of 250,000, they suggest that this would mean that the number of adults with profound intellectual and multiple disabilities will rise, from 78 in 2009 to 105 in 2026, and that the number of young people with profound intellectual and multiple disabilities becoming adults will rise, from 3 per year in 2009 to 5 per year in 2026.

They point out that these rates are likely be higher in those communities that have a younger population, or those that have a higher number of families from Pakistani and Bangladeshi communities (where the incidence of learning disability is higher). These increases are not linked to levels of socio-economic deprivation.

Despite the clear demographic data about the increase in numbers, there has been a limited policy focus on people with profound and multiple learning disabilities, although this is a relatively small and easily identifiable group. They and their families have clear and undeniable needs for practical and emotional support, yet improvements in services have often not materialised. This must be addressed, not least because improvements in medical technology are leading to a significant increase in the number of adults with profound and multiple learning disabilities in the future. The Profound and Multiple Learning Disability (PMLD) Network has stated that there is a serious lack of understanding of the numbers and needs of people with profound and multiple learning disabilities, and that this has resulted in poor planning and monitoring of the support they receive.

In the report, *Raising our sights*, Mansell (2010, p 5) noted that:

> Access to services is becoming an increasing problem. Families report cuts in services, difficulties in getting an assessment and the tightening of eligibility criteria for essential services, despite their needs staying the same or, in many cases, worsening.

Many with learning disabilities face difficulties when accessing general health services, but these difficulties are exacerbated for those with profound and multiple learning disabilities. Undertaking health assessments, for example, can prove difficult due to their frail physiology and communication difficulties. As a result of such difficulties in assessment and diagnosis, mental illness, and developmental disorders, such as autism spectrum disorder, often go unrecognised in this group.

What is it that is preventing people with profound intellectual and multiple disabilities getting the services they need? Family carers themselves have suggested that it is rooted in prejudice, discrimination and low expectations. The person may be considered as 'too disabled' for existing services, and the families themselves just have to get on with it as best they can. Families often experience problems and barriers accessing short breaks or daytime activities because of the degree of their family member's disability.

> 'We had been on a waiting list for overnight residential breaks for two-and-a-half years and I heard that the centre Matthew was waiting to go to was under threat of closure. I felt in a black hole

with no light at the end of the tunnel. I felt I couldn't go on any more.' (Quoted in Mencap, 2006, p 14)

Consequently, families perceive themselves and their sons or daughters being written off as too difficult to support, and too complex to be included in the moves towards personalisation. And yet, there is clear evidence that people who have profound and multiple learning disabilities have a better lifestyle when they have opportunities in their communities and can develop relationships with people other than paid staff. There are examples of services that strive to ensure that people with profound and multiple learning disabilities are part of their local community, not just through using local facilities, but also by building connections to other citizens, creating the opportunity for people to be appreciated for who they are and what they bring (Wightman, 2011).

Many adults with profound intellectual and multiple disabilities have the same interests and like to take part in the same kinds of activities as other community members. It is increasingly the case that people with high support needs are using their individual budgets in imaginative ways to take part in a wide range of leisure, education and employment opportunities (Swift and Mattingley, 2009; Wightman, 2011). Efforts are also being made to increase these opportunities through programmes such as Sport for All and Valuing Employment Now.

It is likely that because of the additional disabilities and health complications that people with profound and multiple disabilities have, they will often need to rest between activities, or will not be well enough to participate fully all of the time. For those living in supported accommodation, it may be appropriate to use their home as the base from which to do things in the community, but for those living with their families, this may be neither practical nor feasible (Mansell, 2010).

People with higher support needs are frequently offered services that are outdated and delivered in congregate, buildings-based and segregated settings (Wightman, 2011). Yet it is the case that families of adults with profound intellectual and multiple disabilities are often concerned about proposals to replace day centres, usually because they are unconvinced about the practical effectiveness and sensitivity of the proposed alternatives. It is therefore important that planners consider making provision for local bases from which people can access different activities. Indeed, the *Raising our sights* report makes a clear recommendation in this regard:

> Local authorities should ensure that they continue to provide somewhere that can be used as a base from which adults with profound intellectual and multiple disabilities can go to different activities during the day. This does not have to be restricted to

people with profound intellectual and multiple disabilities – a place used by a wider range of people might be more interesting and provide more opportunities for social interaction. (Mansell, 2010, p 29)

There are other approaches that can be added to the range of alternatives. Circles of support such as those facilitated by Equal Futures in Scotland can be particularly useful to people with profound and multiple learning disabilities and their families to become more engaged in their communities and to plan for the future.

Planning for the future – Lewis, Marie and Heather's story

Lewis and Marie are brother and sister. They both have multiple physical and sensory disabilities. They share a bungalow in a residential estate on the edge of a large city. Their father passed away 10 years ago, and the house belongs to their mother, Heather. The bungalow and garden are adapted for Lewis and Marie's needs, and there is space for the equipment they need (for example, a ceiling hoist from the en-suite bathrooms through to their bedrooms, special beds and ample storage space for supplies). There is also a bedroom for a support worker to sleep overnight, as they both need round-the-clock support. Lewis also has a Motability car in which he can be driven in his wheelchair.

A local specialist support agency provides staffing, with one-to-one support available for both siblings during the day. Heather plays a central role in selecting, training and working with staff to ensure Lewis and Marie get the support they need.

During the day Lewis attends a nearby day centre provided by social services. Heather is not happy about this, and wants something more personalised. Marie does not use day services, but has a little support from staff to do different things during the day and in the evenings. The service is jointly funded by social services and health. Both also receive ILF money and other benefits.

Heather is concerned about planning for their future, considering two additional options that she thinks might benefit her two adult children:

■ Seeking individual budgets for each of them so that they can have a wider range of inclusive activities – she is worried, however, that the budget will be restricted to a level below what they currently receive, and the net effect will be detrimental to each of them.

■ She is considering offering to give the house to the care provider in return for a guarantee about Lewis and Marie's ongoing security.

Think spot

Take some time to reflect on what your role might be in this situation:

> As Heather's social worker, what role would you have in helping her address these questions?
> Is there any sense in which the arrangements, although relatively well resourced, may tend to result in the brother and sister's needs being conflated and not being addressed individually and separately, and that other accommodation and support options should be considered if everything is up for grabs?
> Are there other ways you could assist Heather to feel more secure about the future?
> How could you sensitively help her to review her will, to check if she has set up suitable discretionary trusts and established powers of attorney?
> Would they benefit individually (or jointly?) from the creation and maintenance of an enduring circle of support? How would you go about establishing a circle or circles if that was deemed a desirable course of action?

The Learning Disabilities Foundation Report, *A life in the community* (Swift and Mattingley, 2009), describes an action research project promoting citizenship for people with high support needs. Some of the key messages from this project were:

■ Circles of support, where a group of people come together to plan around a person and implement ideas, offer an effective way of finding out what a person with high support needs might like changed in their life.
■ Having their own pot of money (and the support to use it) leads a person with high support needs to have more choice and control about what they do, when they do it, and how they do it.
■ For people with high support needs to meet and spend time with people other than paid staff, support staff need to work in a different way and develop skills to be good community connectors.
■ Commissioners and care managers have a key role to increase these opportunities through personalised funding as well as funding services that have a community connecting role.

Swift and Mattingley (2009) found that:

> ... circles of support proved a cost effective way of coordinating planning and action for and around an individual. However, commissioners and care managers did not always recognise and value the work with circles of support to help people with care needs have a better life in the community. In particular, many of the good outcomes achieved in the project were driven by families and non-paid supporters, sometimes with help and advice from others (such as from a specialist in self employment).
>
> Of the people taking part in the project, two thirds had an identifiable circle of support. These varied in composition, in the leadership of them and the role they played in the life of the person at the centre of the circle. However, there was a clear association between the presence of a circle and the achievement of goals, not least because goals were more likely to be clearly stated where a circle was operating. (Swift and Mattingley, 2009, p 10)

It is still the case that adults with profound intellectual and multiple disabilities are unlikely to be successful in gaining any kind of employment. Mansell (2010) points out that families and professionals are sceptical of the possibilities of employment for these men and women. Despite the scale of the challenges involved, others continue to be idealistic about their prospects:

> ... it has to be recognised that for some people with highly complex needs, such as those with profound and multiple learning disabilities or who are medically dependent, paid employment poses particular challenges, although it remains an aspiration. (PMLD Network, 2009, p 4)

Where people with profound and multiple learning disabilities do have the chance to engage in employment, it is likely to be only one of a range of activities and opportunities that they experience. It will enhance their life in a number of ways, not just through the job activity, but also through the contact and interaction with those around them.

Conclusion

Despite problems of definition, people with complex needs can be characterised as having a multiplicity of inter-related, and often severe, needs that require a comparable complexity of services and professionals cooperating to meet those needs.

Prior to the national closure programme of NHS long-stay 'mental handicap' hospitals, and the emergence of the paradigm of supported living in the community, routine use has been made of institutional resources to meet the multi-layered and complex needs of people with learning difficulties who come into contact with the criminal justice system, the mental health system or who have profound and multiple difficulties. Sometimes such institutional placements were intended to be holding ones while planning for more suitable options took place, but the short-term often became permanent. People with complex needs often find themselves in services where staff and resources are geared to one aspect of their needs, with the result that they are offered outdated and segregated resources, with staff ill-trained to meet their needs. Recent research indicates that personalised funding and individualised planning can be harnessed to allow people with high support needs to participate in community living, and we now have successful examples of this being achieved on which to draw (Wightman, 2011) .

In Part Three, and the final chapter of the book, we take some of these themes of complexity, as illustrated in Simon's story, into a broader discussion that reviews the main issues raised in the book; the challenges they pose in practice; and how social workers might respond positively. We conclude with a commentary on the challenges for social work that lie ahead.

Part Three
Conclusion

11 Conclusion: challenges for social work practitioners – staying person-centred and community-focused, and managing risk

> In this chapter we narrate five different perspectives on Simon's story, followed by a commentary on related practice considerations. We then reflect on why it is that practitioners struggle to keep a person-centred, community-centred, positive risk-taking focus in these particular areas of work. We conclude by highlighting some future challenges for social work services in terms of the impact of austerity on welfare, the renewed initiatives to integrate health and social care, and the failure to deal with continued institutionalisation.

One story, five perspectives

Simon had always lived at home and attended a local school with an attached special class. Despite his mum's reservations, he moved into supported accommodation in his early twenties. He has been volunteering as part of a gardening project in a nursery run by a national learning disability charity, and has also 'recruited' a support worker to find ways he could 'hang out' with the now ageing Goths and terminal Punks down on the green, in the centre of town. With eyebrow studs, a wild hairstyle and the right t-shirts, he really looks the part. The support staff have been really supportive in helping him buy the right gear. However, they have recently become concerned about his friendship with a roadie with one of the punk bands, Steve, who is a heavy drinker, has been known to dabble in drugs, and has a history of petty theft from supermarkets. Tonight, there's a really big gig at a club in town. There's going to be 'one hell of a party' afterwards, and Simon has rehearsed his lines....

Simon's perspective

The really exciting thing since I left home is that I'm now officially a roadie with one of the bands. I love it – I'm bigger than most of my mates, and lifting amps and speakers is easy. My support workers have been great up to now, but there's going to be a scene when I tell Dave I'm not going back to the group home after the gig. I'm just going to tell him straight…. "It's my choice; it's got nothing to do with you. I'm a grown man; I make my own decisions. I'm going with my mates to the party and Steve has said he'll look out for me. You're not coming and that's it."

Elsie, Simon's mother's perspective

I thought the services were here to support us as a family. It was hard enough getting through the boy leaving home and going into a flat, but now it's all getting out of hand. He's got an eyebrow stud for goodness sake … and frankly I'm really worried about him getting caught up in drink and drugs through these weird looking people he is now spending most of his time with. I've told the staff and the social worker that I'm not happy, especially about Steve. Since then, the two of them have been spending quite a bit of time together. He's started drinking and seems short of money while Steve seems to have a lot of cash for a roadie. I want it stopped, but they treat me like an old fuddy duddy. They think I know nothing about Simon and what he really needs. But I'm his mum, and I know that he always sees the good in people, and doesn't realise when people are taking a loan of him. He believes Steve when he says he'll pay back the money he's lent him. I don't want him keeping bad company; I've been told that that Steve was charged with stealing alcohol from the minimarket and that Simon was with him, but they only got a warning. I've told Simon and the staff at the home in no uncertain terms that I think this whole situation is a disgrace. I'm really ashamed – we are law-abiding folk. These professionals don't seem to realise what they are putting me through, but I'm putting a stop to it once and for all. I'm seeing my lawyer to tell him that if this is how it's going to be, then I want Simon back home where I can make sure he is safe. He needs a guardian, and whatever this so-called advocate has to say on the subject, it's going to be me….

Dave, the support worker's perspective

I really like Simon. We're both 23 and we have a lot in common. Okay so his taste in music is a bit dodgy – but it sure beats the perennial Jim Reeves and Jimmy Shand! Anyway, tonight we had a crisis. Simon refused to come back to the house at the end of the gig in the pub, and said he was going to a party with the rest of the Goths. I said that I couldn't let him do that. And it wasn't that I had to finish my shift or anything – it was just that he insisted on going with his so-called friends – and without me. But I've got responsibilities here. It's no comfort that Steve will be there, as he's the one who took him on a nicking spree for vodka and beer a few weeks ago. I had to make it clear that I thought this was 'too risky', that he could not afford to get into more trouble after the police warning, and that it would land me in a lot of bother. So I ended up with no alternative but to get Geoff Jones, the on-call senior manager, out to help me take him back. Needless to say, Mr Jones was not a happy bunny – the unwritten rule round here is that you try your damnedest not to disturb the on-call manager – you just get on with it, unless it's a really dire emergency. Well, between us we 'coaxed' Simon into coming home. He went silent on us, then, when the boss had gone, Simon trashed his room big style. After that he spent what was left of the night 'ranting'. I was worried about his state of mind – not to mention the neighbours – and so the following morning I called out the CPN (community psychiatric nurse), who was able to give him something to calm him down. There's going to be trouble....

Dorota, the social worker's perspective

I have heard from the provider, Integrated Experiences Ltd, that we need to have an emergency review in relation to my client Simon. They say he is presenting challenging behaviour, and they are not too sure if they can cope with him. They say they are not geared up for such specialist provision, that is, his challenging behaviour, which has led to involvement with the police and the local mental health team. On the other hand, Simon's mum has been niggling away at me for the last few months. She thinks Simon is being allowed (maybe even encouraged) to 'run wild'. She says she wants him home and is talking about guardianship. Since the appearance of Steve in Simon's life, she says she has 'plenty of evidence' for taking back control of Simon's life – and says her lawyer agrees. Not surprisingly, she is slipping back into her old over-protective behaviour. I really thought we had got over that three years ago when Simon left home, but recent events involving the police have undone all that progress. In some ways this is a crisis, but I also think there may be an opportunity here. I need to do some careful work with Elsie in the hope of buying us some time to make a considered and multi-disciplinary decision, and my proposal would be that we look for a direct payment, or use the new provision for self-directed support to establish a mixture of arranged services and an individual budget. I had thought we could establish a single tenancy for Simon, but budgets are tight, and my colleagues are wary in case any flat might get taken over by his 'so-called mates' and become a 'drinking den'. I know I'm exaggerating, but my mind keeps going back to the tragic murder of Steven Hoskin. Integrated Experiences won't be happy about supporting a single tenancy in the circumstances, and my worry is that I don't think my senior will back me up.

Jim, the advocate's perspective

I've known Mike since we were at art college and played in a band together. When I got a permanent graphics job back in the area, we met up for coffee and he told me about the Citizen Advocacy Initiative where he now works after the funding ran out for his hospital arts project. I should have known better – by the end of the second coffee, I was being recruited as a possible advocate for this young guy, Simon. I like the sound of Simon – he's got style! Mind you, he's got conflict in his life with people who seem to have his best interests at heart, but they're just not Simon's interests. There's a bit of a crisis at the moment about where he's living and how he chooses to spend his time. If we hit it off, and if Simon gives me the okay, I'll try and help him get his point of view across (without trashing his room), and hope we might become long-term buddies. I'm told he has recently got into trouble for the first time, and am hoping that my presence might be a timely shot across the bows of Steve and his cronies. As I see it, I think the social worker is trying to get a good deal for Simon, but she's in an awkward position; I can say things that she and Dave can't say to their employers. Simon's mum is going to take a lot of persuading ... but despite being into this music scene, I am a 'proper person' with a respectable job, and maybe that will help....

Some practice reflections

Notwithstanding the extensive debate about 'what is social work?' (Asquith et al, 2005; Payne, 2006; Cree and Myers, 2008), there is a degree of consensus that it involves supporting disadvantaged and marginalised people in an 'holistic' way that requires skills in negotiating the interface of the systems, services, communities and families that make up people's lives.

With good reason, Dorota has been well pleased with her work 'in this case'. She managed to persuade Elsie to acknowledge Simon as an adult by allowing him to move out of the family home, to take up some voluntary work, and she had found a person–centred provider with young staff able to share some of Simon's interests and to begin to integrate him into a group of non-disabled young people. One staff member shared his music interests, had supported him to become a roadie with a group, while another had even found an advocate for Simon who shared this interest. Her next stage of finding Simon a single tenancy through a direct payment or individual budget has been thrown into doubt by the emergence of an 'undesirable' roadie friend. Getting the individual budget should be straightforward enough as it is now an entitlement, but getting a single tenancy may not be so easy to get support for.

Dorota is already engaged with a range of 'systems', and seems to have developed constructive working relationships with them all to date. However, it seems she is going to need time and skill to work with Simon's mother and possibly the service provider. Her concern about her senior's position is not unusual as managers are located at the tension points between the user's 'interests', service resources and risk-taking policies. The interface with the community may be the one that is most elusive for Dorota, both in terms of her skills and the caseload time at her disposal. That said, she could consider how to ally herself proactively with the advocate without undermining his independence. The advocate could be the key player here, especially as he is a *citizen* advocate, where relationships are long term, and in addition to direct support in decision making, potentially offer access to the advocate's own social network. This provides a base from which to build community involvement and connections through someone who lives and is a known face in the neighbourhood, in a manner that a social worker could not undertake.

In the UK, the statutory context of social work has also meant that social workers are practised in managing the conflicts and dilemmas thrown up by the care and control aspects of their role. With the exception of compulsory measures in mental health services, and guardianship in learning disability and dementia services, the tensions facing social workers in community care are more likely to concern protection, over-protection and the promotion of personal development through risk taking. Promoting self-determination for Simon in a way that is at odds with the views of the person who knows him best, and who has a primary and enduring concern for his wellbeing, namely, his mother, and who realistically is likely to continue to be the most important person in his life, requires time and skill. Assuming Dorota has the skills, she may require determination, collegial and professional support to persuade her own managers to find time in her workload to avoid the line of 'least resistance', and to seek solutions beyond pragmatic service ones, such as group living.

Then there is the public protection issue to be addressed – both with regard to Simon himself, and potentially to neighbours and local shops on the receiving end of his 'challenging' behaviours. It is likely that Simon would meet the three-point eligibility test for intervention under the Adult Support and Protection (Scotland) Act 2007 that gives social workers certain powers of intervention, especially in circumstances of 'duress', as possibly applicable to his friend Steve. The heightened profile of safeguarding has been further reinforced, not only within the context of human rights legislation, but in response to increasingly personalised services through direct payments and self-directed support.

If Simon's outbursts become a pattern, this may bring him into the ambit of mental health and criminal justice services. Neither of these systems has traditionally seen learning difficulties as their main area of expertise. Neither does the bulk of staff in these services have the right training or experience to best support them. Similarly, workers with knowledge of learning difficulties are unlikely to be confident in such related areas. This is the 'silo effect' of service structures, and Dorota will need to put considerable energy into working across these boundaries, liaising with social workers located in these systems as well as with other professionals.

It will be helpful to Simon that he is well known to services in planning to avert a criminal justice referral or outcome. As with offending, challenging behaviour is more likely to be presented by men, especially in the age range 15–35, in those having a more severe intellectual difficulty and in those who have additional impairments. Recent studies suggest that between 12–17 per cent of people with a learning disability will display behaviour that is challenging to services. Approximately 40–60 per cent of these will show more severe problems, including physical aggression, self-injury and destructiveness towards the environment.

While Dorota does not see Simon as having mental health problems, she is aware (in line with Emerson's definition, 1995) that if his 'challenging behaviour' continues, he might be categorised this way. This presents Dorota with a dilemma – how to access the expertise of the community mental health team, with its specialist nursing and psychologist resources that could give the provider the confidence and skills to continue to support Simon, without attaching a label to him.

While person-centredness has created a clear focus and philosophy for how support is provided in the community, supporting people with complex support needs has largely been by-passed in that process. There is still a pattern of people with learning disabilities and complex care needs being the subject of out-of-area placements, due either to a breakdown in current local services, or a complete absence of services locally that can respond to their specific needs. The high cost of individualised support arrangements, combined with budget restrictions, has also seen the re-emergence of congregate services, albeit in apparently more benign forms, such as new versions of core and cluster services. Social workers in Dorota's position need to be alert to the reinvention of the institutions they have spent several decades replacing with more personal and individualised support arrangements. Although Elsie, Simon's mother, states her intention to take him back home, she may not be well placed to manage more assertive behaviour, particularly as she gets older.

The alternative to out-of-area placements for many of these people is typically a life in locked wards on the remnants of old long-stay hospital sites, or in medium secure units around the country, often referred to as forensic units. In most cases, these forensic units are run by the NHS, and in many cases, people live very isolated lives that fail to reach any of the quality measures of *Valuing People* (DH, 2001a) or *The same as you?* (Scottish Executive, 2000) or *The keys to life* (Scottish Government, 2013).

The impact of the 'managerialist' trend in practice, whereby social workers were required to become care managers commissioning services and arguably rationing rather than delivering them, has had its impact on the profession's traditional interpersonal skill set (Lymbery, 2001; Jordan, 2004; Ferguson, 2007, 2012). Yet this is exactly the professional expertise that is required in order to implement the government's personalisation agenda based on user-led assessment, with a focus on 'outcomes' and not only needs. Navigating the tensions between personal outcomes that can be agreed to by families and met by local communities, and in collaboration with multiple agencies, all of which is implicit in the personalisation agenda, especially in a time of financial cut-backs, is not only challenging, but requires a re-thinking of the repertoire of professional skills that draws not only on professional expertise, but also on creative, defensible risk taking and innovation.

It seems to us that 'risk taking' in its multiple guises is the pivotal point around which social workers must learn to operate expertly: risk that 'promotes' personal development; risk that is 'informed' by the views of family, friends, other professionals and the individual at the centre; risk that 'safeguards' and strives for a balance between autonomy and protection; risk taking that tackles 'risk-averse' practices and policies; and being alert to the risk of sliding back into institutional practices and ways of thinking, especially under the pressure of austerity measures in public welfare. This is not a professional agenda for the faint-hearted; the tick-box mentality must give way to creativity, courage tempered with, but not overwhelmed by, realism, resilience and digging in for the long haul. It will not be possible to deliver a Rolls-Royce service all the time, but we should be striving for that when we can.

Think spot

In view of what you have read about current good practice, how would you assess Dorota's performance as the responsible social worker, along ▶

the parameters of self-determination, person-centredness, community connectedness, and in particular, how might you respond to this as an issue about managing risk?

Self-determination
> Is capacity an issue or not?
> Is vulnerability a consideration?
> How do these considerations impinge on decision making?

Person-centredness
> What evidence is there that Simon has been at the centre of decisions made about his future?
> Is Simon being helped to acquire the skills of informed decision making?
> What supports for decision making are in place?

Community connectedness
> How well is Simon connected with ordinary people in the community?
> What connections does he have with people other than those paid to be with him?

Risk management

Taking full account of risks is a vital part of good person–centred support for people with complex support needs. There are four primary areas to consider in risk management – damage or harm to self; damage or harm to staff; to people in the community; and damage to goods and property. Among the questions we might ask to assess risk are:

■ What risks exist?
■ How great are they?
■ What will the person lose if the risk isn't taken?
■ What can be done to minimise the risk if the decision to do something is taken?
■ How likely is that to happen in the context of the support that they receive, or that it is planned for them to receive?

Of course risks will change over time and within different contexts. Risk assessments therefore need to be regularly reviewed and updated to reflect people's development and context/environment (Kinsella, 2000). The task will often be one of risk minimisation rather than risk management. One potential negative consequence of this is that in asking questions about how to reduce risk, questions about the desired outcomes for the person, and how they can be supported to achieve them safely, are forgotten.

Clearly there are risks to Simon due to inexperience as he mixes with a new group of people whose offer of 'friendship' he is not well placed to judge, yet how is he going to learn about how to make these judgements in the absence of experience? There is a risk that the provider will become increasingly unwilling to tolerate Simon's outbursts, that these outbursts, if ongoing, will be reframed as 'challenging behaviour' rather than an understandable reaction to disappointment, and his mother's determination to seek guardianship has become a very real risk to hard-won control of his lifestyle.

Dorota knows that the mental health and criminal justice systems are not necessarily well placed to take on Simon's needs for some of the reasons discussed below. Yet there is expertise in the mental health team that could assist the support staff to develop skills and strategies for responding to such behaviour. The community policeman involved in Simon's warning seemed to have a good understanding of learning disabilities, and could possibly be helpful in getting Simon to consider the risks he is running. Dorota's own management is likely to respond by becoming risk-averse, especially after the Steven Hoskin case and other extreme examples of hate crime. Dorota believes the best way forward would be to call a multi-disciplinary meeting, not simply a placement review, and that prior to that she could work on a number of options to minimise the risk. This might involve:

- establishing a circle of support, getting Jim and Simon to explore whether other roadies, fans and group members might join, thereby 'neutralising' any negative influence that Steve might have; the circle might explore any other interests that Simon has that might be activated and reinforced;
- talking with Jim about what opportunities there might be within his own network for Simon to meet new people and to investigate new interests;
- working with Simon on other accommodation options, if required;
- talking to the support team about a period of grace for Simon, and about getting some specialist input from the challenging behaviour team;
- talking with relevant colleagues about the new and more nuanced definition of 'capacity' and the options with adult protection (see Chapter Nine), which may be more relevant, for example, banning orders;
- preparing for the two biggest challenges for Dorota personally – namely, trying to find a way of working in alliance with Elsie rather than in opposition, and persuading Dorota's senior to hold fire on any risk-averse planning.

Dorota seems to have decided that the events of the last few months can be reasonably constructed as predictable features of a transitional phase from young person to adult; from making some foolish decisions out of inexperience to being supported in a learning curve about both the rights and responsibilities of adult life; and from being overly protected at home to taking *defensible* risks in the community. Unafraid to deploy the emergent policy imperative of co-production in discussion with her managers, Dorota will work with Simon and 'collaborate' with colleagues from other agencies and significant people in Simon's life, to re-frame these problems as 'learning opportunities' for Simon in taking the massive steps into adult life and into the community.

Keeping an individualised, person-centred and community involvement focus

Matching aspirations to resources

The history of services and policy development in the field of disability serves to remind us that maintaining the vision of a 'better life', and the professional practice required to achieve this, is a continuous battle. There is no final 'victory', the terrain is constantly shifting in the face of service delivery pressures, resources that are always insufficient and currently under pressure, and in the face of persistent, negative and 'scapegoating' attitudes in society about disability.

The coincidence of the introduction of personal budget policies, such as self-directed support, with the current period of austerity that is deeper and more prolonged than even the Depression of the 1930s, makes for turbulent waters for practitioners to navigate. Given the significant tension between the high aspirational nature of the policies and the fear of risk taking by managers and frontline workers, how can social workers maintain idealism and a commitment to social justice, and resist the development of new forms of congregate care?

There is some evidence that assessments are being distorted to fit individual needs into available resources. Professionals and politicians need to be honest about the 'shortfall in funding'. Peter Beresford (2014), for example, suggests a public acknowledgement that:

- admits that the level of resource is important to achieving better outcomes;
- stops requiring practitioners to work in ways that deny this;
- records when need is not met.

This requires social workers to continue to practice in the model of existing successful outcomes achieved through person-centred planning, direct payments and self-directed support. However, and importantly, it requires the creation of working alliances with not only their managers and politicians, but also with people with learning difficulties and their families. This is not straightforward as it involves not only working at an organisational level that may be resistant, but also at an individual level, with service users who may be in vulnerable and hazardous situations. However, some 'champions' of good services can usually be flushed out from the organisational undergrowth, and people with learning difficulties themselves often have strengths and resources that can be mobilised with support from professionals who take the time to ask and look.

Challenge of demography

The changing demographic profile of disability services is characteristic of population trends in the population as a whole. Although this should ease the challenge, ageism in services and society in general is as entrenched as it is proving to be in relation to learning disability. Thanks to advances in medicine, public health, and, it should surely be acknowledged, to the evolution of attitudes and the human rights agenda, people with moderate and mild learning difficulties are surviving into old age, and those with multiple and profound difficulties are surviving into adulthood. This challenges professional assumptions, skills and services with regard to self-determination, independence and choice in different ways from those that professionals are used to meeting.

Remaining person-centred and outcomes-driven

Helping people to achieve their potential through person-centred methodologies, and by adopting a strengths- rather than deficit-based approach in decision making, is well established in practice and in the literature. However, appropriate tools for self-assessment, such as the outcomes-focused Talking Points approach extensively used in Scotland (Cook and Miller, 2012), are underdeveloped, as are the links between such outcomes-led approaches and wider care management and commissioning approaches. What this adds up to for frontline practitioners is a tough operating environment, requiring not only skills, but also sheer determination to keep faith with these aspirations in an often, although not necessarily cynical, hostile environment.

While it has long been acknowledged that we need to move away from a dominant medical model, we also need to find ways to integrate good clinical support within a person-centred approach. It is important to achieve shared and agreed approaches, and not paper over the cracks – because it will most frequently be at crisis points that the differences of perspective will be exposed, and yet can least be afforded.

Working in partnership

The construction of 'better lives' for a group of people who have been historically and systemically marginalised and disenfranchised in our society cannot be tackled by one professional alone. Sustained changes on many levels and in all sectors are required. So professional energy has to be targeted, not only on intervention with the individuals themselves, but in fostering partnerships across boundaries, between specialist and mainstream providers. And then, drawing on the strength and commitment of advocacy groups, learning how to share power with those who rely on services, working out how the work can be informed by the views of people with learning difficulties and their family carers in ways that reach beyond consultation to collaboration and co-production.

At the same time, people with learning disabilities need to grow into their responsibilities as they are afforded citizenship. The Michael Batt Foundation includes the following rules for working with people who have offended, but which are relevant to services across the board:

- We cannot tolerate physical violence toward the people who support you.
- If you damage property, you must replace or repair it.
- We cannot allow the law to be broken in properties we own.
- Anything stolen will be replaced from your own money.
- You must understand and respect the needs of your neighbours to live their lives peacefully.
- Treat the people who support you as you would like to be treated yourself.

We do not know whether such ground rules were in place between Simon, the service provider and Dorota, but it is in Simon's long-term interests as he establishes his place in the adult world to understand in concrete terms the relationship between being given choice and taking responsibility for his choices and behaviour. This is detailed and time-consuming work. It is unlikely that social workers would undertake this themselves, but they need to understand the process, and support the care workers doing it.

Balancing risk and autonomy

It is not uncommon, particularly retrospectively, for those professionals promoting person-centred services and community involvement to be caricatured as ignoring risk, and those promoting specialist, congregated services as completely risk-averse. Professionals are faced with the enormous challenge of maintaining a balance between positive and defensible risk taking and conservative risk-averse policies and procedures. In our view, what is required is good, specialist input, within the context of a good community-based and person-centred service. Insistence by social workers on the provision and use of relevant tools such as PRAMS (Progress Recording and Monitoring System) (Titterton, 2005) and Risk Assessment and Protection Planning (JIT, 2007), for managing and reviewing risk in a systematic and dynamic way, has to be a good starting place.

We might speculate that these challenges may be to do with the fact that the most important priority in many services, especially those with a forensic focus, is to keep the community at large safe. Perhaps mixed or contradictory messages have been given by the government in, on the one hand, promoting independence as a key principle, and on the other, generating a strong ethos of safety before all else. Negative public perceptions of, and attitudes to, disability continue to be problematic, despite potentially being subject to 'hate crime' legislation.

That said, surely there is the potential to respond to the values within the policy guidance papers *and* to keep our communities safe. All public sector services have a legal duty to provide 'reasonable adjustments' for people with learning disabilities. These include removing physical barriers to accessing services, but importantly, they also include changing the ways in which services are delivered, and ensuring that policies, procedures and staff training all enable services to work equally well for people with learning disabilities. The National Development Team for Inclusion (NDTi, 2012) report, *Reasonably adjusted?*, clarifies how these adjustments can be achieved and embedded into practice for people with autism and people with learning disabilities in mainstream mental health services. Further, it also argues that such reasonable adjustments improve service quality for everyone, and as all of us at some time are likely to draw on services for ourselves or someone we know, we all have an investment in that.

We think Simon's story reflects most of the social work practice issues raised throughout this book:

■ The need to access support and services without becoming stereotyped by the acquisition of a service or diagnostic label (as discussed in Chapter One).

- The influence of historical paradigms that result in service staff seeing people's disabilities and delimiting people's options, and inappropriately re-inventing failed models (as discussed in Chapter Two).
- The value of access to a support network, person-centredness and an outcome focus (as discussed in Chapter Three).
- The benefits to be gained and empowerment that can result from taking up direct payments (as discussed in Chapter Four).
- The role of the social worker in supporting the young person through the stages of transition to adulthood (also discussed in Chapter Four).
- The role of the social worker in supporting the person to live in their own place while working with the family carer to deal with ongoing anxieties about this (as discussed in Chapter Five).
- Consideration of alternatives to the day centre (as discussed in Chapter Six).
- Preparing for the prospect of someone returning to the parental home, and this presenting serious difficulties as the parent/carer gets older (as discussed in Chapter Eight).
- The social worker's role in managing the balance between risk management and the promotion of independence, and supporting the role of independent advocacy (as discussed in Chapter Nine).
- Awareness of the dangers of silo working vis-à-vis learning disability, mental health and criminal justice services (as discussed in Chapter Ten).

While Simon's story doesn't address the issues of sexuality and indeed, parenting, there is every chance that these issues will have to be addressed in the future. Social workers need to be ready to address these contentious issues, whether they present immediately or not.

Future challenges

There are some very significant developments in the political and policy context that are already having an impact on the lives of people with learning difficulties that we think will present even greater challenges in the near future. These include the impact of austerity and of the integration of health and social care, and the continuing failure to deal with institutionalisation.

Impact of austerity

In response to the financial crisis of 2008, the government decided to make significant cuts in public spending. By 2015, there will have been a 10.8 per cent cut, but the critical point from the perspective of people with learning difficulties and their families is that these cuts will not fall evenly across all areas. Although the NHS and pensions are protected, local government and benefits budgets are to be cut by 50 per cent, even though they only account for 26.8 per cent of all central government expenditure (see Duffy, 2013, for a detailed exposition of the figures). Given that services for adults (excluding the NHS) are primarily funded by local government, this is a serious and worrying situation that is summed up in the Haringey Learning Disabilities Partnership Board report (2014, p 2):

> ... people to have an "ordinary" life and be included in society, as it means they will become more isolated, their health will worsen, and family carers will not be able to cope.

This report records the views of service users, carers and staff, and reveals the level of stress and distress accumulating as a consequence. In real terms, these cuts mean a loss of income of £4,410 for people with disabilities and £8,832 for people with severe disabilities, as opposed to £467 for most other people. Effectively, 2 per cent of the population is bearing 29 per cent of the total cuts.

It is hard not to conclude that people with disabilities have been 'targeted', especially when the government has been resistant to undertaking a cumulative impact assessment (Duffy, 2014). Further, there is a worry that the prominence given to such 'targeted' cuts in the public arena will possibly resurrect negative images of people with learning difficulties as a burden, or worse, 'demonise' them (a clear example of this can be found in the substantially greater media coverage of benefits fraud, in comparison to the coverage of tax fraud, which is 15 times greater). An adapted extract from Duffy's report below itemises some of these 'targeted cuts'.

Attacks on the rights of disabled people

- Someone with severe disabilities faces cuts *19 times greater* than the average person by a combination of benefit, housing and social care cuts.
- Social care faces the deepest cuts of all – local services for people with severe disabilities, including the elderly, are being *cut by 33 per cent* by 2015.
- The ILF is being closed down – *19,373* people with severe disabilities will now lose their direct entitlement for money to support their independence.[1]
- The UK is the *third most unequal country* in the developed world. The new benefit system disconnects income from growth (and even inflation).

- Cuts in Housing Benefit and the introduction of the 'Bedroom Tax'[2] are further impoverishing disabled people and forcing people to leave their own homes. A total of *420,000 disabled people* or their families will each lose an average of *£728 per year*.
- Disability Living Allowance (DLA), which helps people who have serious health conditions and disabilities to live independently, is to be replaced with Personal Independence Payments (PIP) – *500,000 people* will lose individual entitlements worth an average of *£3,000 per year*.
- The Employment Support Allowance (ESA) has been designed to save *£2 billion* by introducing means testing.
- The government's Work Programme has had a very low success rate, helping only *5 per cent* of disabled people to find work.
- Since 2010 there has been a *200 per cent* increase in tribunals appealing social security decisions. Citizens' Advice recently reported a *67 per cent* increase in disability benefit problems.

Source: Adapted from Duffy (2014)

Impact of the integration of health and social care

In a review of the current evidence on health and social care integration, Petch (2012) states that although policies in Scotland (and elsewhere in the UK) are clearly to be driven and measured by their success in delivering positive outcomes for the person, the evidence to date about health and social care integration is not hopeful about delivering on this. Petch notes that evaluation of partnership working has tended to focus on the organisational processes, rather than on whether the partnership is effective in enabling individuals to achieve desired outcomes. She states that the evidence from Northern Ireland, 'one of the most structurally integrated and comprehensive models of health and personal social services in Europe' (Heenan and Birrell, 2006, p 48), is that structural change has not delivered the predicted benefits, and that health domination appears to persist. There is a limited record of innovation, with little evidence of the progressive development of personalisation, direct payments and individual budgets.

In a telling summary, Petch states that structural integration has failed to deliver the aspirations set for it, and that there is, as yet, no robust evidence for positive financial benefit.

Failure to deal with continuing institutionalisation

The implications for the matters under review in this book are worrying. With such deep cuts, it seems inevitable that families will be less able to cope, that admissions to institutions like Winterbourne View will increase, and that social isolation and vulnerability to harm may be intensified.

Jim Mansell (2011), writing about Winterbourne View, stated:

> ... this isn't just about wicked staff or weak management. It is about the wrong model of care – people with challenging behaviour being shunted off to these institutions because their local health and social services have not got their act together to provide the kind of support they need locally.

In an open latter to the Prime Minister, a group of 86 leading advocacy organisations, professionals and academics in the field stated:

> ... there is no place for hospitals such as Winterbourne View. Beyond a very small number of beds integrated with other local services for short-term assessment and treatment and a small number of others linked to forensic needs, the provision of learning disability hospitals is wrong. The model does not work and should be made unnecessary by competent local services. (NDTi, no date)

In reply, the Prime Minister gave assurances that action was underway to ensure that lessons would be learned:

> A joint plan of action is needed both locally and nationally to drive improvements in services and determine how the lessons from Winterbourne View can influence future policy and practice ... [the government] ... is committed to taking all necessary action to minimise the chance of such terrible event recurring. (quoted in BILD, no date)

However, when the Bubb report, *Winterbourne View – Time for change*, was published in 2014 (NHS England, 2014), nearly 2,600 people with learning disabilities or autism and additional mental health needs still lived in inpatient settings. The government's 2012 key response to the Winterbourne View report was the commitment to end such inappropriate placements by June 2014. The Bubb report has come at a critical time. More people are being admitted to assessment and treatment units than are being discharged, and people with a learning disability and their families feel they were made a promise and have been hugely let down. Three years on from the Winterbourne View scandal, little seems to have really changed.

Responding to the report, BILD (2014) supported the focus on people's rights, but pointed out that it is it a damning indictment of our society, and particularly the health and social care sector, if those charged with supporting people with learning disabilities have to be reminded to 'pledge' their support to uphold the human rights of every citizen. The report contains few firm commitments to action, and indeed, comments contained in the report could have been made in 2001 relating to the government's policy to close all long-stay 'mental handicap' hospitals, or indeed, after the Ely Hospital scandal of 1969.

Speaking for people with learning disabilities in England, Gary Bourlet, from People First,[3] said:

> The report is full of good words. But there's not much here that hasn't been said before. We need someone to take charge of making change happen. And that person should be working alongside someone with a learning disability. We call that co-working. And we need a timetable as well.

Yet again, we see an ineffective institutional model that is resilient to change, and are reminded that social work and other professions cannot afford to be complacent, that institutional services belong to the past, and that social workers need to be vigilant and resist their reappearance in planning options. It is worth noting that although personalisation promotes choice and control, the exercise of this choice and control may, in reality, be restricted by cuts that diminish the range of options from which to choose. Self-directed support and having a personal budget may have become a right, but capped budget ceilings may mean that people cannot afford the creative alternative they really want. Cuts result in people being slotted in inappropriately into available vacancies in existing services. Austerity therefore leads not only to limited specialist services, but also, just as importantly, to depleted universal services.

Despite the challenging developments listed above, there are many aspects that give hope about the future. Across the UK there are clear values-led policy frameworks embraced by all the stakeholders, based on:

■ policy commitment to person–centredness
■ policy commitment to human rights
■ a legal framework to help in managing the tension between risk and autonomy.

These policies provide the springboard for us, as social workers, to maintain a passion for change – and this time around, the leaders of the movement for change are most likely to be people with learning disabilities themselves. There are many inspiring examples of people with learning difficulties working for change at a national and local level. This has already taken the form of people with learning difficulties taking senior roles in care provider organisations. The Thera group, for example,[4] is committed to employing paid directors with the lived experience of learning disability in all of its subsidiaries. We know, too, of people in co-working roles in government policy and other similar working groups. We also know of people with learning difficulties who are contributing to their local communities in the role of elected council members.

However, if such improvements are to be sustained, they must go hand in hand with a broader understanding of how deeply entrenched attitudes to disability in our society really are. History warns us that resilience to change in practice, policy and legislation is such that people with disabilities remain at risk of death and abuse in our services and in our communities. Practitioners must not lose sight of this, and should engage with an agenda of creating better lives as well as better services.

Notes

[1] ILF monies will be incorporated into the local authority budget but will not necessarily be ring-fenced when the scheme closes in June 2015.

[2] The Scottish government has acquired powers to mitigate the impact of the 'Bedroom Tax' in Scotland.

[3] See http://peoplefirstltd.com/ and http://peoplefirstscotland.org

[4] See www.thera.co.uk/leadership

References

ADSS (Association of Directors of Social Services) and (NAPSAC) National Association for the Protection from Sexual Abuse of Adults and Children with Learning Disabilities (1996) *Advice for social services departments on abuse of people with learning disabilities in residential care* (www.opengrey.eu/item/display/10068/378170).

ADSW (Association of Directors of Social Work) (2009) *Personalisation: Principles, challenge and a new approach* (http://lx.iriss.org.uk/sites/default/files/resources/personalisation_principleschallengesandanewapproach).

Age Concern (2007) *Working with older people with learning disabilities: Lessons from an Age Concern pilot programme*, London: Age Concern (www.ageuk.org.uk/documents/en-gb/for-professionals/equality-and-human-rights/16_0208_working_with_older_people_with_learning_disabilities_lessons_from_an_age_concern_pilot_programme_2008_pro.pdf?dtrk=true).

Ager, A., Myers, F. and Kerr, P (2001) 'Moving home: social integration for adults with intellectual disabilities resettling into community provision', *Journal of Applied Social Research*, vol 14, pp 392-400.

Asquith, S., Clark, C. and Waterhouse, L. (2005) *The role of the social worker in the 21st century: A literature review*, Edinburgh: Scottish Executive.

Atkinson, D. and Williams, F. (1990) *Know me as I am*, London: Hodder Education.

Aunos, M., Feldman, M. and Goupil, G. (2008) 'Mothering with intellectual disabilities: relationship between social support, health and well-being, parenting and child behaviour outcomes', *Journal of Applied Research in Intellectual Disabilities*, vol 21, no 4, pp 320-30.

Bartnik, E. (2008) 'Active citizenship and community engagement - Getting serious about more positive pathways to relationships and contribution.' *Intellectual Disability Australia*, vol 29, no 2, pp 3-7.

Bartnik, E. (2010) 'Developing personalised and creative community living options: a West Australian example of influencing systems change', *Intellectual Disability Australasia*, vol 31, no 3, pp 3-8.

Bartnik, E. and Chalmers, R. (2007) 'Local area co-ordination: supporting people with disabilities', in S. Hunter and P. Ritchie (eds) *Co-production and personalisation in social care*, Research Highlights 49, London: Jessica Kingsley Publishers, pp 19-38.

Bass, M. and Drewett, R. (1996) *Supported employment for people with learning disabilities*, Social Care Research Findings 86, York: Joseph Rowntree Foundation.

BASW (British Association of Social Workers) (2002) *Code of ethics for social workers*, Birmingham: BASW.

Bayley, M. (1973) *Mental handicap and community care: A study of mentally handicapped people in Sheffield*, London: Routledge & Kegan Paul.

BBC News (2011) 'Four arrests after patient abuse caught on film, 1 June (www.bbc.co.uk/news/uk-13548222).

Beamer, S. with Brookes, M. (2001) *Making decisions. Best practice and new ideas for supporting people with high support needs to make decisions*, London: Values into Action.

Beattie, R.B. (1999) *Implementing inclusiveness, realising potential (Beattie Committee Report)*, Edinburgh: Scottish Government

Beck, U. (1992) *Risk society: Towards a new modernity*, London: Sage Publications.

Bellamy, G.T., Wilson, D.J., Adler, E. and Clarke, J.Y. (1980) 'A strategy for programming vocational skills for severely handicapped youth', *Exceptional Education Quarterly*, vol 1, no 2, pp 85-97.

Beresford, P. (2014) 'Personal budgets: how the government can learn from past mistakes', *The Guardian*, 28 February (www.theguardian.com/public-leaders-network/2014/feb/26/social-care-failures-personal-budgets).

Bewley, C. (1997) *Money matters*, London: Values into Action.

Beyer, S. and Kilsby, M. (1996) 'The future of employment for people with learning disabilities: a keynote review', *British Journal of Learning Disabilities*, vol 24, pp 134-7.

Beyer, S. and Robinson, C. (2009) *A review of the research literature on supported employment: A report for the cross-government Learning Disability Employment Strategy Team*, Cardiff and London: Centre for Learning Disabilities, School of Medicine, Cardiff University and Department of Health, *Valuing People Now*.

Beyer, S., Kilsby, M. and Lowe, K. (1994) 'What do ATCs offer in Wales?: A survey of Welsh day services', *Mental Handicap Research*, vol 7, no 1, pp 16-40.

Bigby, C. (1997) 'Later life for adults with intellectual disability: a time of opportunity and vulnerability', *Journal of Intellectual and Developmental Disability*, vol 22, issue 2, pp 97-108 (www.tandfonline.com/doi/abs/10.1080/13668259700033331#.VTDaCmaz4os).

Bigby, C. (2004) *Ageing with a lifelong disability: A guide to practice, program, and policy issues for human services professionals*, London: Jessica Kingsley Publishers.

Bigby, C. (2010) 'A five-country comparative review of accommodation support policies for older people with intellectual disability', *Journal of Policy and Practice in Intellectual Disabilities*, vol 7, no 1, pp 3-15.

Bigby, C. and Atkinson, D. (2010) 'Written out of history: invisible women in intellectual disability social work', *Australian Social Work*, vol 63, pp 4-17.

BILD (British Institute of Learning Disabilities) (2014) *BILD and the Stephen Bubb report*, Kidderminster: BILD.

BILD (no date) 'Responses to the abuse of people with learning disabilities and autism at Winterbourne view', Kidderminster: BILD (www.bild.org.uk/news-and-whats-on/winterbourne-view/).

Blatt, B. and Kaplan, F. (1974) *Christmas in purgatory: A photographic essay on mental retardation*, Boston, MA: Allyn & Bacon (www.disabilitymuseum.org/lib/docs/1782card.htm).

Booth, T. (2000) 'Parents with learning disabilities, child protection and the courts', *Representing Children*, vol 13, no 3, pp 175-88 (http://disability-studies.leeds.ac.uk/files/library/Booth-parents-with-lea-diff.pdf).

Booth, T. and Booth, W. (1997) *Exceptional childhoods, unexceptional children*, London: Family Policy Studies Centre.

Booth, T. and Booth, W. (1998) *Growing up with parents who have learning difficulties*, London: Routledge.

Booth, T. and Booth, W. (2003) *Self-advocacy and supported learning for mothers with learning difficulties* (www.supported-parenting.com/projects/SLPpaper Final copy.pdf).

Booth, T. and Booth, W. (2007) 'Parental competence and parents with learning difficulties', *Child & Family Social Work*, vol 1, no 2, pp 81-6 (http://onlinelibrary.wiley.com/doi/10.1111/j.1365-2206.1996.tb00011.x/abstract).

Booth, T., Booth, W. and McConnell, D. (2004) 'Parents with learning difficulties: care proceedings and the family courts: threshold decisions and the moral matrix', *Child and Family Law Quarterly*, vol 16, no 4, pp 409-21.

Booth, T., Booth, W. and McConnell, D. (2005) 'The prevalence and outcomes of care proceedings involving parents with learning difficulties in the family courts', *Journal of Applied Research in Intellectual Disabilities*, vol 18, pp 7-17.

Booth, W. and Booth, T. (1993) 'Accentuate the positive: A personal profile of a parent with learning difficulties', *Disability, Handicap & Society*, vol 8, no 4, pp 377-92.

Booth, W. and Booth, T. (1998) *Advocacy for parents with learning difficulties*, Brighton: Pavilion Publishing.

Bournewood Judgement (2004) *H.L. v United Kingdom* (Application no 45508/99) (www.1cor.com/1315/?form_1155.replyids=952).

Bovaird, T. and Loeffler, E. (2012) 'From engagement to co-production: the contribution of users and communities to outcomes and public value', *Voluntas*, vol 23, pp 1119-38.

Bovaird, T. and Loeffler, E. (2013) *The role of co-production for better health and well-being: Why we need to change*, Governance International, Co-production in Health and Social Care, Birmingham: Governance International.

Bowcott, O. (2012) 'Victims of disability hate crime are still being let down, report claims', *The Guardian*, 21 May (www.theguardian.com/society/2015/may/21/disability-hate-crime-police-probation-prosecutors-failing-victims-report-claims).

Boyle, D., Clark, S. and Burns, S. (2006) *Hidden work: Co-production by people outside paid employment*, York: Joseph Rowntree Foundation.

BPS (British Psychological Society) Professional Affairs Board (2000) *Learning disability: Definitions and contexts*, London: BPS.

Braddock, D., Emerson, E., Felce, D. and Stancliffe, R.J. (2001) 'Living circumstances of children and adults with mental retardation in the United States, Canada, England and Wales and Australia', *Mental Retardation and Disabilities Research Review*, vol 37, no 2, pp 155-84.

Brearley, P.C. (1982) *Risk in social work*, London: Routledge & Kegan Paul.

Brignell, V. (2010) 'When the disabled were segregated', *New Statesman*, 15 December (www.newstatesman.com/society/2010/12/disabled-children-british).

Brober, G. and Roll-Hansen, N. (eds) (1996) *Eugenics and the welfare state: Sterilization policy in Denmark, Sweden, Norway and Finland*, Lansing, MI: Michigan State University Press.

Brown, H. (1999) 'Abuse of people with learning disabilities: layers of concern and analysis', in N. Stanley, J. Manthorpe and B. Penhale (eds) *Institutional abuse*, London: Routledge, pp 89-109.

Brown, H. and Hunter, S. (2015: forthcoming) 'Reflections on the evolving context of adult protection and safeguarding in the UK: legislation, regulation and professional practice', in G. Palattiyil, M. Chakrabati and D. Sidhva (eds) *International social work*, London: Routledge.

Brown, H. and Smith, H. (1994) *Normalisation: A reader for the nineties*, London: Tavistock/Routledge.

Brown, H. and Stein, J. (1998) 'Implementing adult protection policies in East Kent and Sussex', *Journal of Social Policy*, vol 27, no 3, pp 371-96.

Buckinghamshire County Council (1998) *Independent Longcare Inquiry*, Buckingham: Buckingham County Council.

Butler, I. and Drakeford, M. (2003) *Social policy, social welfare and scandal: How British public policy is made*, Basingstoke: Palgrave.

Cafe, R. (2012) 'Winterbourne View: abuse footage shocked nation', BBC News, 26 October (www.bbc.co.uk/news/uk-england-bristol-20084254).

Caldwell, J. (2007) 'Experiences of families with relatives with intellectual and developmental disabilities in a consumer directed support program', *Disability & Society*, vol 22, no 6, pp 549-62.

Caldwell, J. and Heller, T. (2007) 'Longitudinal outcomes of a consumer-directed program supporting adults with developmental disabilities and their families', *Journal of Intellectual and Developmental Disability*, June, vol 45, no 3, pp 161-73.

Callahan, M. (Marc Gold & Associates) (2002) 'Employment: from competitive to customized', *TASH Connections Newsletter*, vol 28, no 9, pp 16-19.

Cambridge, P. (1998) 'The physical abuse of people with learning disabilities and challenging behaviours: lessons for commissioners and providers', *Tizard Learning Disability Review*, vol 3, no 1, pp 18-27.

Carson, D. (1996) 'Risking legal repercussions', in H. Kemshall and J. Pritchard (eds) *Good practice in risk assessment and risk management, vol 1*, London: Jessica Kingsley Publishers, pp 3-12.

Carson, D. (2008) 'Editorial: Justifying risk decisions', *Criminal Behaviour and Mental Health*, vol 18, pp 139-44.

Challis, D. and Davies, B. (1986) *Case management in community care*, Aldershot: Gower.

CHANGE (2012) *You and your baby*, Edinburgh: NHS Education.

Chetty, K., Dalrymple, J. and Simmons, H. (2012) *Personalisation and human rights*, Sheffield: The Centre for Welfare Reform.

CIPFA (Chartered Institute of Public Finance and Accountancy) (2007) *Direct payments and individual budgets: Mananging the finances*, London: CIPFA.

Clark, S. and Broad, R. (2011) *Local area coordination in England*, Leeds: Inclusion North and Inclusive Neighbourhoods (http://inclusiveneighbourhoods.co.uk/what-is-local-area-coordination/).

Collins, J. (1995) 'Moving forward or moving back? Institutional trends in services for people with learning difficulties', in T. Philpot and Ward, L. (eds) *Values and visions. Changing ideas in services for people with learning difficulties*, Oxford: Butterworth-Heinemann Ltd, pp 95-105.

Community Care (2007) 'Direct payments, personal budgets and individual budgets', 5 January (www.communitycare.co.uk/2007/01/05/direct-payments-personal-budgets-and-individual-budgets/).

Community Care (2012) 'The state of personalisation 2012' (www.communitycare.co.uk/the-state-of-personalisation-2012/#.U2dysBzxaYQ).

Connors, C. and Stalker, K. (2002) *Interchange 75: Children's positive experiences of disability: A positive outlook*, Edinburgh: Scottish Executive.

Cook, A. and Miller, E. (2012) *Talking Points – Personal outcomes approach: Practical guide*, Edinburgh: Joint Improvement Team/Scottish Government.

Corden, A. (1997) *Supported Employment, People and Money, Social Policy Reports No. 7*, York: Social Policy Research Unit, University of York.

Corker, M. and French, S. (eds) (1999) *Disability discourse*, Buckingham: Open University Press.

Council of Europe (1953) *European Convention on Human Rights*, Strasbourg: Council of Europe.

Cree, V. and Myers, S. (2008) *Social work: Making a difference*, Bristol: Policy Press.

Cummins, J. and Miller, C. (2007) *Co-production and social capital. The role that users play in improving local services*, London: Office of Public Management.

DAA News Network (2011) *The Netherlands: Personal budgets decimated by cuts* (www.daa.org.uk/index.php?page=left-daa-news-network&daa-cat=123).

Davies, M., McGlade, A. and Bickerstaff, D. (2002) 'A needs assessment of people in the Eastern Health and Social Services Board (Northern Ireland) with intellectual disability and dementia', *Journal of Learning Disabilities*, vol 6, no 1, pp 23-33.

Davis, A. (1996) 'Risk work and mental health', in H. Kemshall and J. Pritchard (eds) *Good practice in risk assessment and risk management*, London: Jessica Kingsley Publishers, 109-20.

DCA (Department of Constitutional Affairs) (2007) *Mental Capacity Act 2005 Code of practice*, London: The Stationery Office.

DH (Department of Health) (1971) *Better services for the mentally handicapped*, London: DH.

DH (2001a) *Valuing People: A new strategy for learning disability in the 21st century*, Cm 5028, London: The Stationery Office.

DH (2001b) *Family matters: Counting families in*, London: DH.

DH (2002) *Local Authority Circular (2002)13: Fair access to care services: guidance on eligibility criteria for adult social care*, London: DH (http://webarchive.nationalarchives.gov.uk/20080814090418/http://dh.gov.uk/en/Publicationsandstatistics/Lettersandcirculars/LocalAuthorityCirculars/AllLocalAuthority/DH_4004734).

DH (2003) *Fair Access to Care Services – Guidance on eligibility criteria for adult social care*, London: DH.

DH (2009a) *Valuing People Now: A new three-year strategy for people with learning disabilities*, London: DH.

DH (2009b) *Safeguarding adults: Report on the consultation on the review of No Secrets*, London: DH.

DH (2010a) *Personalisation through person-centred planning*, London: DH.

DH 2010b) *A vision for adult social care: Capable communities and active citizens*, London: DH.

DH (2010c) *Prioritising need in the context of Putting People First: A whole system approach to eligibility for social care – Guidance on eligibility criteria for adult social care, England 2010*, London: DH.

DH (2011a) *Pathways to getting a life: Transition planning for full lives*, London: DH.

DH (2011b) *Think local, act personal*, London: DH.

DH (2012a) *Reforming the law for adult care and support: The government response to LC report 326*, London: DH.

DH (2012b) *Transforming care: A national response to Winterbourne View Hospital, DH review: Final report*, London: DH, December.

DH (2012c) *Caring for our future: Reforming care and support*, Cm 8378, London: DH.

DH and DfES (Department for Education and Skills) (2007) *Good practice guidance on working with parents with a learning disability*, London: The Stationery Office.

DHSS (Department of Health and Social Security) (1969) *Report of the Committee of Inquiry into allegations of ill-treatment of patients and other irregularities at the Ely Hospital*, Cmnd 3975, Cardiff: DHSS.

DHSS (1974) *Report of the Committee of Inquiry into the ill-treatment of patient at South Ockendon Hospital (1974)*, London: HMSO.

Disability Rights UK (2014) *Attitudes to disabled people since Paralympics*, 9 July (www.disabilityrightsuk.org/news/2014/july/attitudes-disabled-people-paralympics).

Douglas, M. (1992) *Risk and blame: Essays in cultural theory*, London: Routledge & Kegan Paul.

Dowson, S. (1998) *Certainties without centres? A discussion paper on day services for people who have learning difficulties*, London: Values Into Action.

Duffy, S., Waters, J. and Glasby, J. (2010) 'Personalisation and adult social care: future options for the reform of public services', *Policy & Politics*, vol 38, no 4, pp 493–508.

Duffy, S. (2011) *A fair society and the limits of personalisation*, Sheffield: The Centre for Welfare Reform.

Duffy, S. (2012) *An apology*, Centre for Welfare Reform, (www.centreforwelfarereform.org/librar y/authors/simon-duffy/an-apology.html).

Duffy, S. (2013) *A fair society? How the cuts target disabled people*, Sheffield: The Centre for Welfare Reform.

Duffy, S. (2014) *Counting the cuts*, Sheffield: The Centre for Welfare Reform.

Duffy, S., Waters, J. and Glasby, J. (2010) *Personalisation and the social care 'revolution': Future options for the reform of public services*, Policy Paper 3, Birmingham: In Control, Health Services Management Centre, University of Birmingham, January (www.birmingham.ac.uk/Documents/college-social-sciences/social-policy/HSMC/publications/PolicyPapers/Policy-paper-3.pdf).

Elvish, J., Hames, A., English, S. and Wills, C. (2006) 'Parents with learning disabilities: an audit of referrals made to a learning disability team', *Learning Disability Review*, vol 11, no 2, pp 26-33.

Ely Hospital Inquiry (1969) *Ely Hospital, Cardiff: Inquiry findings*, House of Lords Debates, 27 March, vol 300, cols 1384-93 (http://hansard.millbanksystems.com/lords/1969/mar/27/ely-hospital-cardiff-inquiry-findings).

Emerson, E. (1995) *Challenging behaviour: Analysis and intervention in people with learning disabilities*, Cambridge: Cambridge University Press.

Emerson, E. (2009) *Estimating future numbers of adults with profound multiple learning disabilities in England*, Lancaster: Centre for Disability Research, Lancaster University.

Emerson, E. and Baines, S. (2010) *Health inequalities and people with learning disabilities in the UK*, Learning Disabilities Observatory.

Emerson, E. and Hatton, C. (2005) 'Deinstitutionalisation', *Tizard Learning Disability Review*, vol 10, no 1, pp 36-40.

Emerson, E. and Hatton, C. (2008a) *People with learning disabilities in England*, Lancaster: Centre for Disability Research, Lancaster University.

Emerson, E. and Hatton, C. (2008b) *Estimating the future need for adult social services for people with learning disabilities in England*, Lancaster: Centre for Disability Research, Lancaster University.

Emerson, E. and Hatton, C. (2011a) *People with learning disabilities in England 2010*, Learning Disability Observatory.

Emerson, E. and Hatton, C. (2011b) *Estimating the future need for adult social services for people with learning disabilities in England: An update*, Improving Health and Lives, Learning Disability Observatory (www.improvinghealthandlives.org.uk).

Emerson, E., Baines, S., Allerton, L. and Welch, V. (2012) *Health inequalities and people with learning disabilities in the UK: 2012*, Improving Health and Lives, Learning Disabilities Observatory (www.options-empowers.org/wp-content/uploads/2013/02/Improving-Health-and-Lives-health-inequalities-and-people-with-learning-disabilities-in-the-UK-annual-report.pdf).

Emerson, E., Malam, S., Davies, I. and Spencer, K. (2005) *Adults with learning difficulties in England 2003/4* (http://webarchive.nationalarchives.gov.uk/20130107105354/http:/www.dh.gov.uk/en/Publicationsandstatistics/Publications/PublicationsStatistics/DH_4120033).

Etmanski, A. (2000) *A good life – For you and your relative with a disability*, Vancouver, BC: Planned Lifetime Advocacy Network.

Etmanski, A. (2010) *Planning for a good life in an uncertain future*, Vancouver, BC: Planned Lifetime Advocacy Network.

Etmanski, A., Cammack, V. with Rowley, D. (2015: forthcoming) *Safe and Secure: Six steps on the path to a good life for people with a learning disability*, Grantham: Planned Lifetime Advocacy Network/Thera Trust.

EUSE (European Union of Supported Employment) (2006) Information booklet and quality standards, Ireland: EUSE (www.euse.org).

Fairbairn, G.J. (1991) 'Complexity and the value of lives – some philosophical dangers for mentally handicapped people', *Journal of Applied Philosophy*, vol 8, no 2, pp 211-17.

Feldman, M., Cruz, V., Hay, J., McConnell, D. and Tardif-Williams, C. (2012) 'A right to parent: Supports for parents with intellectual disabilities and their children', in D. Griffiths, F. Owen and S. Watson (eds) *Human rights agenda: An action plan to advance the rights of persons with intellectual disabilities*, Kingston, NY: NADD Press, pp 129-38.

Ferguson, I. (2007) 'Increasing user choice or privatizing risk? The antinomies of personalization', *British Journal of Social Work*, vol 37, no 3, pp 387-403.

Ferguson, I. (2012) 'Personalisation, social justice and social work: a reply to Simon Duffy', *Journal of Social Work Practice*, vol 26, no 1, pp 55-73.

Fife Council (2009) *Corporate governance – risk management, Report to the Standards and Audit Committee*, Kirkcaldy, Fife Council.

Fitzpatrick, J. (2006a) *Thinking ahead in Fife*, Glenrothes: Fife Council.

Fitzpatrick, J. (2006b) *Housing and support jigsaw: Home ownership – One of the keys*, Birkenhead: Paradigm.

Flynn, M. (2007) *The murder of Steven Hoskin: A serious case review*, Truro: Cornwall Adult Protection Committee.

Flynn, M. (2012) *Winterbourne View Hospital: A serious case review*, Bristol: South Gloucestershire Council Safeguarding Committee.

Flynn, M. and Hurst, M. (1992) *This year, next year, sometime...? Learning disability and adulthood*, London and York: National Development Team and Social Policy Research Unit, University of York.

Forbat, L. (2006) 'An analysis of key principles in Valuing People: implications for supporting people with dementia', *Journal of Intellectual Disabilities*, vol 10, no 3, pp 249-60.

Forbat, L. and Atkinson, D. (2005) 'Advocacy in practice: the troubled position of advocates in adult services', *British Journal of Social Work*, vol 35, no 3, pp 321-35.

Foundation for People with Learning Disabilities (2012) *Learning difficulties and ethnicity: Updating a framework for action*, London: Foundation for People with Learning Disabilities.

Fox, A. (2012) *Personalisation: Lessons from social care*, London: RSA.

Franklin, J. (ed) (1998) *The politics of a risk society*, Cambridge: Polity Press.

Freud, D. (2007) *Reducing dependency, increasing opportunity: Options for the future of welfare to work. An independent report to the Department for Work and Pensions*, London: Department for Work and Pensions.

Gallimore, A., Hay, L. and Mackie, P. (2008) *What do those with multiple and complex needs want from health, social care and voluntary sector services?*, Musselburgh: East Lothian CHP.

Gath, A. (1988) 'Mentally handicapped people as parents', *Journal of Child Psychology and Psychiatry*, vol 29, no 6, pp 739-44.

Gilchrist, A. (2009) *The well connected community: A networking approach to community development*, Bristol: Policy Press.

Gillespie, J. and Duffy, S. (2008) *Community capacity and social care*, Wythall: In Control.

Glasby, J. (2011) *Rights, responsibilities, risk and regulation: Whose risk is it anyway? Risk and regulation in an era of personalization*, York: Joseph Rowntree Foundation.

Glasby, J. and Littlechild, R. (2009) *Direct payments and personal budgets: Putting personalisation into practice*, Bristol: Policy Press.

Glendinning, C., Challis, D., Fernandez, J., Jacobs, S., Jones, K., Knapp, M., Manthorpe, J., Moran, N., Netten, A., Stevens, M. and Wilberforce, M. (2008) *Evaluation of Individual Budgets Pilot Programme, Final report*, York: Social Policy Research Unit, University of York.

Glenn, S. and Lyons, C. (1996) 'Employment and people with learning difficulties', *European Journal of Supported Employment and Vocational Rehabilitation*, issue 2.

Goffman, E. (1961) *Asylums: Essays on the social situation of mental patients and other inmates*, New York: Doubleday.

Gold, M. (1980) *Try another way: Training manual*, Champaign, IL: Research Press.

Goldsmith, S. and Burke, C. (2012) *The accomplished community – Building inclusive communities*, London: Foundation for People with Learning Disabilities.

Goodinge, S. (2000) *A jigsaw of services: Inspection of services to support disabled adults in their parenting role*, London: Social Services Inspectorate.

Grant, S. (2013) 'Councillor again claims disabled babies should be killed – so public toilets could stay open', Western Morning News, 11 May (www.westernmorningnews.co.uk/Councillor-claims-disabled-babies-killed-public/story-18956686-detail/story.html).

Gravell, C. (2012) *Loneliness and cruelty: People with learning disabilities – Their experience of harassment, abuse and related crime in the community. Ongoing Inquiry*, London: Lemos & Crane.

Greig, R. (2008) 'Editorial: Themed issue, Planning challenges for UK learning disability services', *Tizard Learning Disability Review*, vol 13, issue 3, pp 2-3.

Gunn, M.J. (1996) *Sex and the law* (4th edn), London: Family Planning Association, quoted in D. Rowley (2007) 'Commentary on Rix: Language and labels: vehicles for change?', *Ethical Space, The International Journal of Communication Ethics*, vol 3, no 4, Special Edition: Health, Care and Communication Ethics.

Hagner, D.D. and Dileo, D. (1993) *Working together: Workplace culture, supported employment and persons with disabilities*, Cambridge, MA: Brookline Books.

Haringey Learning Disabilities Partnership (2014) *Report on the cuts in Haringey to service to adults with learning disabilities*, London: Haringey Council.

Haringey Local Children's Safeguarding Committee (2009) *Serious case review of Baby Peter*, London: Haringey Council.

Haringey Local Safeguarding Children Board (2010) *Serious case review 'Child A'*, November, London: Department for Education.

Hassiotis, A., Parkes, C., Jones, L., Fitzgerald, B. and Romeo, R. (2008) 'Individual characteristics and service expenditure on challenging behaviour for adults with intellectual disabilities', *Journal of Applied Research in Intellectual Disabilities*, vol 21, no 5, pp 438-45.

Hatton, C. (2012) 'Intellectual disabilities – classification, epidemiology and causes', *Clinical Psychology and People with Intellectual Disabilities*, vol 97, p 1.

Hatzidimitriadou, E. and Milne, A. (2005) 'Planning ahead: Meeting the needs of older people with intellectual disabilities in the United Kingdom', *Dementia*, vol 4, no 3, pp 341-59.

Healthcare Commission (2008) *A life like no other*, London: Healthcare Commission.

Heenan, D. and Birrell, D. (2006) 'The integration of health and social care: the lessons from Northern Ireland', *Social Policy and Administration*, vol 40, no 1, pp 47-66.

Heller, T. and Caldwell, J. (2005) 'Impact of a consumer-directed family support program on reduced out-of-home institutional placement', *Journal of Policy and Practice in Intellectual Disabilities*, vol 2, issue 1, March, pp 63–65.

Henwood, M. and Hudson, B. (2007) *Here to stay? Self-directed support: Aspiration and implementation*, London: Department of Health.

Heslop, P., Mallett, R., Simons, K. and Ward, L. (2002) 'Bridging the divide at transition', *What happens for young people with learning difficulties and their families*, Kidderminster, BILD.

Heslop, P., Mallett, R., Simons, K. and Ward, L. (2003) 'Bridging the divide at transition: what might make it better?', *Climb Update*, vol 2, no 1.

Higgins, L. and Mansell, J. (2009) 'Quality of life in group homes and older persons' homes', *British Journal of Learning Disabilities*, vol 37, no 3, pp 207-12.

HM Government (2007) *Putting People First: A shared vision and commitment to the transformation of adult social care*, London: HM Government.

HM Government (2009) *Valuing People Now: Jobs for people with learning disabilities*, London: HM Government.

HMSO (1957) *Royal Commission on the law relating to mental illness and mental handicap*, London: HMSO.

HM Treasury and Department for Education and Skills (2007) *Aiming High for Disabled Children: Better support for families*, London: HM Treasury.

Hogg, J. and Lambe, L. (1998) *Older people with learning disabilities: A review of the literature on residential services and family caregiving*, London: Foundation for People with Learning Disabilities.

Holland, A.J., Hon, J., Huppert, F.A., Stevens, F. and Watson, P. (1998) 'Population based study of the prevalence and presentation of dementia in adults with Down's syndrome', *British Journal of Psychiatry*, vol 172, pp 493–8.

Home Office/DH (Department of Health) (2000) *No Secrets: Guidance on developing and implementing multi-agency policies and procedures to protect vulnerable adults from abuse*, London, DH.

House of Commons and House of Lords Joint Committee on Human Rights (2008) *A life like any other? Human rights of adults with learning disabilities*, London: The Stationery Office.

Hudson, B. (2006) 'Making and missing connections: learning disability services and the transition from adolescence to adulthood', *Disability & Society*, vol 21, no 1, pp 47–60.

Hunter, S. and Ridley, J. (2007) 'Supported employment in Scotland: some issues from the research and implications for development', *Tizard Learning Disability Review*, vol 12, no 2, pp 3–13.

Hunter, S. and Ritchie, P. (2007) *Co-production and personalisation in social care*, Research Highlights, London: Jessica Kingsley Publishers.

Hunter, S., Pearson, C. and Witcher, S. (2012a) 'Self-directed support: preparing for delivery', Insights 18, Glasgow: Institute for Research and Innovation in Social Services.

Hunter, S., Manthorpe, J., Ridley, J., Cornes, M. and Rosengard, A. (2012b) 'When self-directed support meets adult support and protection: findings from the evaluation of the SDS test sites in Scotland', *Journal of Adult Protection*, May, vol 14, no 4, pp 206–15.

Ingham, N. (1999) *Gogarburn lives*, Edinburgh: Living Memory Association (www.livingmemory.org.uk/shop.html).

IPCC (Independent Police Complaints Commission) (2011) *IPCC report into the contact between Fiona Pilkington and Leicestershire Constabulary 2004-2007: Independent investigation final report*, London: IPCC.

Ipsos MORI (2011) *Users of social care personal budgets*, London: Ipsos MORI.

Janicki, M.P., McCallion, P., Force, L., Bishop, K. and LePore, P. (1998) 'Area agency on ageing outreach and assistance for households with older carers of an adult with a developmental disability', *Journal of Ageing and Social Policy*, vol 10, pp 13–36.

JIT (Joint Improvement Team) (2007) *Working together to improve adult protection: Report on Phase 2*, Edinburgh: Scottish Government.

Johnson, K., Walmsley, J. and Wolfe, M. (2010) *People with intellectual disabilities: Towards a good life?*, Bristol: Policy Press.

Jordan, B. (2004) 'Emancipatory social work? Opportunity or oxymoron?', *British Journal of Social Work*, vol 34, no 1, pp 5–19.

Kalsy, S., McQuillan, S., Adams, D., Lloyd, V., Basra, T., Konstantinidi, E., Broquard, M., Peters, S. and Oliver, C. (2005) 'A proactive psychological strategy for determining the presence of dementia in adults with Down syndrome: preliminary description of service use and evaluation', *Journal of Policy and Practice in Intellectual Disabilities*, vol 2, issue 2, pp 116–25.

Kelley, J. and Walmsley, J. with Wolfe, M. (2010) *People with intellectual disabilities: Towards a good life?*, Bristol: Policy Press.

Kemshall, H. (2002) *Risk, social policy and welfare*, Buckingham: Open University Press.

Kendrick, M.J. (1994) 'Personal and public leadership challenges', in V.J. Bradley, J.W. Ashbaugh and B.C. Blaney (eds) *Creating individual supports for people with developmental disabilities*, Baltimore, MD: Paul H. Brookes Publishing Company.

Kendrick, M.J. (2002) 'Some observations on the American advocacy scene', in B. Gray and R. Jackson (eds) *Advocacy and learning disability*, London: Jessica Kingsley Publishers, pp 189–205.

Kennedy, J., Sanderson, H. and Wilson, H. (2002) *Friendship and community: Practical strategies for making connections in communities*, Accrington: North West Training and Development Team.

Kennedy, J., Munro, K., Ritchie, P. and Smith, A. (1997) *Community living. Implications for people and agencies*, Edinburgh: SHS (Scottish Human Services).

KeyRing (no date) *KeyRing – Where independence does not equal isolation* (www.keyring.org/DocumentDownload.axd?documentresourceid...).

King's Fund (1980) *An ordinary life: Comprehensive locally based services for mentally handicapped people*, London: King's Fund.

Kinsella, P. (2000) *A person-centred risk assessment*, Liverpool: Paradigm.

Kinsella, P. (2002) *Report of review of KeyRing*, unpublished, Paradigm.

Kinsella, P. (2005) 'Life without walls – stories of successful deinstitutionalisation', *Tizard Learning Disability Review*, vol 10, no 1, pp 41–5.

Laing, J. and McQuarrie, D. (1992) *Fifty years in the system: One man's struggle to prove his sanity*, London: Corgi.

Laming, H. (2003) *The Victoria Climbié Inquiry*, Cm 5730, London: The Stationery Office (www.victoria-climbie-inquiry.org.uk/).

Le Grand, J. (1991) 'Quasi-markets and social policy', *The Economic Journal*, pp 1256-67.

Leadbeater, C. (2004) *Personalisation through participation: A new script for public services*, London: Demos.

LDAS (Learning Disability Alliance Scotland) (2010) *Stuck 869*, Dalkeith: LDAS.

Lennox Castle Stories (2012) (www.lennoxcastlestories.co.uk).

Llewellyn, P. (2011) 'The needs of people with learning disabilities who develop dementia: a literature review', *Dementia*, May, vol 10, no 2, pp 235-47.

Lupton, D. (1999) 'Risk and sociocultural theory', in *Risk and sociocultural theory: New directions and perspectives*, Cambridge: Cambridge University Press, pp 1-11.

Lymbery, M. (2001) 'Social work at the crossroads', *British Journal of Social Work*, vol 31, pp 369-84.

Lymbery, M. and Morley, K. (2012) 'Self-directed support and social work practice', *Social Work in Action*, vol 24, no 5, pp 135-27.

MacIntyre, G. and Stewart, A. (2008) *Parents with learning disabilities – The lived experience: A study for equal say*, Glasgow: Equal Say.

McCallion, P., McCarron, M. and Force, L. (2005) 'A measure of subjective burden for dementia care: the Caregiving Difficulty Scale – Intellectual Disability', *Journal of Intellectual Disability Research*, vol 49, issue 5, pp 365-71.

McConkey, R. (2005) 'Views of people with intellectual disabilities of their present and future living arrangements', *Journal of Policy and Practice in Intellectual Disabilities*, vol 1, pp 115-25.

McConkey, R., McConaghie, J., Barr, O. and Roberts, P. (2006) 'Views of family carers to the future accommodation and support needs of their relatives with intellectual disabilities', *Irish Journal of Psychological Medicine*, vol 23, no 4, pp 140-4.

McConkey, R., Slevin, E. and Barr, O. (2004) *Audit of learning disability in Northern Ireland*, Belfast: Department of Health, Social Services and Public Safety.

McConnell, D., Llewellyn, G. and Fronato, L. (2002) 'Disability and decision-making in Australian care proceedings', *International Journal of Law, Policy and the Family*, vol 16, pp 270-99.

McCormack, B., Kavanagh, D., Caffrey, S. and Power, A. (2005) 'Investigating sexual abuse: findings of a 15-year longitudinal study', *Journal of Applied Research in Intellectual Disabilities*, vol 18, pp 217-27.

McGaw, S. and Newman, T. (2005) *What works for parents with learning disabilities?*, Ilford: Barnardo's.

McKnight, J. (1995) *Community careless: Community and its counterfeits*, New York: Basic Books.

McLimons, A. (2007) 'Language, labels and diagnosis: an idiot's guide to learning disability', *Journal of Intellectual Disabilities*, January, vol 11, no 3, pp 257–66.

Magrill, D. (2007) *Supporting older families: Making a real difference*, London: Mental Health Foundation.

Mank, D. (1994) 'The underachievement of supported employment: a call for reinvestment', *Journal of Disability Policy Studies*, vol 5, no 2, pp 1-24.

Mansell, J. (2010) *Raising our sights: Services for adults with profound intellectual and multiple disabilities*, Canterbury: Tizard Centre, University of Kent.

Mansell, J. (2011) 'Bristol care home: a failure on every level', *The Guardian*, 1 June (www.theguardian.com/commentisfree/2011/jun/01/bristol-care-home-failure-every-level).

Manthorpe, J. and Alaszewski, A. (1998) Special issue on risk: 'Editorial', *Health and Social Care in the Community*, vol 8, no 1, pp 1-3.

Manthorpe, J. and Samsi, K. (2012) 'Inherently risky? Personal budgets for people with dementia and the risks of financial abuse: findings from an interview-based study with adult safeguarding co-ordinators', *British Journal of Social Work*, 27 March, pp 1-15.

Manthorpe, J., Walsh, M., Alaszewski, A. and Harrison, L. (1997) 'Issues of risk practice and welfare in learning disability services', *Disability & Society*, vol 12, no 1, pp 69-82.

Manthorpe, J., Stevens, M., Rapaport, J., Harris, J., Jacobs, S., Challis, D., Netten, A., Knapp, M., Wilberforce, M. and Glendinning, C. (2009) 'Safeguarding and system change: early perceptions of the implications for adult protection services of the English individual budgets pilots – a qualitative study', *British Journal of Social Work*, vol 39, no 4, pp 1465-80.

Marmot, M., Banks, J., Blundell, R., Lessof, C. and Nazroo, J. (eds) (2003) *Health, wealth and lifestyles of the older population in England: ELSA 2002*, ELSA (English Longitudinal Study of Ageing (http://bit.ly/Vm5MX2).

Martin, J. (1984) *Hospitals in trouble?*, London: Routledge.

Means, R., Morbey, H. and Smith, R. (2002) *From community care to market care? The development of welfare services for older people*, Bristol: Policy Press.

Mencap (2000) *Living in fear*, London: Mencap.

Mencap (2001) *No ordinary life: The support needs of families caring for children and adults with profound and multiple learning disabilities*, London: Mencap.

Mencap (2002) *The housing timebomb*, London: Mencap.

Mencap (2006) *Breaking point – Families still need a break: A report on the continuing problem of caring without a break for children and adults with severe and profound learning disabilities*, London: Mencap.

Mencap (2007) *Death by indifference*, London: Mencap.

Mencap (2012) *Death by indifference: 74 deaths and counting*, London: Mencap.

Mencap (2014) 'Facts about learning disability' (www.mencap.org.uk/about-learning-disability/about-learning-disability/facts-about-learning-disability).

Miller, E. (2012) *Individual outcomes: Getting back to what matters*, Edinburgh: Dunedin Academic Press.

Ministry of Health (1968) *Local authority training centres for mentally handicapped adults: Model of good practice*, London: HMSO

Ministry of Justice (2009) *Mental Capacity Act 2005 Deprivation of liberty safeguards: Code of Practice to supplement the main Mental Capacity Act 2005 Code of Practice*, London: The Stationery Office.

Ministry of Justice, HM Prison Service and NOMS (National Offender Management Service) (2014) *Multi-agency public protection arrangements* (www.gov.uk/government/publications/multi-agency-public-protection-arrangements-mappa--2).

Mitchell, D., Traustadóttir, R., Chapman, R., Townson, L., Ingham, N. and Ledger, S. (2006) *Exploring experiences of advocacy by people with learning disabilities: Testimonies of resistance*, London: Jessica Kingsley Publishers.

Murphy, G.H. and Mason, J. (1999) 'People with developmental disabilities who offend', in N. Bouras (ed) *Psychiatric and behavioural disorders in developmental disabilities and mental retardation*, Cambridge: Cambridge University Press, pp 226-46.

National Assembly for Wales (2001) *Fulfilling the promises: Report to the National Assembly for Wales. Proposals for a framework for services for people with learning disabilities*, Cardiff, Learning Disability Advisory Group, National Assembly for Wales.

National Development Group (1977) *Day services for mentally handicapped adults*, Pamphlet no 5, London: Department of Health and Social Services.

NDT (National Development Team) (1992) *Survey of supported employment services in England, Scotland and Wales*, Manchester: NDT.

NDTi (National Development Team for Inclusion) (2012) *Reasonably adjusted? Mental health services and support for people with autism and people with learning disabilities*, Bath: NDTi.

NDTi (2013) *Better life outcomes:Delivering support and aspiration for disabled young people*, London: Preparing for Adulthood programme.

NDTi (no date) 'A national response to the abuse of people with learning disabilities', Bath: NDTi (www.ndti.org.uk/news/latest-press-releases/press-releases-from-2011/a-national-response-to-the-abuse-of-people-with-learning-disabilities2/).

Needham, C. and Carr, S. (2009) *Co-production: An emerging evidence base for adult care transformation*, Research Briefing 31, London: Social Care Institute for Excellence.

Needham, C. (2011) *Personalising public services: Understanding the personalisation narrative*, Bristol: Policy Press.

NHS England (2014) *Winterbourne View – Time for change: Transforming the commissioning of services for people with learning disabilities and/or autism (The Bubb Report)*, London: NHS England.

NHS Scotland (2004) *Health needs assessment report – People with learning disabilities in Scotland*, Edinburgh: NHS Scotland.

Nirje, B. (1969) 'The normalisation principle and its human management implication', originally published in R. Kugel and W. Wolfensberger (eds) *Changing patterns in services for the mentally retarded*, Washington, DC: President's Committee on Mental Retardation.

Northern Ireland Executive (2005) *Equal lives: Review of policy and services for people with a learning disability in Northern Ireland*, Belfast: Northern Ireland Executive.

Northern Ireland Executive (2011) *Learning disability service framework*, Belfast: Northern Ireland Executive.

O'Brien, J. and Lyle, C. (1987) *Frameworks for accomplishment: A workshop for people developing better services*, Decatur, GA: Responsive Systems Associates.

Oliver, M. (1983) *Social work with disabled people*, Basingstoke: Macmillan.

Outside the Box (2005) *Moving on to adult life,* Glasgow: Outside the Box Development Support.

Pannell, J. and Harker, M. (2010) *Finding a place to live: Help with your plans*, Liverpool: Housing and Support Partnership/Housing Options.

Payne, M. (2006) *What is professional social work?*, Bristol and Birmingham: Policy Press/British Association of Social Workers.

Peace, S., Kellaher, L. and Willcocks, D. (1997) *Re-evaluating residential care*, Buckingham: Open University Press.

People First (Scotland) (2012) *Citizen's Grand Jury report*, Edinburgh: People First (Scotland) (http://peoplefirstscotland.org/files/2012/10/citizensgrandjuryreportweb.pdf).

Perske, R. (1972) 'Dignity of risk and the mentally retarded', *Mental Retardation* and *Intellectual and Developmental Disabilities* (previously *Mental Retardation*), vol 10, no 1, February.

Pestoff, V. (2006) 'Citizens as co-producers of welfare services: preschool services in eight European countries', *Public Management Review*, vol 8, no 4, pp 503-20.

Petch, A. (2012) *Integration of health and social care*, IRISS Insights 14, March, Glasgow: Institute for Research and Innovation in Social Services.

PMLD (Profound and Multiple Learning Disabilities) Network (2009) *How does Valuing People Now aim to improve things for people with profound and multiple learning disabilities (PMLD)?*, PMLD Network.

PMSU (Prime Minister's Strategy Unit), DWP (Department for Work and Pensions), DH (Department of Health), DfES (Department for Education and Skills) (2005) *Improving the life chances of disabled people* (http://webarchive.nationalarchives.gov.uk/+/http:/www.cabinetoffice.gov.uk/media/cabinetoffice/strategy/assets/disability.pdf).

Poll, C. (2007) 'Co-production in Supported Housing: KeyRing Living Support Networks and Neighbourhood Networks', in Hunter, S. and Ritchie, P. (eds) *Co-Production and Personalisation in Social Care, Research Highlights*, London: Jessica Kingsley Publishers, pp 49–66.

Poll, C., Duffy, S., Hatton, C., Sanderson, H. and Routledge, M. (2006) *A report on In Control's first phase 2003-2005*, London: In Control.

Portes, J. and Reed, H. (2014) 'Austerity has hit women, ethnic minorities and the disabled most', *The Guardian*, 31 July (www.theguardian.com/commentisfree/2014/jul/31/austerity-women- ethnic-minorities-disabled-tax-welfare).

Postle, K. (2002) 'Working "between the idea and the reality": ambiguities and tensions in care managers' work', *British Journal of Social Work*, vol 32, no 3, pp 335-51.

Poxton, R. (2010) *All means all – Interim evaluation report*, London: Foundation for People with Learning Disabilities.

Pring, J. (2013a) 'Colin Brewer: there is a good argument for killing some disabled babies', Disability News Service, 10 May (www.disabilitynewsservice.com/colin-brewer-there-is-a-good-argument-for-killing-some-disabled-babies/).

Pring, J. (2013b) 'Transcript of Collin Brewer interview', Disability News Service, 8 July (www.disabilitynewsservice.com/transcript-of-collin-brewer-interview/).

Rachels, J. (1986) *The end of life: Euthanasia and morality*, Oxford: Oxford University Press.

Rankin, J. and Regan, S. (2004) *Meeting complex needs: The future of social care*, London: Turning Point and Institute for Public Policy Research.

RCN (Royal College of Nursing) (2013) *Meeting the health needs of people with learning disabilities*, London: RCN.

Rhodes, B. (2010) *Much more to life than services: Unleashing the potential of personalisation in social care*, Peterborough: Fastprint Publishing.

Ridley, J. (2001) 'Supported employment and learning disability', in C. Clark, *Adult day services and social inclusion*, Research Highlights, London: Jessica Kingsley Publishers, pp 158–80.

Ridley, J. and Jones, L. (2002) *Direct 'what': A study of direct payments to mental health service users*, Edinburgh: Scottish Executive Central Research Unit.

Ridley, J., Hunter, S. and Infusion Co-operative (2005) *Go for it! Supporting people with learning disabilities and/or autistic spectrum disorder in employment*, Edinburgh: Scottish Executive.

Ridley, J., Spandler, H., Rosengard, A., Little, S., Cornes, M., Manthorpe, J., Hunter, S., Kinder, T. and Gray, B. (2011) *Evaluation of self directed support test sites in Scotland*, Edinburgh: Scottish Government Social Research (http://clok.uclan.ac.uk/2888/4/0121078.pdf).

Ritchie, P., Jones, C. and Broderick, L. (no date) *Ways to work*, Edinburgh: SHS (Scottish Human Services).

Robertson, J., Emerson, E., Hatton, C., Elliott, J., McIntosh, B., Swift, P., Krijnen-Kemp, E., Towers, C., Romeo, R., Knapp, M., Sanderson, H., Routledge, M., Oakes, P. and Joyce, T. (2005) *The impact of person centred planning*, Lancaster: Institute for Health Research, Lancaster University.

Rose, D. (2012) 'After the Paralympics: has anything changed for disabled people?', BBC News Magazine, 13 December (www.bbc.co.uk/news/magazine-20693647).

Routledge, M. (2000) 'Collective responsibilities, fragmented systems: transition to adulthood for young people with learning disabilities', *Tizard Learning Disability Review*, vol 5, no 4, pp 17-26.

Rowley, D. (2007) 'Commentary on Rix: language and labels: vehicles for change?', *Ethical Space, The International Journal of Communication Ethics*, vol 3, no 4, Special Edition: Health, Care and Communication Ethics.

Ryan, T. (1996) 'Risk management and people with mental health problems', in H. Kemshall and J. Pritchard (eds) *Good practice in risk assessment and risk management*, London: Jessica Kingsley Publishers, pp 93-108.

Ryan, A., Taggart, L., Truesdale-Kennedy, M. and Slevin, E. (2014) 'Issues in caregiving for older people with intellectual disabilities and their ageing family carers: a review and commentary', *International Journal of Older People Nursing*, vol 9, no 3, pp 217-26.

SCIE (2010) *Enabling risk. Ensuring safety: Self-directed support and personal budgets*, Report 36, London: SCIE.

SCLD (Scottish Consortium for Learning Disability) (2009) *Scottish good practice guidelines for supporting parents with learning disabilities*, Glasgow: SCLD.

Scottish Executive (2000) *The same as you? A review of services for people with learning disabilities*, Edinburgh: The Stationery Office (www.gov.scot/Resource/Doc/1095/0078271.pdf).

Scottish Executive (2001) *New Directions - Review Of The Mental Health (Scotland) Act 1984 (The Millan Report)*, Edinburgh: Scottish Executive.

Scottish Executive (2002) *It's everybody's job to make sure I'm alright, Report of the Child Protection Audit and Review*, Edinburgh: Scottish Executive (www.gov.scot/Publications/2002/11/15820/14009).

Scottish Executive (2004) *Working and learning together to build stronger communities*, Edinburgh.

Scottish Executive (2007) *National guidance on self-directed support, primary and community care directorate adult care and support – change team*, Edinburgh: Scottish Executive.

Scottish Government (2004) *Report of the Inspection of Scottish Borders Council Social Work Services for People Affected by Learning Disabilities*, Edinburgh: Scottish Government

Scottish Government (2013) *The keys to life*, Edinburgh: Scottish Government.

Scottish Government (no date) 'Public protection – Multi-agency public protection arrangements (MAPPA)', Edinburgh: Scottish Government (www.gov.scot/Topics/Justice/policies/reducing-reoffending/sex-offender-management/protection).

Scourfield, P. (2007) 'Social care and the modern citizen: client, consumer, service user, manager and entrepreneur', *British Journal of Social Work*, January, vol 37, no 1, pp 107-22.

Seed, P. (1987) *Day care at the crossroads*, Tunbridge Wells: DJ Costello Publishers.

Shakespeare, T. and Watson, N. (2002) 'The social model of disability: an outdated ideology?', *Journal of Research in Social Science and Disability*, vol 2, pp 9-28.

SHS (Scottish Human Services) (1995) *The Changeover Programme*, Edinburgh: SHS.

Simons, K. (1998) *Living support networks – An evaluation of the services provided by KeyRing*, Brighton and York: Pavilion/Joseph Rowntree Foundation.

Simpson, M. and Hogg, J. (2001) 'Patterns of offending among people with intellectual disability: a systematic review. Part I: methodology and prevalence data', *Journal of Intellectual Disability Research*, vol 45, issue 5, pp 384-96.

Singer, P. (1979) *Practical ethics*, Cambridge: Cambridge University Press.

Slevin, E., Taggart, L., McConkey, R., Cousins, W., Truesdale-Kennedy, M. and Dowling, S. (2011) *A rapid review of literature relating to support for people with intellectual disabilities and their family carers when the person has: Behaviours that challenge and/or mental health problems; or they are advancing in age*, Belfast: Public Health Agency, University of Ulster.

Snow, J. (1992) *What's really worth doing and how to do it: A book for people who love someone labelled disabled*, Toronto, ON: Inclusion Press.

SSI (Social Services Inspection) Unit (1998) *Moving into the mainstream: The report of a national inspection of services for adults with learning disabilities*, London: Department of Health.

Stainton, T. and Boyce, S. (2004) '"I have got my life back": user's experience of direct payments', *Disability & Society*, vol 19, no 5, pp 443-4.

Stalker, K. (1998) 'The antinomies of choice in community care', in S. Baldwin, *Needs assessment and community care*, Oxford: Butterworth Heinemann.

Stalker, K. (2001) 'Inclusive daytime opportunities for people with learning difficulties', in C. Clark, *Adult day services and social inclusion*, London: Jessica Kingsley Publishers, pp 46-66.

Stalker, K. (2003) 'Managing risk and uncertainty in social work', *Journal of Social Work*, vol 3, no 2, pp 211-33.

Stalker, K. and Harris, P. (1998) 'The exercise of choice by adults with intellectual disabilities: a literature review', *Journal of Applied Research in Intellectual Disabilities*, vol 11, no 1, pp 60-76.

Stanley, N., Manthorpe, J. and Penhale, B. (eds) (1999) *Institutional abuse: Perspectives across the life course*, London: Routledge.

Steele, D. (1991) 'Survey reveals gulf between work aspirations and success', *Community Living*, July.

Strathclyde Regional Council (1993) *Social work day services review: No mean service*, Strathclyde Regional Council.

Strydom, A., Hassiotis, A., King, M. and Livingston, G. (2009) 'The relationship of dementia prevalence in older adults with intellectual disability (ID) to age and severity of ID', *Psychological Medicine*, vol 39, no 1, pp 13-21.

Styan, J. (2004) *Connecting to citizenship: Social policy recommendations to address isolation and loneliness*, Vancouver, BC: Planned Lifetime Advocacy Network.

Suto, W., Clare, I. and Holland, A. (2005) 'Maximising capacity to make financial decisions', *Tizard Learning Disability Review*, vol 10, no 3, pp 4-10.

Swain, P. and Cameron, N. (2003) '"Good enough parenting": parental disability and child protection', *Disability & Society*, vol 18, no 2, pp 165-77.

Swift, P. and Mattingley, M. (2009) *A life in the community: An action research project promoting citizenship for people with high support needs*, London: Learning Disabilities Foundation.

Szivos, S. (1992) 'The limits to integration', in H. Brown and H. Smith (eds) *Normalisation: A reader for the nineties*, London: Routledge, pp 112-30.

Taggart, L., Truesdale-Kennedy, M., Ryan, A. and McConkey, R.L. (2012) 'Examining the support needs of ageing family carers in developing future plans for a relative with an intellectual disability', *Journal of intellectual disabilities*, vol 16, no 3, pp 217-34.

Tarleton, B. (2004) *The road ahead? Information for young people with learning difficulties, their families and supporters at transition*, Bristol: University of Bristol, Norah Fry Research Centre.

Tarleton, B., Ward, L. and Howarth, J. (2006) *Finding the right support? A review of the issues and positive practice in supporting parents with learning difficulties and their children*, Bristol and London: Norah Fry Research Centre, University of Bristol and The Baring Foundation.

Taylor, J. and Taylor, D. (1986) *Mental handicap: Partnership in the community*, London: Office of Health Economics/Mencap.

Thatcher, M. (1971) *Speech to National Society of Mentally Handicapped Children. Bristol April 16th*, Thatcher Archive. DES release, (www. margaretthatcher.org/document/102105).

Thomas, C. (2004) 'Developing the social relational in the social model of disability: a theoretical agenda', in C. Barnes and G. Mercer (eds) *Implementing the social model of disability: Theory and research*, Leeds: The Disability Press, pp 32-47.

Thompson, A. and Taggart, L. (2014) 'Planning for the future for family carers of adults with intellectual disabilities (ID): training–the-trainers: A pilot study', *Journal of Applied Research in Intellectual Disabilities*, vol 27, no 4, p 348.

Titterton, M. (2005) *Risk and risk taking in health and social care*, London: Jessica Kingsley Publishers.

Titterton, M. (2011) 'Positive risk taking with people at risk of harm', in H. Kemshall, *Good practice in assessing risk: Current knowledge, issues and approaches*, London: Jessica Kingsley Publishers, pp 30-47.

Traustadottir, R. and Sigurjonsdottir, H. (2008) 'The "mother" behind the mother: generations of mothers with intellectual disabilities and their family support networks', *Journal of Applied Research in Intellectual Disabilities*, vol 21, issue 4, pp 331-40.

Tymchuk, A. and Andron, L. (1990) 'Mothers with mental retardation who do, or do not, abuse or neglect their children', *Child Abuse and Neglect*, vol 14, pp 313-23.

UN (United Nations) (1948) *The Universal Declaration of Human Rights*, New York: UN.

UN (2007) *Convention on the Rights of Persons with Disabilities*, New York: UN.

Understanding Intellectual Disability and Health (nd) *Key Highlights of Research Evidence on the Health of People with Learning [Intellectual] Disabilities* (first published 2002 by the Valuing People Support Team) (www.intellectualdisability.info/mental–health/research-evidence-on-the-health-of-people-with-learning-intellectual-disabilities?searchterm =key+highlights+).

Valuing People Support Team (2003) Information pack for transition champions (www.valuingpeople.gov.uk/Transition.htm).

Walker, C. and Magrill, D. (2002) 'Living with older family carers: planning with families and preparing for the future', in Foundation for People with Learning Difficulties, *Today and tomorrow: The report of the Growing Older with Learning Disabilities Programme*, London: Foundation for People with Learning Disabilities, pp 57-69.

Walker, C. and Walker, A. (1998) *Uncertain futures: People with learning difficulties and their ageing family carers*, Brighton: Pavilion Publishing.

Walmsley, J. (2002) 'Principles and types of advocacy', in B. Gray and R. Jackson (eds) *Advocacy and learning disability*, London: Jessica Kingsley Publishers, pp 24-37.

Ward, C. (2012a) *Older people with a learning disability*, BILD Factsheet, Kidderminster, British Institute of Learning Disabilities.

Ward, C. (2012b) *Perspectives on ageing with a learning disability*, York: Joseph Rowntree Foundation.

Ward, L.J. (2008) 'Supporting parents with learning disabilities and their children', Community Care Inform (www.ccinform.co.uk).

Warnock, H.M. (1978) Special educational needs, *Report of the Committee of Enquiry into the education of handicapped children and young people (The Warnock Report)*, Cmnd 7212, London: HMSO.

Waterson, J. (1999) 'Redefining community care social work: Needs or risk led?', *Health and Social Care in the Community*, vol 7, no 4, pp 276-9.

Webb, S.A. (2006) *Social work in a risk society*, Basingstoke: Macmillan.

Welsh Assembly Government (2007) *Statement on policy and practice for adults with a learning disability*, Cardiff: Welsh Assembly Government.

Welsh Office (1983) *All Wales Strategy for the development of services for mentally handicapped people*, Cardiff: Welsh Office.

Welsh Office (1984) *All Wales Strategy for the development of services for mentally handicapped people: Associated guidance*, Cardiff: Welsh Office.

Wertheimer, A. (1992) *Real jobs initiative (1990–1992): An evaluation*, Manchester: National Development Team.

Wertheimer, A. (1996) *Changing days: Developing new day opportunities with people who have learning difficulties*, London: King's Fund.

Weston, J. (2001) *A blue print for supported employment in Scotland*, Scottish Union for Supported Employment (www.susescotland.co.uk/media/19204/blueprintfullfinal.pdf).

WHO (World Health Organization) (2000) *Ageing and intellectual disabilities – improving longevity and promoting healthy aging: Summative report*, Geneva: World Health Organization.

Wightman, C. (2011) *Connecting people*, London: Foundation for People With Learning Disabilities.

Wilkinson, H., Kerr, D. and Cunningham, H. (2006) 'Learning disability and dementia: are we prepared?', *Journal of Dementia Care*, vol 14, no 3, pp 17-19.

Williams, C. (1995) *Invisible victims: Crime and abuse against people with learning disabilities*, London: Jessica Kingsley Publishers.

Williams, P. and Schoultz, B. (1979) *We can speak for ourselves*, London: Souvenir.

Williams, V., Abbott, D. and Rodgers, J. (2007) *Money, rights and risks: A scoping review of financial issues for people with learning disabilities in the UK*, Bristol: Norah Fry Centre, University of Bristol.

Wilson, A. (2003) '"Real jobs", "learning difficulties" and supported employment', *Disability & Society*, vol 18, no 2, pp 99–115.

Winter, N., Holland, A.J. and Collins, S. (1997) 'Factors predisposing to suspected offending by adults with self-reported learning disabilities', *Psychological Medicine*, vol 27, pp 595–607.

Witcher, S., Stalker, K., Roadburg, M. and Jones, C. (2000) *Direct payments: The impact on choice and control for disabled people*, Edinburgh: Scottish Executive Central Research Unit.

Wolfensberger, W. (1969) 'The origin and nature of our institutional models', in R. Kugel and W. Wolfensberger (eds) *Changing patterns in services for the mentally retarded*, Washington, DC: President's Committee on Mental Retardation, pp 63–143.

Wolfensberger, W. (1972) *The principle of normalization in human services*, Toronto, ON: National Institute on Mental Retardation.

Wolfensberger, W. (1983) 'Social role valorization: a proposed new term for the principle of normalization', *Mental retardation*, vol 21, no 2, pp 234–39.

Wolfensberger, W. (1997) *A multi-component advocacy and protection scheme*, Toronto: Canadian Association for the Mentally Retarded.

Wolfensberger, W. (2005) *The new genocide of handicapped and afflicted people* (3rd edn), Syracuse, NY: Training Institute for Human Service Planning, Leadership and Change Agentry, Syracuse University.

Wood, C. (2011) *Tailor made*, London: Demos.

Wood Committee (1929) *Report of the Mental Deficiency Committee: A Joint Committee of the Board of Education and Board of Control (The Wood Report)*, London: HMSO (www.educationengland.org.uk/documents/wood/index.html).

Wood, C. and Grant, E. (2012) *Tracking the lives of disabled families through the cuts*, London: Demos.

Wormald, J. and Wormald, S. (1914) *A guide to the Mental Deficiency Act, 1913* (www.publichealthjrnl.com/article/S0033-3506%2813%2980234-X/abstract).

Young, S. and Strouthos, M. (1997) *First steps to parenthood*, Brighton: Pavilion.

Index